ELEVATING
IMPACT

To Pietro and the
team at FotC —
thanks for all that
you do!
Jackie Green

ELEVATING IMPACT

CASE STUDIES IN SUSTAINABLE BUSINESS AND SOCIAL ENTREPRENEURSHIP

Edited by Jacen Greene

Elevating Impact: Case Studies in Sustainable Business and Social Entrepreneurship
© 2019 The School of Business, Portland State University

ISBN13: 978-1-947845-12-1

Impact Entrepreneurs
The School of Business, Portland State University
KMC 533 | 615 SW Harrison St
Portland, Oregon 97201
503.725.3747
https://www.pdx.edu/impactentrepreneurs/

Cover design by Kristen Ludwigsen
Interior design by Stephanie Anderson

References to website URLs were accurate at the time of writing. Neither the author nor Portland State University School of Business is responsible for URLs that have changed or expired since the manuscript was prepared.

Printed in the United States of America

Table of Contents

Introduction to the Case Collection   ix

Case Abstracts and Awards   xiii

ALTIS: A Microfinance Startup in Nepal   23
Oikos Case Writing Competition Finalist (Social Entrepreneurship Track), 2010
By Jacen Greene and Scott Marshall, Ph.D.

Burgerville: Instilling a Sustainable Culture   41
By Sully Taylor, Ph.D., James Begg, Colin Gallison, Will Sandman, and Benjamin Werner

Clean Water Grow™: "Go or No Go?"   67
Oikos Case Writing Competition 2nd Place (Social Entrepreneurship Track), 2014
By Scott Marshall, Ph.D., and Simon Ngawhika

Columbia Forest Products: Pursuit of Sustainability in a Changing Market   89
Oikos Case Writing Competition 3rd Place (Corporate Sustainability Track), 2009
By Scott Marshall, Ph.D., Zachary Anderson, Matthew Flax, Daniel Gambetta, Jacen Greene, and Madeleine E. Pullman, Ph.D.

Country Natural Beef: A Maturing Co-op at the Crossroads   107
By Madeleine E. Pullman, Ph.D., Victoria Villa-Lobos, and Zhaohui Wu, Ph.D.

Friends of the Children: Strategies for Scaling Impact   137
Oikos Case Writing Competition 2nd Place (Social Entrepreneurship Track), 2016
By Jacen Greene, Nicki Yechin Lee, and Eric Nelsen

Hopworks Urban Brewery: A Case of Sustainable Beer   153
Oikos Case Writing Competition 1st Place (Corporate Sustainability Track), 2015
By Madeleine E. Pullman, Ph.D., Jacen Greene, Devin Liebmann, Nga Ho, and
    Xan Pedisich

Portland Roasting Company: Farm Friendly Direct   183
Oikos Case Competition 1st Place (Corporate Sustainability Track), 2010
By Madeleine E. Pullman, Ph.D., Brandon Arends, Mark Langston, Greg Price,
    and Greg Stokes

SeQuential: Sustainability and Growth in the Biofuels Business   225
By Dave Garten, Jacen Greene, Carolyn Niehaus, and Devdeep Aikath

Tropical Salvage's Growth Strategy: From Recession to Expansion 253
Oikos Case Writing Competition 3rd Place (Social Entrepreneurship Track), 2011
By Scott Marshall, Ph.D., Lisa Piefer, and Erin Ferrigno

ELEVATING IMPACT

INTRODUCTION TO THE CASE COLLECTION

When most people think of Oregon business, they think of the two largest firms located in the state, Nike and Intel. But business in Oregon is larger and more complex than that picture. The latest firm to target a billion dollars in annual revenue is Tillamook Creamery, a dairy farmers' cooperative, and this mix of technology, apparel, and food products reflect some of the state's most dynamic business sectors. Oregon's business history mirrors that of the rest of the Pacific Northwest, with a shift from the long-term sustainability of Native American usage to an emphasis on extractive industries and intensive agriculture following the arrival of Euro-American settlers. Forestry, fishing, mining, ranching, and farming dominated for decades, but these industries began to see diminishing returns due to resource depletion and environmental degradation in the 20th Century. Some rural economies were able to shift to tourism, while Portland experienced a tech boom focused on semiconductor design, manufacturing, and testing led by Intel and Tektronix — the "Silicon Forest."

In the early 21st Century, a cluster of athletic and outdoor apparel firms gained prominence in Portland, including Columbia Sportswear, Nike, Adidas North America, and numerous smaller companies. Tech startups focused on cloud computing grew to prominence and drove a second tech boom. Meanwhile, companies like New Seasons, the world's first B Corp-certified grocer, and Burgerville, one of the first U.S. fast-food chains with an employee union, demonstrated a rising prominence of sustainability as a core business strategy. A new cluster of firms emerged in Portland, not associated with any specific industry, but instead driven by a shared commitment to creating social and environmental benefit through business. By 2018, Oregon had more than 110 certified B Corps, with nearly 90 of them located in Portland alone. Partially in response in this trend, Portland State University (PSU) and the University of Oregon created sustainable business programs that quickly achieved top national and international rankings.

This collection of ten case studies, selected from the first ten years of the case writing program in PSU's School of Business, captures an incredible cross-section of this movement. The cases were written by PSU faculty, students, and staff based on interviews and direct interaction with the organizations and executives profiled. Two of the cases have won the international Oikos Case Writing Competition, several were finalists, and all of them have been tested in undergraduate and graduate classrooms. Every organization profiled here is headquartered in Oregon or southwest Washington, although many have international supply chains or impact. From a Nepalese microfinance spinoff of the global development and relief NGO Mercy Corps, to a business startup launched by a local public water utility, to the sustainability efforts of major regional fast-food company Burgerville, these cases demonstrate sustainability and social entrepreneurship principles across sectors.

Although "sustainability" in business is commonly understood to mean development and economic activity that "meets the needs of the present without compromising the ability of future generations to meet their own needs," as defined by the UN's Brundtland Commission,[1] "social entrepreneurship" is frequently misunderstood. Three interlocking concepts are often grouped together as social entrepreneurship: social innovation, social entrepreneurs, and social enterprise. Social innovation is "A novel solution to a social problem that is more effective, efficient, sustainable, or just than existing solutions and for which the value created accrues primarily to society as a whole rather than private individuals."[2] This definition also captures environmental sustainability, albeit (like the Brundtland definition) through an anthropocentric lens. A social innovation may be generated or adapted by a social entrepreneur.

Social entrepreneurs are individuals who *play the role of change agents in the social sector, by:*

- *Adopting a mission to create and sustain social value (not just private value),*
- *Recognizing and relentlessly pursuing new opportunities to serve that mission,*

1   World Commission on Environment and Development. Our Common Future: Report of the World Commission on Environment and Development. Oxford: Oxford University Press, 1987.
2   Phills Jr., James A., Kriss Deiglmeier, and Dale T. Miller. "Rediscovering Social Innovation." Stanford Social Innovation Review, Fall, 2008.

- *Engaging in a process of continuous innovation, adaptation, and learning,*
- *Acting boldly without being limited by resources currently in hand, and*
- *Exhibiting heightened accountability to the constituencies served and for the outcomes created.*[3]

This definition from J. Gregory Dees extends entrepreneurship theory to include those who use entrepreneurial mindsets and approaches to generate social benefit. Social entrepreneurs may use a social enterprise as the mechanism to deliver the social value which they create.

Kim Alter describes a social enterprise as "any business venture created for a social purpose — mitigating/reducing a social problem or a market failure — and to generate social value while operating with the financial discipline, innovation and determination of a private sector business."[4] This relates closely to the official UK government definition of a social enterprise as "a business with primarily social objectives whose surpluses are principally reinvested for that purpose in the business or in the community, rather than being driven by the need to maximize profit for shareholders and owners."[5] Although a social innovation can take many forms, and social entrepreneurs can work within any sector, a social enterprise is strictly a business with a primary mission of addressing social and environmental issues — not a business that simply adopts some sustainability practices.

The cases in this book include clear examples from all four categories: cutting-edge models of sustainable business, the development and delivery of social innovations, leading social entrepreneurs, and highly effective social enterprises. The common thread is the use of business models to generate and deliver lasting social and environmental benefit. I hope that you find the following cases as useful as we have in training the next generation of business, nonprofit, and government leaders, using examples of some of the most innovative organizations in Oregon.

Supplemental videos for most of the cases, and digital teaching notes for all of the cases, are available for free to educators. To request additional content, please contact the editor, Jacen Greene, at jacen@pdx.edu, or contact PSU's School of Business at sbinfo@pdx.edu.

---

3   Dees, J. Gregory. "The Meaning of Social Entrepreneurship." 1998. Revised 2001. https://centers.fuqua.duke.edu/case/wp-content/uploads/sites/7/2015/03/Article_Dees_MeaningofSocialEntrepreneurship_2001.pdf
4   Alter, Kim. "Social Enterprise Typology." Inter-American Development Bank, 2003. Revised 2007. https://www.globalcube.net/clients/philippson/content/medias/download/SE_typology.pdf
5   Department of Trade and Industry. "Social Enterprise: A Strategy for Success." Government of the United Kingdom, July 2002. https://webarchive.nationalarchives.gov.uk/20061211103748/http://www.cabinetoffice.gov.uk/third_sector/social_enterprise/strategy_background/

CASE ABSTRACTS AND AWARDS

ALTIS: A Microfinance Startup in Nepal (2010)

Oikos Case Writing Competition Finalist (Social Entrepreneurship Track), 2010

By Jacen Greene and Scott Marshall, Ph.D.

This case describes the issues and dilemmas facing Sanjay Karki, a social entrepreneur working to initiate a microfinance operation in rural agricultural areas of Nepal. Although the Nepalese government supported microfinance models, a recent civil war had severely disrupted government services and worsened poverty. The case covers the recent history of Nepal, the condition of the country's capital markets, the ALTIS concept, and the competitive landscape.

Sanjay Karki possessed the necessary expertise, a high level of motivation, and many key stakeholder relationships to help him establish a microfinance enterprise separate from his employer, Mercy Corps. He had carefully considered the funding needs, financial and technical service components of the client model, and the initial management structure. However, there remained a number of issues he had yet to fully consider, and he had not yet developed a clear strategic plan for implementing the enterprise.

The reader is in the position to analyze the external circumstances that both provided greater opportunity (i.e., a need exists) and created significant barriers to success. Further, the reader is called on to assess the degree to which

Sanjay has considered the roles of different stakeholders and how to effectively engage each of them in the launch of ALTIS. The case is designed to highlight the inherent uncertainties of new enterprise launch, the particular challenges of starting a social enterprise in a developing country, and the role of a variety of stakeholders in influencing the potential success of such a startup.

Burgerville: Instilling a Sustainable Culture (2012)

By Sully Taylor, Ph.D., James Begg, Colin Gallison, Will Sandman, and Benjamin Werner

From a single store to a regional chain, Burgerville (BV) had differentiated from other national chains by maintaining a strong relationship with its customers, supply partners, employees and the community. This case study delves into Burgerville's commitment to instilling a sustainability culture by assessing the impact of the company's mission to "Serve with Love." The analysis in this study covers Burgerville's strategic changes in:

- Product development — BV's commitment in using locally and seasonally sourced ingredients throughout its menu.
- Supply chain management — BV's approach to maintaining strong relationships with suppliers, and preferentially purchasing from Food Alliance certified producers.
- Use of renewable energy — BV's purchase of wind power credits equal to 100% energy use in its restaurants and corporate headquarters.
- Recycling and composting — BV's commitment to providing recycling and composting stations. In addition, nearly all of BV's packaging materials come from 100% renewable materials.
- Employee relations — BV's commitment to offering healthcare benefits to any employee working more than 20 hours per week.
- Training — BV's commitment to training employees at all levels to convey its core beliefs in sustainability and community.
- Transparency — BV's commitment to educating customers about exactly what they are eating by providing specific nutritional information on each receipt.

Burgerville's commitment in implementing these strategic changes had shaped its reputation as the alternative place to go for quality, local, fast food.

Clean Water Grow™: Go or No Go? (2014)

Oikos Case Writing Competition 2nd Place (Social Entrepreneurship Track), 2014

By Scott Marshall, Ph.D., and Simon Ngawhika

The $43 billion US wastewater treatment industry was a landscape in which the high costs of capital construction and the need for economies of scale featured prominently. The US Environmental Protection Agency estimated that between 2004 and 2024, over $200 billion needed to be spent upgrading and expanding America's wastewater infrastructure.

One significant challenge in maintaining treatment infrastructure was the build-up of struvite. Struvite accumulates inside treatment facility pipe networks, reducing capacity and increasing operating and maintenance costs. But discharging the components of struvite — the nutrients nitrogen and phosphorous — into the environment also has negative consequences. Concentrated amounts can cause significant harm to aquatic ecosystems.

Clean Water Services (CWS) was the public wastewater utility for Washington County, Oregon, USA, providing sewage and stormwater treatment services to more than 500,000 homes and businesses. Responsible for the health and management of a public good, the 83-mile long Tualatin River, CWS was subject to regulation over the temperature and quality of the water it discharged into the natural environment.

This case follows Clean Water Services in its pilot test of a home garden fertilizer product that was linked to the environmental benefits and operational efficiencies gained through an innovative treatment technology. In 2009, CWS implemented a groundbreaking solution to the challenge of struvite, one that also had the potential to turn a waste stream into a revenue stream. An advanced 'nutrient recovery technology' removed the nutrients that form struvite and pollute the environment if discharged, recycling them into an effective, safe to handle garden fertilizer. In mid-2012, the CWS Board gave the green light to produce Clean Water GROW™, its own brand of fertilizer, and test its commercial viability in the local consumer market.

This case educates students on the challenge of finding innovative ways to operate and maintain wastewater infrastructure in the face of population growth and increased pressure on natural systems. It provides detail on the development and commercial pilot of the GROW fertilizer product, and the packaging, pricing and distribution options that were analyzed. It asks students to conduct the crucial steps of analyzing the implications of marketing mix options in terms of break-even quantity and return on investment, and recommending a 'go' or 'no go' decision to the CWS board.

Columbia Forest Products: Pursuit of Sustainability in a Changing Market (2009)

Oikos Case Writing Competition 3rd Place (Corporate Sustainability Track), 2009

By Scott Marshall, Ph.D., Zachary Anderson, Matthew Flax, Daniel Gambetta, Jacen Greene, and Madeleine E. Pullman, Ph.D.

From its humble beginnings as a small, shuttered plywood mill, Columbia Forest Products had grown to be one of the largest players in the U.S. hardwood plywood products market. This case follows the company's introduction of a new sustainable plywood product in an extremely competitive and economically challenging market. At the time detailed in the case, the construction of new homes had fallen across the United States.

The fate of Columbia Forest Products (CFP) was tightly bound to the US housing market. CFP had over a 40% market share in hardwood plywood products, most of which went into new home construction. Further, over the past three years, CFP had embarked on a journey into sustainability. This journey was marked most profoundly by the introduction of PureBond© non-formaldehyde plywood in 2006. A first in the industry, PureBond© provided significant health benefits to CFP employees and customers by removing a known carcinogen from its products. It also had been a catalyst for CFP to pursue a more comprehensive, sustainability-inspired strategy. But in the midst of the dreadful housing market in the US, CFP's executive team wondered if further pursuit of a sustainability strategy would be detrimental to their company's competitiveness.

The threat of domestic and international competition is ever present, and the company was well aware that the advantage provided by PureBond© was only temporary. CFP's domestic competition would be able to offer competitive non-formaldehyde products in 1 ½ to 2 years. It would likely take China and other overseas manufacturers another year, at least, to offer comparable products.

Another consideration was CFP's reputation. It had spent many years building recognition for its sustainability initiatives. By further pursuing a sustainability-based strategy, CFP invited greater public scrutiny. CFP needed to be clear on how it committed itself to sustainability and the reputation that it built as a result. There was always the potential that well intentioned and ambitious sustainability efforts could turn into PR disasters.

This case describes the issues and dilemmas facing the company in deciding to adopt a sustainability strategy. The case is designed to highlight decisions related to strategy, adverse industry reactions, public policy and health claims, etc. In addition, it provides an example of a product developed through bio-mimicry. The case can draw on the following frameworks: Porter's Five Forces Model, Resource Based Theory, and Systems Dynamics.

Country Natural Beef: A Maturing Co-op at the Crossroads (2010)

By Madeleine E. Pullman, Ph.D., Victoria Villa-Lobos, and Zhaohui Wu, Ph.D.

This case describes the issues and challenges facing a natural beef cooperative in a turbulent moment in their industry. With a severe economic downturn, increasing certification/standards demands from various stakeholders, and their management group in transition, the organization was faced with decisions which would have significant impact on their viability. The case highlights decisions related to overall organizational design, sustainability challenges in supply chain relationship management and new product innovations, and the changing landscape in the food industry. The case discusses the following management topics:

- Entrepreneurship and Family Business
- Marketing & New Product Innovations
- Supply Chain Management and Operations Strategy
- Sustainability, Rural Development, Cooperatives

This case was made possible through the generous cooperation of Country Natural Beef Cooperative by their time and providing information for this case, and Agriculture of the Middle by providing funding for this study.

Friends of the Children: Strategies for Scaling Impact (2016)

Oikos Case Writing Competition 2nd Place (Social Entrepreneurship Track), 2016

By Jacen Greene, Nicki Yechin Lee, and Eric Nelsen

Friends of the Children, a nonprofit organization in Portland, Oregon, was founded in 1993 by retired entrepreneur Duncan Campbell to serve youth at the highest risk of teen parenting, incarceration, or dropping out of school. Each youth client was matched with a paid mentor from first grade through the end of high school. The costs of this intervention were high, but the outcomes were extremely impressive in each of the three risk areas. The total benefits to society of Friends of the Children's intervention was estimated at $7 for every $1 spent on the program.

In the United States alone, 2.25 million children under the age of five lived in extreme poverty, one of the key markers of Friends of the Children's target clients. The organization had written an award-winning business plan to scale their impact nationwide, but needed $25 million to fully fund the new strategy. Key elements of the plan included launching new chapters, hiring more development staff, separating the roles of local chapters from that of the national organization, engaging with additional affiliate partners, and more effectively sharing their model and impact with other organizations, policymakers, and the public.

As Friends of the Children embarked on this ambitious funding campaign and scaling strategy, national President Terri Sorensen faced a series of challenges and potential tradeoffs unique to leading a rapidly-growing nonprofit with social enterprise characteristics. In this case, students are tasked with analyzing a scaling strategy and contrasting the effectiveness of alternative approaches, evaluating the suitability of different funding models (including social impact bonds) for the selected strategy, and performing a simple social return on investment analysis to measure impact.

Hopworks Urban Brewery: A Case of Sustainable Beer (2015)

Oikos Case Writing Competition 1st Place (Corporate Sustainability Track), 2015

By Madeleine E. Pullman, Ph.D., Jacen Greene, Devin Liebmann, Nga Ho, and Xan Pedisich

Founded in 2007 in Portland, Oregon, Hopworks Urban Brewery was a sustainability-focused brewpub that produced certified organic beer. The State of Oregon was the second largest producer of hops, a main ingredient in beer, in the United States, and also had more craft breweries per capita than any other state. The metro area of Portland, home to over 2 million people, had over 84 craft breweries within its borders.

The craft brewing industry had grown rapidly in the United States over the previous decade, with an annualized growth rate of 9.6% from 2009–2014 and a $14.3 billion market in 2013. Craft brewers are small enterprises, producing fewer than six million barrels of beer per year, employing both traditional and innovative brewing methods, and focusing on quality products and connecting with their local community.

To date, Hopworks had thrived in this competitive environment, producing over 12,000 barrels of beer per year while staying carbon neutral and diverting 98.6% of their total waste from landfills. Hopworks' top quality beers had won prestigious national awards. Additionally, Oregon's Governor had honored the brewery for its achievements as a sustainable business. However, to expand, Hopworks was faced with a number of key decisions that affected its sustainability, both economically and ecologically. Christian Ettinger, founder and brewmaster of Hopworks, had to make strategic decisions about capital investments, labor allocations, and even the future of their organic certification as he executed a growth plan in line with their sustainable values. In this case, students will be challenged with analyzing all aspects of a sustainability-focused business and considering the many choices a craft brewer, or any small business owner, faces.

Portland Roasting Company: Farm Friendly Direct (2010)

Oikos Case Competition 1st Place (Corporate Sustainability Track), 2010

By Madeleine E. Pullman, Ph.D., Greg Stokes, Price Gregory, Mark Langston, and Brandon Arends

This case describes the issues and dilemmas facing a company in their efforts to differentiate their product through a social sustainability program. Over the years, Portland Roasting Company had built a strong reputation with their sustainability efforts, particularly amongst their peers in the specialty coffee industry. There was some question as to whether this reputation had been visible to consumers and if consumers saw the value proposition. The case covers the history of coffee, the specialty coffee industry, the supply chain and roles of different participants, and the competitive landscape.

Furthermore, most of the competitive eco-labels and certification schemes are discussed. The reader is asked to decide the appropriate method for conveying the company's social sustainability efforts to the marketplace, and beyond that, to consider how one might measure and monitor social programs in the developing world. The case is designed to highlight decisions related to marketing and operations strategy, pros and cons of certification, and particularly social sustainability versus the other aspects of sustainability.

SeQuential: Sustainability and Growth in the Biofuels Business (2018)

By Dave Garten, Jacen Greene, Carolyn Niehaus, and Devdeep Aikath

SeQuential, a vertically-integrated biodiesel company based in Portland, Oregon, pursued a more sustainable supply and production strategy than many competitors by securing inputs from used cooking oil (UCO) rather than new crops. A fragmented U.S. biodiesel industry produced more than 1.25 billion gallons of the fuel in 2016 from a mix of virgin materials and UCO, but the environmental impact of crop-based biodiesel was increasingly controversial. Meanwhile, UCO collection had grown rapidly in recent years, and with strong forecasted growth, offered a potential additional revenue stream for vertically-integrated biodiesel firms.

The price of the UCO used to produce SeQuential's biodiesel and the fuel itself were driven by commodity indices, creating a highly volatile market. In addition, industry profitability was heavily reliant on government support. This support was manifested through funding for Renewable Identification Numbers (RINs) and tax credits. The recent election of a U.S. President publicly opposed to climate change mitigation, and the re-election of a sympathetic U.S. Congress, worsened perennial uncertainty around the renewal of these policies.

Tyson Keever, President and CEO of SeQuential, had guided the company through a period of major growth and vertical integration by overseeing a series of regional mergers and acquisitions. As a result, the company now faced growing pains linked to employee turnover, operational integration and efficiency, and instilling a culture of sustainability in all SeQuential employees. At the same time, SeQuential was developing a new strategy for future growth, while attempting to mitigate increased regulatory and market uncertainty. In this case, students are tasked with developing a series of strategic, mission-aligned growth proposals that address these challenges.

Tropical Salvage's Growth Strategy: From Recession to Expansion (2011)

Oikos Case Writing Competition 3rd Place (Social Entrepreneurship Track), 2011

By Scott Marshall, Ph.D., Lisa Piefer, and Erin Ferrigno

Tim O'Brien, Founder of Tropical Salvage, was ready to launch a growth strategy for his company. He had spent ten years building the sourcing, production, and marketing capabilities of Tropical Salvage. And he had worked successfully with a not-for-profit partner to establish the Jepara Forest Conservancy to further the social and environmental missions that had provided the primary motivation for the company.

O'Brien had many key business decisions to make to actualize his growth strategy, including how to finance a new branded retail store, the best ways to build brand awareness of the products, and whether or not to extend the product offerings. The inspiration for Tropical Salvage came to O'Brien during a week of trekking in Indonesia in 1998. O'Brien had encountered stunning biodiversity juxtaposed with wasteful exploitation of natural resources and underutilization of craft traditions. As his travels continued he noticed old wooden structures being replaced by more secure structures built from concrete and rebar. In many instances no plan existed to re-use the old beams, boards, and poles. The idea for Tropical Salvage struck — salvaging wood from deconstructed buildings can be a significant source of raw material for hardwood furniture production.

O'Brien started Tropical Salvage based on a conviction that "a reasonable and promising market-oriented strategy can contribute to positive change in a part of the world beset by extraordinary challenges." Tropical Salvage uses only salvaged, or rediscovered, wood to build its line of furniture. The company uses a variety of wood salvage strategies, including demolishing old buildings, bridges and boats, recovering logs from rivers and lakes, mining entombed trees from the ground, and taking trees from diseased plantation timber. Salvaged wood is cut into lumber, treated for insects, and kiln-dried. From the kiln, woodcrafters construct the furniture. The product catalog includes roughly 150 different models and the company also builds one-of-a-kind custom pieces and furnishings built to commercial specifications. Tropical Salvage's products are sold in its own warehouse as well as through retail partnerships in the US and Canada.

Although O'Brien was convinced he needed to expand through branded retail, he was aware of some significant challenges. First, there was an abundance of quality salvageable wood in Indonesia, but as Tropical Salvage sought additional sources it would need to ensure efficient salvage and transport processes to maintain the high margins that were important to its expansion efforts. Second, Tropical Salvage lacked a formal computer-based system to track and control its incoming and outgoing inventory. This approach might be strained with the introduction of one or more branded retail locations. Third, increased demand for its furniture was necessary in order for Tropical Salvage to expand its operations. O'Brien considered marketing to be his greatest challenge. And, finally, O'Brien needed to determine how to finance the expansion — through retained earnings, debt financing, or venture capital. Each option presented different pros and cons, and he needed to weigh each before moving forward.

This case study provides students with the opportunity to analyze a social enterprise operating in an intensely competitive global industry. Background is provided on the competencies of the company, the competitive dynamics in the industry, and the challenges and opportunities presented by O'Brien's intended approach to growing his business. Students will be tasked with looking at many facets of the business — sourcing, operations, marketing, distribution and finance — to derive recommended actions.

ALTIS
A Microfinance Startup in Nepal

Oikos Case Writing Competition Finalist (Social
Entrepreneurship Track), 2010

By Jacen Greene and Scott Marshall, Ph.D.

ALTIS Case Study

In Sanjay Karki's role as Deputy Director for the Nepal office of Mercy Corps,
an international non-profit organization providing disaster relief, civic organization, and economic development services, he had worked on a number of
poverty reduction programs. One of the most promising innovations in poverty alleviation was the concept of microfinance, the provision of small-scale
loans and other financial services to poor entrepreneurs. Although the government of Nepal quickly embraced microfinance models and created supporting institutions, a decade-long civil war ending in 2006 had severely disrupted
government services, even while worsening poverty. In the *terai*, or plains, of
Nepal, government and non-profit microfinance institutions were able to access population densities and transportation infrastructure necessary for successful operations, but in the rugged and undeveloped mid-mountain and
high-mountain regions, little was being done to help the poor.

Karki had considered launching a for-profit social enterprise focusing on
agricultural microfinance and technical services for the rural poor, one formed
with the assistance of Mercy Corps that could extend the reach of Mercy Corps

programs. Such an organization might be better positioned than the government and private, for-profit institutions that had previously failed to deliver essential financial services. However, starting a social enterprise was risky even in developed nations, and in a geographically rugged, developing nation recovering from a recently ended civil war, it seemed nearly impossible. Aside from the normal questions of market size, which customers to target, what products and services to provide, how to obtain startup funding, and how to manage competition, Karki faced the near total collapse of the national financial system. And yet, some of the very same conditions that increased the difficulty of starting a new business or securing funds spoke to the desperate need for basic financial services. Confronting some of the most daunting challenges to business formation in the world, could a social enterprise bridging the worlds of for-profit and non-profit institutions succeed in helping impoverished farmers improve their livelihoods?

Nepal

Nepal, stretching along the southern slope of the Himalayas between India and the Tibetan plateau, rises from subtropical lowlands to the snowcapped peaks of the tallest mountains on Earth (see Exhibit 1). Although until recently it was the only officially proclaimed Hindu state in the world,[6] Nepal has a rich heritage of ethnic, linguistic, and religious diversity. Nepal's history was strongly influenced by its position between China and India, or as the first King of Nepal famously put it, "a yam between two rocks."

Ten years of civil war between Maoist insurgents and the royal government of Nepal, culminating in the dissolution of parliament by the king, was resolved in 2006 with the signing of a peace treaty and establishment of an interim constitution restoring democratic rule. In 2008, the newly elected Constituent Assembly of Nepal abolished the monarchy, ending more than two centuries of hereditary rule, and proclaimed a federal democratic republic. The nation's first President, Dr. Ram Baran Yadav, was elected in July of that year; the new Prime Minister, Pushpa Dahal, was a Maoist.

The new government faced lingering political instability as well as severe social and economic pressures. With an unemployment rate of 46%, and year-on-year inflation approaching 8%,[7] the economic situation was dire. Gross

---

6   Central Intelligence Agency, "Nepal."
7   Ibid.

national income per capita in Nepal was US$290.[8] Nepal had a poverty rate of 31%[9] (those living on less than $0.22 a day, per the national poverty line), placing it among top 20 poorest nations in the world.[10] Although the Kathmandu valley had a poverty incidence of only 3%, other urban areas averaged 10% and the rate in the countryside was much higher, demonstrating the lack of effective poverty alleviation programs outside of cities.[11] More than eight out of ten Nepalese lived in rural areas and remained dependent on agriculture for their livelihoods,[12] although the agricultural sector accounted for less than half of the nation's GDP of US$8.05 billion[13] (see Exhibit 3). It was clear that economic development would need to take into account the importance of rural agriculture to the people of Nepal. Still recovering from the civil war, the government faced major difficulties in meeting the needs of Nepalese citizens. The rural financial sector, in particular, had suffered a near-collapse during the war, and the need for financial services in the mid-mountain and high-mountain regions of Nepal was almost entirely unmet. A major market existed for a social enterprise designed to offer low-cost financial instruments to the poor of Nepal.

The Marketspace

In 2006, banks and NGOs in Nepal that served the rural poor accounted for only 2.36% of total financial sector assets, with US$60.6 million in lending.[14] Nepal had only six domestic banks, and the number of branch offices per 100,000 people had declined to a mere 1.73 due to emergency closures during the civil war, with most branches and ATMs located only in cities10[15] (see Exhibit 4). Bank deposits and lending showed a linked decline during the same period (See Exhibit 5), and it was estimated that more than 70% of Nepal's people had no access to commercial banks at all. [16] Poor and rural Nepalese faced a crippling inability to access financial services necessary for the most basic aspects of daily life. What few financial services were traditionally

---

8   The World Bank, "Getting Finance in South Asia 2009."
9   Ibid.
10   Josh Dewald, Interview.
11   Ibid.
12   ANZDEC, "Nepal Commercial Agricultural Development Project, Final Report."
13   The World Bank.
14   Ibid.
15   Ibid.
16   Bloomberg, "Nepal Asks Lenders to Expand Branches as Maoist Hostility Ends."

available to the rural poor were provided by money lenders or merchants who charged exorbitant interest rates, undermining the effectiveness of such loans in wealth creation and poverty reduction.

Government attempts to expand access to credit were hampered by political instability and endemic corruption. Although Nepal's central bank, Nepal Rastra, had introduced corporate governance guidelines in 2005, little progress had been made in achieving those goals.[17] Commercial banks were required to grant loans or equity of a value between 0.25% and 3% of total loan portfolios to the "deprived sector" of low-income households, but the lack of financial infrastructure in remote areas hampered the program.[18] Nepal Rastra had also established five Regional Rural Development Banks to provide financial services to the rural poor, with mixed results. A number of non-profit organizations had formed microfinance banks or stepped in directly to address the financial needs of the poor (see Exhibit 6). Mercy Corps, in particular, had developed a series of offerings that Karki hoped to develop further and integrate as complementary services in his new organization.

Mercy Corps

Founded in 1979 by Dan O'Neil and Ellsworth Culver as an extension of O'Neil's *Save the Refugees Fund* for survivors of the Cambodian genocide, the non-profit Mercy Corps embraced principles of sustainable development with an emphasis on civic engagement and market-driven efforts (see Exhibits 7 and 8). Headquartered in Portland, Oregon, the organization had delivered over $1.3 billion in aid to more than 107 countries by 2009,[19] with country directors or representatives in each country spearheading program development and fundraising in partnership with local organizations, colleague agencies, and the United Nations. Mercy Corps specifically targeted nations and communities in transition following major natural or social disasters, with efforts ranging from material relief and assistance to the development of long-term civic and economic programs.

The turmoil in Nepal following the end of the civil war, the abolition of the monarchy, and the establishment of a democratic republic fit well within the scope of Mercy Corps' mission to aid societies in transition. Mercy Corps Nepal was established near the end of 2005, and by the time ALTIS was in

---

17   The World Bank.
18   Asia Resource Center for Microfinance, "Nepal Country Profile."
19   Mercy Corps, "Financials."

the process of formation, Mercy Corps had been engaged in a number of projects and partnerships to address unmet needs in agriculture-dependent communities. Mercy Corps partnered with the Youth Initiative for Peace and Reconciliation to create youth groups for job training and conflict resolution, worked with the University of Washington to map the value chain of high-value commodities and improve production processes, and partnered with Nirdhan Utthan Bank Ltd. (NUBL) to expand access to microfinance services in agricultural communities.[20]

The partnership with NUBL helped Mercy Corps meet some of the critical need for microfinance lending and other financial services in remote agricultural communities, but Karki saw that lending services worked best when coupled with technical assistance. By linking Mercy Corps' financial and value chain services together in packaged products, and by moving toward a for-profit model, he hoped to provide a constant revenue stream to drive a greater scale of projects while providing a targeted portfolio of complementary services. He would call the new organization ALTIS, or Agricultural Lending and Technical Services Company.

The ALTIS Model

ALTIS was conceived as a non-profit company that would offer microloans coupled with technical and agricultural training targeted to the specific needs of small, rural farms (see Exhibits 9 and 10). Loan interest rates would be capped at slightly less than existing microfinance institutions in Nepal, but higher than the 12%–14% average rate from government-subsidized development banks. Although it was necessary for ALTIS to charge a higher rate of interest than government-subsidized banks, Karki expected little direct competition in the chronically underserved, remote communities where the company hoped to do business. ALTIS would also be the only agricultural lending institution in Nepal to offer embedded technical services and the first to specifically target high-value crops.[21]

ALTIS's non-profit structure would allow the company to target communities with the greatest need rather than the greatest market potential, to reinvest all profits in expansion, to seek funding from sources not normally available to for-profit companies, and to creatively employ government and non-profit

---

20   Ibid.
21   Josh DeWald.

partnerships. Once the company became self-sufficient, it could reorganize as a for-profit social business (see Exhibit 11) relying predominately on internal revenue to cover operational costs and fund future expansion.[22]

Karki estimated that ALTIS would need approximately US$4.16 million in startup capital for the first four years, after which the organization would be expected to quickly achieve profitability (See Exhibit 12). By the tenth year of operation, ALTIS was expected to have a net worth of roughly US$6.75 million, with annual loan disbursements totaling more than US$12 million and total benefits to the agricultural sector of Nepal in excess of US$22 million per year. (All budget estimates altered to maintain confidentiality.)

Starting with a central office and a pair of branch offices, ALTIS was expected to expand to a total of five branch offices within the first five years. Board members were to be drawn from ALTIS, Mercy Corps, the Nepal Ministry of Agriculture and Cooperatives, the Bankers Association of Nepal, Nirdhan Utthan Bank and Nepal Rastra Bank. It was expected that strategic partnerships could be formed with board member organizations, in addition to the Federation of Nepalese Chambers of Commerce and Industry's Agro-Enterprise Center, the Rural Microfinance Development Center, and the Rural Self-Reliance Fund.[23]

By partnering with local NGOs, government institutions, industry organizations and for-profit companies, Karki hoped to avoid antagonizing potential competitors and draw on a diversity of experience and expertise to guide the growth of the company. How long such cooperative partnerships could be maintained without devolving into serious competition if ALTIS established a profitable model for serving remote communities, however, remained unknown. ALTIS also faced a number of entrenched alternatives that could either complement or supplant ALTIS operations.

Potential Competitors

Governmental Institutions

National Co-operative Bank, Limited (NCBL): NCBL was established to provide banking and financial services to Nepal's 7500 cooperatives, with membership comprising nearly 25% of the nation's population. In addition to

---

22   Mercy Corps, "ALTIS Internal Concept Note."
23   "ALTIS Internal Concept Note."

providing loans, NCBL was structured to serve as an interface between Nepal Rastra Bank, international financial and aid institutions, and cooperatives. The bank was capitalized with 160 million paid-up shares of capital at 1000 rupees each, with an additional 160 million issued but unpaid shares and 320 million authorized but unissued shares.[24]

Agricultural Development Bank, Limited (ADBL): A government-owned bank with a charter to provide lending to small farmers in addition to traditional commercial financial activities, at the time of this case ADBL accounted for more than 67% of Nepal's institutional credit supply. Under the Small Farmer Development Program, households with a per capita income of fewer than 2500 rupees or land holdings of less than half a hectare were eligible to receive credit for income-generating activities, participate in group savings programs, and receive business and financial training. An institutional development program to assist with the establishment of self-sufficient farmers' cooperatives was later created to address the lack of growth and high costs of the Small Farmer Development Program. A subsidiary of ADBL, the Small Farmer's Development Bank, was formed in 2002 to further address the needs of rural farmers, with a goal of eventually transferring ownership to farmers' cooperatives.[25]

Microfinance Banks

Nirdhan Utthan Bank, Limited: Nirdhan Utthan was formed as a banking subsidiary of the poverty reduction non-profit Nirdhan (see Exhibits 12 and 13). Nirdhan Utthan provided a large variety of loans, as well as banking, microinsurance, and remittance services, but was active in only a quarter of the Nepal's districts.[26]

Swabalamban Bikas Bank, Limited: Swabalamban Bikas was an offshoot of the Centre for Self-Help Development, a non-profit organization dedicated to providing financial services in the underserved hill regions of Nepal. In 2006, Swabalamban Bikas had a gross loan portfolio of US$1,010,436, assets of $2,276,200, savings of $494,548, and equity of $705,775.[27]

Informal Organizations

It was estimated that although roughly 30% of Nepal's citizens had access to traditional financial institutions, only 18% of the population actually borrowed

---

24 National Co-operative Bank Limited, coopbank.com.np.
25 Agricultural Development Bank Limited, adbl.gov.np.
26 Nirdhan.com
27 Banking With The Poor network, bwtp.org.

from such sources.[28] The remainder of the nation's credit needs were served by the informal sector, with 55% of such loans provided by family and friends, 26% by moneylenders, and the remainder by a mix of informal groups.[29] None of these groups offered the financial, agricultural, and technical services often packaged with loans offered by microfinance institutions, and a lack of transparency in loan rates and terms could have crippling consequences on a family's financial stability.

Conclusion

ALTIS seemed to present a unique opportunity to serve the financial needs of poor, rural farmers in Nepal. Traditional governmental and business models had failed to address the needs of the rural poor, and non-profit organizations found it difficult to maintain long-term planning and scale up programs due to their dependence on (sometimes fickle) outside funding. Forming ALTIS as a non-profit to broaden funding sources and provide some tax benefits until the company was able to become self-sufficient, then shifting to a for-profit, social business model seemed to offer the best potential, but the company was still highly dependent on a number of major partnerships. Had Karki only substituted the demands of investors for the demands of partners? Was a hybrid model combining aspects of both non-profit and for-profit models the best way to reduce the extensive risk faced by entrepreneurs in developing nations, or would the combination prove too unwieldy? Would ALTIS be a yam, or a rock?

---

28   Nepalese Economic Review, "Determinants of Formal Credit Market Participation in Nepal."
29   Ibid.

Exhibits

Exhibit 1: Map of Nepal

Source: Map by OCHA, CC BY 3.0 (https://creativecommons.org/licenses/by/3.0/)

Exhibit 2: Population of Nepal, Millions

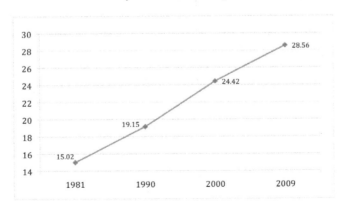

Source: derived from Central Intelligence Agency, The World Bank.

Exhibit 3: Sector Contribution to GDP in Nepal, by Value Added

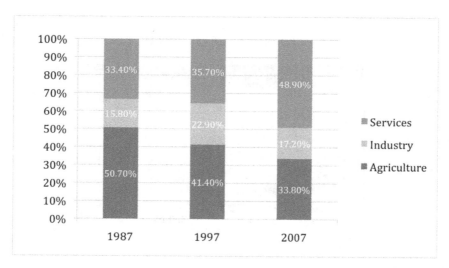

Source: derived from The World Bank, "Nepal Fact Sheet."

Exhibit 4: Bank Branch and ATM Penetration per 100,000 People

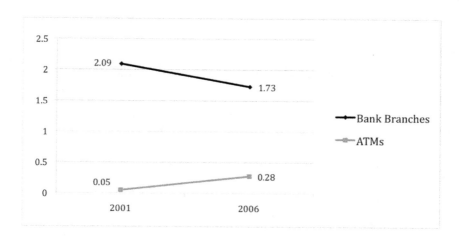

Source: The World Bank, "Getting Finance in South Asia 2009."

Exhibit 5: Deposit and Loan Accounts per 1000 People

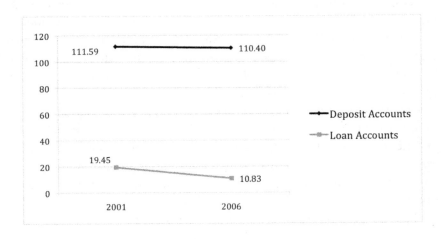

Source: The World Bank, "Getting Finance in South Asia 2009."

Exhibit 6: Microfinance Institutions (MFIs) in Nepal

Institution Type	Number	Inst. Type	Cust. Type	Customers
Grameen Bank replicators / Microfinance Development Banks	12,100 73,120	Self-managed center Groups	Poor rural women	353,715
Savings and Credit Cooperatives / Credit Unions	2,672		Clients	310,771
Small Farmers Cooperative Limited / Small Farmers Development Program	47	Intermediary NGOs	Poor Clients	103,000 247,000
United Nations Development Program Projects	39,229	Self-help groups	Men Women	510,676 523,280
Rural Water Supply & Sanitation Fund Development Board	1260	Women Technical Support Service Groups	Women	63,000
TOTAL				**2,111,442**
Estimated population, 2005				25,296,537
% of population served by MFIs				8.35%
% below poverty line of those served by MFIs				26.10%
Women served by MFIs				1,233,058

Source: Nepal Center for Microfinance, "Strategic Plan 2007/08 – 2009/10"

Exhibit 7: Mercy Corps Strategic Vision, FY 2009

Mercy Corps' **Mission** is to alleviate suffering, poverty and oppression by helping people build secure, productive and just communities across the globe.

Our **Vision for Change**, based on the Universal Declaration of Human Rights, is that peaceful, secure and just societies emerge when the private, public, and civil society sectors are able to interact with accountability, inclusive participation and mechanisms for peaceful change.

Our **Strategy** is to work in countries in transition, where communities are suffering and recovering from disaster, conflict or economic collapse. Our experience demonstrates that during these times of turmoil and tragedy, there exists the possibility for positive change. We add our greatest value as an international relief and development agency by supporting those kernels of positive change with community-led and market-driven action.

To accomplish our mission, we aim to be a world leader in:

(1) *Transforming Transitional Environments Through CommunityLed and MarketDriven Initiatives*

Our foundational work is at the community and country level, where we operate rapid relief, long-term recovery and sustainable development programs. In times of crisis or transition, we seek to enable communities to organize for the change they want to see, catalyze the interaction of civil society, government and business, and prompt market-led economic prosperity. We do this based on our experience working alongside communities around the world that these elements are essential to sustaining the changes communities seek.

We emphasize sustainable solutions that are both specific to the context of each community and scalable for broad impact. These country programs are driven by our significant investments in three areas critical to operationalizing our vision for change: (1) rapid relief assistance that paves the way for longer term recovery programs; (2) initiatives that enable peaceful, community-driven change and linkages between government, business and civic sectors; and (3) market-led development.

(2) *Catalyzing Social Innovations*

We will have the greatest impact on global problems if we are able to identify, replicate and scale the most innovative solutions that arise from our global team of social entrepreneurs and the communities where we work. Mercy Corps is particularly focused on capturing, *"new ideas blending methods from the worlds of business, government and civil society to create social value that is sustainable and has the potential for largescale impact."* We seek to magnify the influence and impact of our community-led market-driven programs by reaching for the largest possible impact, with a focus on financial sustainability.

(3) *Inspiring Global Engagement*

Finally, our experience tells us it is imperative to help create a globally engaged citizenry that can advocate for change and take action in the quest to eliminate global poverty, hunger and conflict. We particularly aim to educate and inspire youth around the world as they represent the hope for the future.

Source: Mercy Corps, "Strategic Planning Framework FY 2009."

Exhibit 8: Mercy Corps Financials

	FY 2008	FY 2007
Support & Revenue		
Proyecto Aldea Global	$2,554,509	$2,526,782
Mercy Corps Scotland	$29,182,552	$34,114,455
Mercy Corps U.S.	$152,883,475	$135,784,173
Material Aid (In Kind)	$59,334,407	$51,148,521
Total Support & Revenue	$243,954,943	$223,573,931
Expenditures Program		
Proyecto Aldea Global	$2,637,883	$2,090,228
Mercy Corps Scotland	$24,583,110	$30,848,398
Mercy Corps U.S.	$175,436,932	$158,463,970
Total	$202,657,925	$191,402,596
Support Services		
General & Administration	$19,144,523	$16,952,176
Resource Development	$11,227,580	$10,862,768
Total	$30,372,103	$27,814,944
Loss	$1,103,410	$2,701,199
Total Expenditures	$234,133,438	$221,918,739
NET	**$9,821,505**	**$1,655,192**

Source: Mercy Corps. "Financials."

Exhibit 9: Rationale for ALTIS

Absence of Technical Capacities

Wider adoption of commercial agriculture requires increased levels of skill and knowledge among farmers as well other stakeholders such as traders, processors, and transporters. The skill and knowledge of actors in the agriculture value chain is inadequate in the changing context of globalization and the WTO. Institutional capacity is also lacking at the local level to foster commercial agriculture.

Lack of Research and Development

The nature of research and development initiatives is still supply-driven and hence less responsive to the needs of clients. Due priority has not been given to the generation and dissemination of location-specific technological packages suitable for the diverse socio-economic and agro-ecological conditions of Nepal. This has resulted in low adoption rates of improved practices.

Decentralized institutional changes are being made to make the extension system farmer-responsible, farmer-accountable and broad-based. However, private sector involvement in agricultural research and extension activities is currently not receiving much attention.

Lack of Funds and/or Access to Capital

The subsistence nature of much production and low levels of savings have resulted in inadequate funding for farming operations. In addition, high interest rates and difficult access to loans has been a bottleneck in the commercialization of the agricultural sector.

Source: Mercy Corps, "ALTIS Business Plan."

Exhibit 10: Sample Technical Services Provided by ALTIS

- Agricultural cash flows and lending cycles
- Varietal selection
- Cultivation
- Disease management
- Post-harvest handling
- Low-cost storage
- Grading and processing
- Business planning
- Collective marketing

- Farmers' groups organizational practices
- Global Partnership for Good Agricultural Practice (GLOBALGAP) standards
- Hazard Analysis and Critical Control Point (HACCP) food safety practices

Source: "ALTIS Internal Concept Note."

Exhibit 11: Aspects of a Social Business

1. Business objective will be to overcome poverty, or one or more problems (such as education, health, technology access, and environment) which threaten people and society; not profit maximization
2. Financial and economic sustainability
3. Investors get back their investment amount only. No dividend is given beyond investment money
4. When investment amount is paid back, company profit stays with the company for expansion and improvement
5. Environmentally conscious
6. Workforce gets market wage with better working conditions
7. ...do it with joy

Source: Muhammad Yunus, "Aspects of a Social Business." Muhammadyunus.org

Exhibit 12: Disguised ALTIS Financials

The following represents a summary of budget support required during the preparatory, inception, and early expansion phases of ALTIS. This includes four years of operational support for ALTIS, until the point at which the institution will be on sound footing for self-sufficiency and expansion, in addition to Mercy Corps facilitation, support, management, monitoring, evaluation and reporting costs.

The budget provided will lead to the creation of a self-supporting company that will have a net worth of over $6.75 million by its tenth year, with annual loan disbursements of at least $12 million. By its tenth year, this company will provide a conservatively estimated macroeconomic benefit to the Nepali agricultural sector of over $21.9 million per year. This macroeconomic benefit will continue and increase annually thereafter.

Source: "ALTIS Internal Concept Note" (figures altered to maintain confidentiality)

Exhibit 13: Nirdhan Utthan Bank Quarterly Balance Sheet, April 2009

ASSETS	Amount in '000 Rupees
Cash and Bank balance	244,432
Receivables	24,415
Inventories	1,402
Investments	94,738
Net Loans Outstanding	976,554
Total Current Assets	1,341,541
Total Long Term Assets	56,066
Less Expenses to be written off	-5,775
Total Assets	**1,403,382**

LIABILITIES	
Inter-Branch Adjustment Account	-23,095
Client Savings	301,500
Other Current Liabilities	51,569
Total Current Liabilities	329,974
Total long Term Liabilities	894,476
Total Liabilities	1,224,450
EQUITY	
Paid up Equity	100,000
General Reserve	11,851
Institutional Development Fund	30,209
Capital Reserve	15,096
Net Profit (Loss) Previous Year	1,196
Net Profit (Loss) Current Year	20,580
Total Equity	178,932
Total Liabilities & Equity	**1,403,382**

Source: Nirdhan.com

Exhibit 14: Nirdhan Utthan Bank Quarterly Income Statement, April 2009

INCOME FROM INVESTMENTS	Amount in '000 Rupees
Interest from Current and Past Due Loan	122,812
Interest from Investment (Bank Deposit)	6,213
Income from Investment	1,930
Other Income	2,785
Total Financial Income	133,740
Interest on Borrowing	-23,301
Interest on Deposits	-10,818
Gross Financial Margin	99,621
Provision for Loan Losses	-5,334
Net Financial Margin	94,287
INCOME FROM OPERATIONS	
Salaries and Allowances	62,382
Office Operating Expenses	14,136
Training Expenses	1,780
Loss Sale of Assets	49
Depreciation	1,025
Total Operating Expenses	79,372
Net Income From Operations	14,915
Grant Income	5,665
Net Income	**20,580**
(no bonuses or tax)	

Source: Nirdhan.com

Bibliography

Agricultural Development Bank Limited. "Publications." http://adbl.gov.np/

ANZDEC. "Nepal Commercial Agricultural Development Project, Final Report." 2003.

Asia Resource Center for Microfinance. "Nepal Country Profile." Accessed 2010. https://www.microfinancegateway.org/sites/default/files/mfg-en-paper-nepal-microfinance-country-profile-2004.pdf.

Banking With The Poor. "Microfinance Resources." Accessed 2010. http://bwtp.org/microfinance-resources/

Bloomberg. "Nepal Asks Lenders to Expand Branches as Maoist Hostility Ends." https://www.bloomberg.com. Accessed 2010.

Central Intelligence Agency. "Nepal." The World Factbook. Accessed 2010. https://www.cia.gov/library/publications/the-world-factbook/geos/np.html.

Dewald, Josh. Interview with the authors. 2010.

Mercy Corps. "About Us." Accessed 2010. https://www.mercycorps.org/about-us/financials.

Mercy Corps. "ALTIS Business Plan." 2009. Internal company document.

Mercy Corps. "ALTIS Internal Concept Note." Company document. 2009.

Mercy Corps. "Strategic Planning Framework FY 2009." 2009. Internal company document.

National Co-operative Bank Limited. "Financials." Accessed 2010. http://coopbank.com.np.

Nepal Ministry of Finance. "Determinants of Formal Credit Market Participation in Nepal." Nepalese Economic Review, n.d.

Nirdhan Utthan Laghubitta Bittiya Sanstha Limited. "Financials." Accessed 2010. http://nirdhan.com/

The World Bank. "Getting Finance in South Asia 2009." Accessed 2010. https://openknowledge.worldbank.org/handle/10986/6546.

Yunus, Muhammad. "Aspects of a Social Business." Accessed 2010. http://muhammadyunus.org/index.php/social-business/social-business

BURGERVILLE
Instilling a Sustainable Culture

By Sully Taylor, Ph.D., James Begg, Colin Gallison, Will Sandman, and Benjamin Werner

Burgerville Case Study

"We spent a whole day in a room, putting words on walls, on flip charts... Near the end of the day we came up with these three words, Serve With Love. How do we serve each other, how do we serve the community we do business in, how do we serve the greater community?"

— Jack Graves, Chief Cultural Officer, Burgerville

Introduction

In 1996, 35 years after opening the doors of the first Burgerville restaurant, headquarters refocused new product development to emphasize locally sourced, seasonal products. Although strong relationships had always been at the core of the Burgerville's supply chain, this move marked the first major step Burgerville would take along the path of becoming leaders in the Quick Serve Restaurant (QSR) industry when it comes to environmental and social sustainability.

Burgerville has evolved over the years from a single shop to a regional chain, but throughout this time a strong commitment to customers, the community, employees, and suppliers has been maintained. This stems from an understanding that relationships and allies are what will maintain continuous operation during slow economic periods. A belief in corporate responsibility and environmental/social sustainability has been a part of the company from the start, before such terms were widely utilized in business. Beyond their environmental efforts, Burgerville is well known for their generous health insurance benefits, even for employees working only part-time.

A major component of adopting and implementing many of the environmental and social stewardship programs at Burgerville is the continued efforts of Jack Graves, Chief Cultural Officer. Jack has been with Burgerville for many years and considers the company his life's work. Jack would be the first one to tell you that he has learned a lot from his mistakes. Trying new things in business was one of the ways Burgerville had gained so much success and Jack knew that to keep the successes coming, Burgerville would have to continue to be innovative and allow room for failures and setbacks.

While shaking hands and seeing old friends at a recent Burgerville vendor appreciation festival, Jack reflected upon the ways he can help to further improve upon the already high standards of social responsibility Burgerville incorporates into its culture. How could they further demonstrate to all stakeholders that they are committed to the individuals and communities who support the company?

The most difficult part of the equation has been getting the story of a company doing all it can for its stakeholders out to customers. Without the marketing budget of larger competitors, the message must often travel from the level of corporate idea makers to individual store managers, to front-line employees before finally getting to the customers themselves. This is no easy task and getting employees to buy in and get excited about their work and the story they are a part of is a critical part of the solution.

Company Profile: Establishment of a Family-Run Business

The Holland Creamery Company (HCC) was founded in 1922 by Jacob Propstra, a Dutch immigrant, to produce butter and other dairy products for local sale. By 1927, product offering had grown to also include milk and ice cream, which were all distributed through local groceries. In the 1930s the creamery began selling sandwiches and prepared foods directly to customers, an effort spearheaded by Jacob's son, George.

After reducing their operational scope through the sale of their ice cream business in 1958, HCC opened the doors of the first Burgerville restaurant in 1961 (Exhibit 1), with George managing the entire business. That same year, founder Jacob Propstra passed away. Over the next two decades, Burgerville continued to grow at a solid pace, adding drive-thru windows to restaurants, establishing the Burgerville patent in all 50 states and opening 10 new restaurants in the 1970's (Exhibit 2).

Today, Burgerville has 39 locations and is known in the Pacific Northwest for their local sourcing, environmental stewardship, and seasonal menu offerings, like hazelnut milkshakes, Walla Walla Sweet onion rings, and sweet potato fries (Exhibit 3).

The Fast Food Industry

Today's fast food restaurants evolved from drive-in restaurants that became common in the 1940's following WWII. This was due to the rise in popularity and accessibility of cars and the increase in disposable income after the war. Early drive-in restaurants used the same basic setup as pre-existing diners and employed short-order cooks to prepare food.

The leap to modern fast food restaurants came in 1948 when Richard and Maurice McDonald decided to work on improving the speed and efficiency of their McDonald's drive-in restaurant. They wanted to "make food faster, sell it cheaper, and spend less time worrying about replacing cooks and car hops."[30] The key, they found, was to implement new ideas about assembly line production: streamlining processes, cutting the menu, shifting from a few skilled workers to many unskilled workers, breaking down the food production process into separate steps, and focusing on mass production. The McDonald's brothers called their new process the *Speedee Service System*. This method proved so effective that it influenced the emergence of a number of imitators and competitors.

The fast food market can be defined as "the sale of food and drinks for immediate consumption either on the premises or in designated eating areas shared with other foodservice operators, or for consumption elsewhere."[31] The market is broken down further by some into four segments: QSR, Takeaways, Mobile & Street Vendors and Leisure Locations. What is commonly referred to as "fast food" actually falls under the heading of QSR.

---

30   Wilson, "How Fast Food Works."
31   Datamonitor, "Fast Food in the United States."

Today the QSR industry is overwhelmingly dominated by major, national chains and spends a total of over $4 billion annually on advertising. By the end of 2010 total US QSR revenue is projected to top $170 billion.[32]

Sustainable Agriculture and Food

Literally, *sustainability* is simply the quality of being sustainable, to have the ability to be perpetuated over time; enduring. But today, *sustainability* and *sustainable development* typically come with a whole host of connotations and assumed meanings. In March 1987, the Brundtland Commission of the United Nations stated that "sustainable development is development that meets the needs of the present without compromising the ability of future generations to meet their own needs." Over time, sustainability has come to include both environment and social sustainability; the ongoing preservation of both our natural environment and social wellbeing. That said, the area is which ideas of sustainability first gained momentum was agriculture.

As farmers and environmentalists began to understand the devastating effect that industrialized farming practices of the late 20th century were having on the environment, they began to explore better practices in order to sustain the continued success of the farming industry. Through this exploration of better practices, the idea of "sustainable agriculture" emerged as the catalyst that is currently driving the broader sustainability movement. "Sustainable agriculture is a method that produces abundant food without depleting the earth's resources or polluting its environment. It is agriculture that follows the principles of nature to develop systems for raising crops and livestock that are, like nature, self-sustaining."[33] While farmers' self-interest was the original driver behind the idea of sustainable agriculture, the practice garnered attention and support within local communities as well.

The popularity of purchasing and consuming sustainable and earth-friendly foods, that had limited exposure to pesticides, began to grow with consumers throughout the United States. Individual consumers also began to associate better tasting, healthy foods, with being locally and/or organically grown. In fact, consumer surveys on local shopping have shown that as many as one in six adults buy local products as often as possible and are willing to pay a higher price, with as much as 30% percent of respondents stating that they

---

32 RNCOS, "US Fast Food Market Outlook."
33 ATTRA, "Sustainable Agriculture."

would purchase local foods if they knew where to find them. As a result of this growing interest in local, sustainable food sources, independent food certification organizations such as the Food Alliance began to emerge throughout the US in the 1990s. This trend was particularly pronounced in the Pacific Northwest where there was a strong history of environmental consciousness.

Many consumers have come to believe that eating healthily, while also taking a stand on environmental and social issues, are worth the added cost. Additionally, purchasing locally grown and sourced foods is beneficial to local economies and communities. This trend is clearly demonstrated through the dramatic increase in famers markets throughout the Northwest region in the past twenty years. "The meteoric growth of farmers' markets in Oregon offers more evidence of the public's interest in local foods. In 1988, there were just 10 farmers' markets around the state. Now, there are more than 90.[34] Going to a farmers' market has become just as much a social event as a food buying experience. There has been a hunger by consumers to reach out to where the food is coming from and connect a face to the source," says Oregon Dept. of Agriculture trade manager Laura Barton. "This has led to more trust in the local grower. At the same time, traditional retailers have taken notice."[35]

"Sustainable" Leadership

Given the growing importance of sustainability in the minds of consumers, firms have been working towards the incorporation of such practices into an array of business activity. The process of transitioning a company towards a more sustainable way of doing business can be very difficult and often requires a shift in thinking. Across all industries, the majority of firms have employed one of two strategies for achieving such a change: 1) Broad transformation across many business units and functions, or 2) Giving a small number of people the role of identifying and executing specific projects and to be the driving force of change.

While the first method of directly instilling the philosophy evenly throughout an organization is sometimes used, the vast majority of organizations have taken the second path and assigned such responsibilities to specific individuals within the company. Historically, this tactic began with lower level employees taking on these responsibilities, for example those involved in system

---

34   Oregon Farmers' Markets Association, "Oregon Farmers' Markets Directory."
35   Pokarney, "Local Foods Find a Bigger Stage."

design or supply chain implementation. However, as the emphasis on sustainability has grown in many companies, the importance of such responsibility has followed suit.

Over time, VP's, executives, or sometimes even entire departments, have been tasked with spearheading sustainability efforts, clearly demonstrating its rise in importance. Many organizations have even taken it to the point of creating positions such as Chief Sustainability Officer (CSO). In some organizations, however, a new trend has begun to take place in recent years. As firms with a developed track record of sustainable practices have begun to feel comfortable with the level of awareness and financial savings that has been achieved, some have decided that there may no longer be a need for such dedicated positions, and are therefore eliminating them or combining them with areas such as compliance (legal) or marketing.

Burgerville Today: Commitment to a Socially Responsible Model

In 1982, George Propstra's son-in-law, Tom Mears was named president of The Holland Inc., furthering the tradition of a family run business; George retired fully in 1992. In the early 1990s, Burgerville was struggling to compete with national chains on price, and decided to try some new tactics in hopes of differentiating themselves.

After going through many physical changes, including remodeling existing stores, Burgerville began to focus on several strategic changes in the mid-nineties. By aiming product development at local and seasonally sourced foods throughout the region the company began to tap into the growing trend towards such products while at the same time becoming a leader in the quick service realm. This change in product sourcing marked the first significant step Burgerville made in what has become their unique and definitive commitment to local farmers, ranchers, and communities alike. A little more than a decade later, Burgerville had cemented their reputation as the place to go for a fast meal constrained local ingredients, a higher quality alternative to more traditional "fast food." Burgerville is also a member and contributor to the Food Alliance, (Exhibit 4) and has contracted with Country Natural Beef to supply all of their beef, a very important input for a hamburger chain, in a socially and environmentally sustainable manner.

Renewable energy has also played a significant part in powering the

Burgerville restaurants. In 2005, local energy giant Portland General Electric approached Burgerville with a proposal: they suggested that the local fast-food chain re-enforce its sustainability ethos with a commitment to make 20% of the energy it consumed wind generated. What Burgerville did next was unprecedented for any fast food chain – the company committed to 100% usage of wind power and wind power credits in all of its restaurants and corporate headquarters and followed through within the year. Furthermore, Burgerville's renewable, 'clean' wind power is supplied by companies within the region that are environmentally sensitive to their locales.[36] By doing this, Burgerville not only invested in local operations and a forward looking energy source that is environmentally friendly, but also encouraged other area businesses to follow in their footsteps and commit to clean energy use. As a further demonstration of their commitment to the environment, Burgerville implemented a Bio-diesel program through which all of their cooking oil is recycled and reused to power bio-diesel run vehicles.

At the same time, Burgerville has committed itself to its employees and communities by introducing a new set of benefits, which would provide affordable healthcare to any employee working more than 20 hours per week. The company's transparency has also been highly recognized and acknowledged throughout local and national media outlets. In order to educate their customers on exactly what they are eating, each receipt that customers receive from their meal is a condensed version of a nutrition label, containing the nutritional information for the specific meal they are about to eat. It also gives suggestions on what they could have done differently to make a more nutritious choice, say, opting for grilled chicken instead of fried.

Burgerville has also adopted one of the most comprehensive recycling and composting programs of any member of the QSR industry. Recycling and composting stations are located in the majority of restaurant dining rooms in order to allow customers to be a part of the process themselves. Further, nearly all packaging materials utilized by Burgerville come from 100% renewable materials assuring that all waste can be recycled or composted through the program they have put in place.

Leadership Evolution at Burgerville

Having married into the Propstra family, Tom joined The Holland's management program in 1966 and managed the first Burgerville in Vancouver, WA.

---

36   Burgerville, "The Business Case."

He stayed committed to the company, making his way up the corporate ranks until he became President and CEO in 1982. He continued to be a main driving force at Burgerville for the next 20+ years.

In 2004, for the first time in the company's history, the decision was made to relinquish control of Burgerville to someone outside of the family and Jeff Harvey was brought on as CEO. Coming from a career in the energy sector, Jeff was perhaps not the most obvious choice for the job. He and Tom Mears had been friends for years, however, and Tom decided that knowing Jeff's values aligned with Burgerville was more important than knowing his professional experience did.

As a result of Tom's selection of CEO there has been the ethical and social values that have been deeply instilled throughout the organization, little change in philosophy has taken. Today, Burgerville remains a leader when it comes to practicing what they preach and promoting social and environmental stewardship through their continued investment in programs such as composting, biodegradable packaging, local sourcing, and affordable healthcare.

Chief Cultural Officer, Jack Graves, is a stalwart of the company, having been with Burgerville for 34 years. He started as the Manager of Burgerville's Centralia restaurant, and served as Vice-President before assuming his current position in 2004. His job title is somewhat unusual, but it represents Burgerville's commitment to a strong company culture, and the maintenance of the core principles upon which the company was founded.

Chief Operations Officer, Janice Williams, also bring years of Burgerville experience to bear. Having started out as an assistance manger she steadily worked her way up, along the way spending time involved with new manager training, in charge of field operations, as a restaurant general manger, as Chief Talent Officer, and recently has had a great deal to do with the development of the company's ongoing management curriculum and training programs.

Chief Financial Officer Kyle Dean is responsible for managing the Burgerville's financial data, financial planning, and record-keeping, as well as financial reporting to upper management. Dean also develops innovative ways to partner with the company's suppliers, economic development entities and the banking community. He also works on internal initiatives that will help people quantify their results and contributions to Burgerville's financial structure.

Alison Dennis was first employed by Burgerville in 2006 in a supply chain management role, where she was responsible for the entire supply chain, sourcing ingredients, and building relationships with local vendors, moving those supplies to restaurants, and managing the company's composting and recycling programs. Alison was then made the Director of Sustainable Programs where she facilitated a range of sustainability initiatives including recycling, composting, and smarter packaging, and helped to put Burgerville on the map as groundbreaker of sustainability in the industry.

The formation of this dynamic leadership team, coupled with a strong emphasis on the environment and community involvement, has helped Burgerville to instill a unique culture throughout the company. Working together as well as with others in the executive team, these thought leaders have left an imprint on everything from the training procedures and basic workforce policies, to restaurant design and marketing efforts. This close working relationship, along with the complete backing of Mears, has allowed for Harvey, Dennis and Graves to establish a clear vision for Burgerville today, and for what needs to be done in order to accomplish their goals for the future.

This vision has been so well developed and internalized that top executives felt that there was no longer a need for the position of Director of Sustainable Programs and in the summer of 2010 let Alison Dennis go after four years in the role. As has occurred in other companies, once the end goal of instilling sustainability values throughout the company was seen as having been accomplished, the position was perceived as redundant. This is testament to Alison's accomplishments at Burgerville; at the time of her leaving, the company was far and away an industry leader in the sustainability realm.

Employees

Burgerville relies heavily on front-line employees to convey their sustainability message and put the company's best foot forward. This emphasis, combined with Burgerville's history of being an active member of the communities in which they are located, have led the company towards a highly relationship-based service model. This applies to not only the way that employees are encouraged to interact with customers, but also the way that Burgerville management tries to interact with employees.

It is a common belief within the Burgerville organization that one of the company's greatest assets is its people. Within a company that takes such pride in conveying its core beliefs in sustainability and community, the most effective way that it can do this, and set itself apart from the pack, is through the employee who serves the customer their bean burger and sweet potato fries. Jack takes great pride in his employees, who he feels are proud and knowledgeable of the company's place within the community and the products that they serve to the customers. "Not long ago, we brought the Country Natural Beef ranchers (Burgerville suppliers) in to all of the restaurants to talk to the employees, who learned a lot and really enjoyed it. The next thing I hear an employee describing the natural process of raising our beef to some customers at the counter. This makes me very proud; employees are one of the best marketing tools we have." Burgerville's training and treatment of employees sets the benchmark for the QSR industry, which has a less than stellar record of such practices. This is testament to the attitude of Burgerville management over the past half century and the value that is placed on employees.

Hiring

In an industry in which turnover and training represent significant operational costs, it is imperative for Burgerville to retain employees and have effective training practices. In a typical employee selection process at Burgerville, a candidate is interviewed by two managers separately. Throughout the interview process, the managers will try to assess the degree to which a potential employee will fit the values that the organization represents. Values taken into account may be the candidate's level of community spirit and giving, but other values are intangible, according to Chris Wegner, manager of Burgerville's Carmen Drive restaurant, "when I'm talking to them, it can be just a feeling I get about who they are as a person."

Within its hiring and training process, Burgerville uses what they call 'The BV (Burgerville) Way'. Less than a formal program, the BV Way encompasses the process of hiring and training employees and ultimately is an effort to align individual values with that of the company mission: to *Serve With Love*. It encourages employees to become genuine ambassadors of Burgerville practices and ideals to the customers and the community.

Burgerville typically has turnover of approximately 400 employees each year, with about half of these being summer workers. This works out to an average of 10 employees per restaurant per year. The hardest age demographic to retain are 18–22 year old students (Exhibit 5). Although many employees do not stay long-term, Burgerville does not feel that time and resources spent training are wasted. Management believes that values instilled at Burgerville can not only enhance the integrity of their company, but can potentially carry the message to other companies as employees move on, as well as into the community where Burgerville will continue to develop a positive relationship.

"Whether you're here for 3 months in the summer or 30 years, you'll leave with some level of understanding and competency around responsible community leadership and take that into wherever you go." — Beth Brewer

Training

In-Store

When a new employee is hired at Burgerville, they receive as 72-page training document and undergo a three and a half hour orientation session. The session is made up of standard fast-food restaurant training: HR practices, health and safety protocols, and restaurant procedures. However, Burgerville adds something more. Within this session, a significant amount of time is spent outlining Burgerville's community and sustainability values, in order for employees to gain a better understanding of the organization's philosophy. Not only is this a large part of the orientation, but as Chris explained, "There are frequently opportunities during regular work shifts to educate and train further around sustainability and our values." It is not uncommon for senior staff to impart their knowledge of Burgerville's unique outlook with their newer colleagues.

One effort to transfer enthusiasm for sustainability efforts to hourly workers involves facilitating direct interactions between suppliers and front-line workers. Employees take "field trips" out to farms where produce is grown to meet the farmers and gain a genuine understanding of relationship between food production and restaurant sales. Likewise, when the ranchers from Country Natural Beef are in town they make an effort to visit restaurant locations and meet the men and woman behind the counter selling their beef as hamburgers.

Burgerville employees start their responsibilities either on the "counter", at the "drive thru" or on the "grill". Obviously, the "counter" and the "drive-thru" are the positions that have the most customer interaction, but employees need to possess a cross section of skills for each position if they wish to move up to the next level, which is a Trainer. As the name suggests, a Trainer is available to help train new employees. Following this position are two key positions; "regular key" and "senior key". There is also a "team manager" that is also paid hourly and the Team Manager is usually a 2-year training program. The 2-year training program is set up to help the "team manager" move into a "store manager" position. The training program can take longer if the Team Manager is happy in that position, and wants to extend the training. Regardless of the position, anything above a trainer position is someone responsible for talking to other Burgerville employees about the stories and concepts they can convey to the customers.

To help the employees convey the concepts to the customers, Burgerville also has suppliers visit the stores. On an annual occasion, the suppliers of beef, Country Natural Beef Co., bring their ranchers to Portland for an appreciation festival. The week before the festival, The Country Natural Beef employees spread out across stores in the Portland area and spend several hours talking with the employees. This gives the Burgerville employees the opportunity to ask questions about the beef, where is comes from and how it gets from the ranch to the store. It is more information for the employees to use to talk to customers about the product and Burgerville's commitment to the community.

Corporate

Burgerville also provides ongoing corporate training and executive coaching through outside consultants. At Burgerville's *Center for Responsible Community Leadership*, courses are taught to not only enable more effective management, but also foster an environment of ongoing betterment. Beth Brewer, Dean of Curriculum, has been the major driving force behind the creation of such courses. As Beth puts it, "there is a strategic focus around development of our people."

The Center was opened in response to internal discussions around how Burgerville could best enable employees to become leaders that would impact the community as well as the company. Currently there are three areas of professional development offered: Operational Excellence (Management Fundamentals), Mission School, and Personal Leadership Development.

Operational Excellence looks at how individuals work together most effectively, how to set and achieve goals, the promotion of best practices, and the promotion of "seamless teams," or the idea of building strong teams within each restaurant. One course what falls under this heading is Management Fundamentals, which deals with many of these issues.

In 2009, the company began an initiative called **Mission School** that is a forum in which leaders of the company come together to explore what being a mission-led company entails, work through challenges as a group, and develop personal leadership abilities within the context of *Serve With Love*. Assistant managers and above are encouraged to participate in Mission School.

Personal Leadership Development is somewhat similar to Mission School, however, it is more about individual learning and development and less about the specifics of one's role at Burgerville. The skills acquired during leadership development training are truly meant to enhance general skills applicable in any company.

At the corporate level, Burgerville promotes a "self managed owner-operator" philosophy, especially for restaurant GMs (Exhibit 6). This means that supporting and coaching store managers to be autonomous problem solvers taking an increased responsibility for store operations is heavily emphasized.

In the end, one of the main goals of leadership development at Burgerville is to create responsible community leaders, according to Jack, "leaders that are flexible and resilient and can continue to lead, and do continue to lead, in the face of change."

Pay/Benefits

Hourly employees in the QSR industry are typically paid minimum wage, and this is true for Burgerville's lowest level employees. Compared to other states, however, Oregon and Washington have the highest minimum wage requirements in the country at $8.50 and $8.55, respectively.[37] On top of this, both full and part time employees at Burgerville receive health insurance, which costs the company roughly $3.50/hour per employee.

In the QSR industry, the existence of a company insurance plan does not typically provide coverage to all employees of an organization. Additionally, many employees who are covered by insurance plans cannot realistically afford the high premiums and co-pays that are associated with them. In 2008, hourly employees received an average of 49% coverage, with only about 54% of employees receiving health benefits at all.[38]

Burgerville's decision in 2005 to provide *affordable* healthcare coverage to all employees working over 20 hours a week for at least 6 months was truly unique within the QSR industry: for $20/month individuals receive full medical, dental and vision coverage with no deductible, a worker and spouse pay $30 monthly, and family plans cost just $90. Health benefits are frequently cited as by far the most appreciated benefit available to employees. As one employee stated, "I'm treated differently because I have an insurance card."

Aside from the philosophy of simply doing the right thing by its people, Burgerville management believes there is also a business case for making sure that employees can receive proper medical care. The national average turnover rate for hourly fast-food workers was around 150% in 2005, according to Jack Graves,x Burgerville's turnover at 128%. After the Dec 2005 introduction of affordable health insurance turnover at Burgerville fell to 54% in 2006. Also, because of the accessibility to healthcare for Burgerville employees, less sick days are taken, and productivity and morale are higher within the restaurants, which lead to happier employees and better customer service.

For Burgerville management, this represents significant cost savings, not to mention the increase in quality services delivered by employees who also

---

37   Burgerville, "People Report."
38   Herrington, "Burgerville (Vancouver)."

remain part of the Burgerville family longer, getting better at their jobs and learning more about Burgerville policies and ideals.

Marketing

Considering Burgerville's position as an industry leader in the fields of sustainability, local sourcing, and community outreach, the company uses its core competencies to create its brand identity, as well as relating that sustainable message to the taste of its food. "The fresher the produce, the better the food will taste, is definitely a message we are working on," says Michele Mather of Burgerville's marketing department. "We are extremely proud of our commitment to sustainability but, in the end, our main product is our food, and we want to let people know how good it is."

Burgerville's record of sustainability and local sourcing dates back to the first day that it opened its doors, and it is something that Burgerville is known for by its consumers in the Northern Oregon/Southern Washington locale. In the marketing mix are the usual outlets of local TV ad campaigns and local radio segments, as well as the loyalty program, The Burgerville Card is designed to entice patrons to spend money in exchange for points ($1 equals one point), and can also be used as a gift card. Burgerville is one of the nation's first QSR chains to offer such a program, which is usually a marketing tool for such industries as retail and airlines. Burgerville.com is a very user-friendly website which highlights its food, restaurants, people, jobs, and the many benefits of eating local and being sustainable. Additionally, Burgerville is active in the social media arena on Twitter and Facebook. Burgerville also participates in voucher programs, such as the 'Chinook Book', a book full of vouchers of local 'green' businesses that encourages buying local and helps to raise money for local charities and schools.

Perhaps the most visible and far-reaching weapon in Burgerville's marketing and outreach artillery is the Nomad, a mobile restaurant. As it describes on the website, "Burgerville favorites like burgers, fries and seasonal milkshakes – the same as you'd enjoy at any of our 39 restaurants – made fresh at special events and popular locations all around our community. Nomad packs up Burgerville's commitment to quality and caring, and takes it on the road, bringing it direct to you." The Nomad has made Burgerville mobile and it has featured at such popular Oregon events as The Bite of Oregon and the Pendleton Roundup. In a marketing coup for the company, it will be the major sponsors of the Portland Timbers soccer team for its entry into Major

League Soccer (MLS), and the Nomad will be a feature at all of the Timbers' home games at PGE Park in downtown Portland. From a marketing perspective, the Nomad focuses more on the selling of food and exposing more customers to its products, as opposed to spreading the work of sustainability and local sourcing.

Storytelling

Burgerville encourages employees to make a connection with customers and teach them about Burgerville's sustainable practices through *storytelling* (Exhibit 7). Storytelling means engaging with customers to transfer enthusiasm concerning sustainable practices. The elements of storytelling at Burgerville revolve around 1) Where to interact with customers (Environments & Opportunity), 2) How to have the conversation (Development & Training), and 3) Burgerville programs designed to help kick-start the process (Tools & Collateral).

Burgerville's Storytelling is perhaps most visible to its customers in the posters that are displayed in all of its restaurants. These are an example of how Burgerville uses their people and their sustainable message to reach out to the consumer. As shown in the Exhibit 8, these posters feature 'a local hero' who is helping Burgerville in their efforts to be more environmentally and socially responsible. These posters relay to customers Burgerville's local commitment and sustainability focus, and relate this to the high quality and taste of the food.

Storytelling is an integral part of Burgerville spreading its message of sustainability, as it humanizes the message, making it feel more local and less corporate. Storytelling creates an interaction between company and customer, and is consistent with Burgerville's local image. Although it can appear as a very natural interaction, it is believed by management to be a highly effective method of marketing the company's sustainability practices.

Customers

With a focus on fast, convenient meals at a low price, QSRs attract a younger, lower-middle income consumer, as well as a substantial family demographic. The taste and quality of the food is also important, which has also lead consumers to care more about where it comes from. Recent trends indicate a strong correlation between organically grown, locally sourced food and superior taste. This trend coupled with publications such as *Fast Food Nation*, which brought into question the sourcing and practices of fast food companies, has meant that the average consumer is taking an increased interest in the practices of the fast food companies.

Consumer perception of fast food is no longer confined to quick-service, drive-thru restaurants and convenience stores. Instead, a dual concept has emerged, consisting of traditional fast food, and of 'food fast,' which is served quickly with a greater emphasis on flavor, quality, and ambiance. Forty-one percent of consumers are reporting that their idea of places offering "fast food" has expanded recently to include fast-casual restaurants such as Panera Bread and full-service restaurants offering carryout and curbside service such as Chili's.[39]

Although Burgerville does not explicitly define its target market, it views its average customer as being slightly older and slightly more educated than the average fast food customer. They define their typical customer as an individual who lives in the Pacific Northwest, cares about sustainability, and is 30–50 years of age. While Burgerville still aims to attract families as a significant portion of their market, youths still make up a significant portion of their clientele. However, in Burgerville's case, the age demographic is skewed towards a slightly older customer. 'Young', in Burgerville's eyes is seen as customers in their twenties and thirties, whereas most other fast food marketing demographics view 'young' customers as teenagers. As with most restaurants, Burgerville relies on a high rate of repeat customers, making it especially important to have a wide-reaching message of sustainability and quality in order to gain first-time customers who will return.

Burgerville Suppliers

Burgerville has four main suppliers: Sysco, Fulton, Franz, and Sunshine Dairy. In 2008–2009, Burgerville purchased about 32.5% of their products, locally sourced from Fulton, 22.9% from Sysco, 10.7% from Sunshine Dairy and 7.7% from Franz Bakery. The rest, 25.7% of the products, were bought from non-local sources. This is a key example of Burgerville's commitment to the community; buying locally keeps the money in the community and supports the very people responsible for Burgerville's profitability. Beef, fish, baked goods and potatoes make up the majority of the locally sourced products.

Burgerville is committed to maintaining strong relationships with their suppliers. Annually, ranchers from Country Natural Beef visit Portland for

---

39   Worldwatch Institute.

a night of fun, dancing and storytelling. Not only is this an opportunity for the ranchers to gather in a social setting, but it also allows them to visit the stores to see where and how their products are served. In addition, they get to meet and give the employees more of an insight into Country Natural Beef, and share information about how they raise the cattle. These kinds of events, along with open channels of communications, help the Burgerville team to maintain a strong relationship with the suppliers. Jack Graves tells a story of a supplier driving 500 miles out of his way to go around a flooded area to deliver some much-needed supplies to the Burgerville restaurant in Centralia, Washington. It is that kind commitment to the company, and to the suppliers, which makes Burgerville special when it comes to sourcing its supplies. It is also central to the company's growth and success, which has taken place over the last 50 years.

Competitor Sustainability Efforts

While sustainability is certainly on the radar of all the major players in the QSR industry, the fact remains that, for most, this is simply an attempt to deflect negative PR when it comes to maintaining best practices. For the majority of QSR companies, especially for those that are larger and publicly held, marketing sustainable practices has been about protecting themselves from watchdog groups that often expose bad corporate practices when it comes to environmental and social issues.

Over the years, Burgerville's competition has increased, diversified, and morphed into a variety of different restaurants. Burgerville's main competitors are McDonald's, Burger King, Wendy's and several others. The company maintains a close watch on what others in the QSR industry are doing, whether it is the creation of new products, pricing levels, or the updating of menu items. They also examine companies in other industries to see how developments in other contexts might provide new insights into successful outcomes.

There is not a definitive sustainability strategy in the QSR industry that has been proven truly successful. Many companies and executive teams tend to feel their way through the issues, looking for guidance wherever they can to determine and define what metrics to measure and to define success. In some cases, it might not be financially viable to invest in a particular area if the benefit is not a significant cost decrease or marked increase in sales. Significant resources are being poured into this area in an attempt to stay current, follow consumer preference trends, and gain a competitive advantage.

Moving Forward

Jack knew that suppliers and employees appreciated Burgerville; it was evident in the long-term relationships that existed with people in both groups. But was that enough to remain competitive and continue to content with national QSR players? He wondered to himself if the diner image the organization decided upon in the mid-nineties properly conveyed Bergerville's goal of trying new things and being committed to social and environmental sustainability. How can the organization better equip their frontline employees to be outstanding storytellers of Bargersville's commitments and culture? Do customers value this commitment and if so, to what extent does it drive return customers? Do Burgerville employees believe in the mission and culture of the organization? How do we attract top of the line employees that do care? How can Burgerville leverage its commitment to sustainability in order to increase revenues while also helping local communities? How can they measure such things?

Exhibits

Exhibit 1: Original Locations

Exhibit 2: Map of Burgerville Locations

Exhibit 3: Burgerville Menu Sample

100% Country Natural Beef

Pepper Bacon Cheeseburger — 5.69
1/4 lb. Country Natural Beef patty, Niman Ranch pepper bacon, Tillamook Cheddar cheese, mayonnaise, onion, pickles, tomato & lettuce on a sesame seed bun.

Half-Pound Colossal Cheeseburger — 6.29
Two 1/4 lb. Country Natural Beef patties, American cheese, Burgerville Spread, ketchup, pickles, tomato & lettuce on a sesame seed bun.

Tillamook Cheeseburger — 3.99
1/4 lb. Country Natural Beef patty, Tillamook Cheddar cheese, mayonnaise, ketchup, pickles, tomato & lettuce on a sesame seed bun.

Colossal Cheeseburger — 3.99
1/4 lb. Country Natural Beef patty, American cheese, Burgerville Spread, ketchup, pickles, tomato & lettuce on a sesame seed bun.

Double Beef Cheeseburger — 2.99
Two small Country Natural Beef patties, American cheese, Burgerville Spread & ketchup on a plain bun.

Original Cheeseburger — 1.69
Small Country Natural Beef patty, American cheese, Burgerville Spread & ketchup on a plain bun.

Original Hamburger — 1.49
Small Country Natural Beef patty, Burgerville Spread & ketchup on a plain bun.

Original Cheeseburger Meal 4.99	INCLUDES REGULAR SIZE FRENCH FRIES & SOFT DRINK	
Original Hamburger Meal 4.79		

Vegetarian

Spicy Anasazi Bean Burger — 5.49
Spicy Anasazi bean patty, Tillamook pepper jack cheese, chipotle mayonnaise, tomato & lettuce on a sesame seed bun.

Yukon & White Bean Basil Burger — 5.19
Yukon & white bean patty, basil aioli, tomato & lettuce on a toasted wheat Kaiser bun.

Make any sandwich a basket

Basket — 3.60
Baskets include regular fries and regular soft drink.

Upgrade fries to a side salad — Add .50

Upgrade soft drink to a regular milkshake or smoothie
Chocolate, vanilla or strawberry — Add 1.40
Specialty or seasonal — Add 2.30

Chicken

Chicken Tenders — 3 pieces **4.29** 4-pieces **5.29**
Golden fried antibiotic-free white meat chicken tenders with your choice of dipping sauce.
Choice of dipping sauce: Burgerville Spread, Country Ranch, Honey Mustard, Blue Cheese with Rogue Creamery Smokey Blue, Smoky BBQ Sauce, Sweet & Sour, Tartar Sauce, Chipotle Mayo, Garlic Aioli.

Rosemary Chicken Sandwich — 5.39
A tender grilled antibiotic-free chicken breast, rosemary aioli & lettuce on a toasted hoagie bun.

Deluxe Crispy Chicken Sandwich — 5.29
Golden fried antibiotic-free chicken breast, Tillamook Cheddar cheese, Niman Ranch pepper bacon, BBQ sauce, tomato, lettuce & Burgerville Spread on a wheat Kaiser bun.

Crispy Chicken Sandwich — 4.29
Golden fried antibiotic-free chicken breast, BBQ sauce, tomato, lettuce & Burgerville Spread on a wheat Kaiser bun.

Turkey

Turkey Club Sandwich — 4.69
Sliced Diestel turkey with nitrite-free bacon, Tillamook Swiss cheese, tomato, lettuce & mayonnaise on a wheat Kaiser bun.

Seasoned Turkey Burger — 4.99
Free-range Diestel ground turkey with mayonnaise, ketchup, pickles, tomato & lettuce on a sesame seed bun.

Wild Alaskan Halibut

Fish & Chips — 3 pieces **9.99** 4-pieces **12.99**
Golden fried halibut pieces served with tartar sauce, fries & lemon wedge.

Fillet Sandwich — 4.99
Golden fried halibut fillet with tartar sauce & lettuce on a plain bun.

Farm Fresh Salads

Choice of dressing: Country Ranch, Blue Cheese with Rogue Creamery Smokey Blue, Honey Mustard, Balsamic Vinaigrette, Raspberry Vinaigrette.

Grilled Chicken Club
Mixed greens, antibiotic-free grilled chicken breast, Tillamook aged white Cheddar cheese, crumbled pepper bacon, red onions & grape tomatoes.
Full **6.99** Half **4.19**

Rogue River Smokey Blue
Mixed greens, dried Oregon cranberries, Rogue Creamery Smokey Blue cheese crumbles, apples & grape tomatoes.
Full **7.49** Half **4.49**

Wild Smoked Salmon & Hazelnut
Mixed greens, sustainably-caught smoked salmon, Oregon roasted hazelnuts, Tillamook aged white Cheddar cheese, red onions & grape tomatoes.
Full **7.49** Half **4.49**

Sides

	Small	Regular	Large
French Fries	1.45	1.95	2.35
Side Salad			2.45

Mixed greens, Tillamook aged white Cheddar cheese, red onions & grape tomatoes.

Burgerville's Signature Dipping Sauce — .40
Country Ranch, Honey Mustard, Blue Cheese with Rogue Creamery Smokey Blue, Smoky BBQ Sauce, Sweet & Sour, Tartar Sauce, Chipotle Mayo, Garlic Aioli, Burgerville Spread is complementary.

Bacon Nitrite-free plain or pepper (1 strip)	1.00
Tillamook Cheese Swiss, Cheddar or pepper jack (1 slice)	.60
Blue Cheese Crumbles Rogue Creamery Smokey Blue	2.00

Drinks

	Regular	Large
Soft Drinks (Coca-Cola products)	1.95	2.35
Fresh-Brewed Iced Tea	1.95	2.35
Lemonade	1.95	2.35
Portland Roasting Coffee	1.45	1.75
Ghirardelli Hot Chocolate	2.75	
Orange Juice	1.95	
Bottled Water	1.65	
1% Milk or Fat Free Chocolate Milk	1.45	

Desserts
Your choice of local Sunshine Dairy ice cream or YoCream nonfat frozen yogurt.

Sundaes Your choice of topping with whipped cream	1.95
Vanilla Ice Cream Cone	1.45
Cookies Chocolate Chunk, Oatmeal Raisin, Lemon, White Chocolate Cherry	.89

Milkshakes & Smoothies
Choose a milkshake made with local Sunshine Dairy ice cream or a smoothie made with YoCream nonfat frozen yogurt.

	Small	Regular	Large
Chocolate, Vanilla or Strawberry	2.95	3.35	4.35
Specialty or Seasonal	3.65	4.25	5.25

Specialty milkshakes are topped with real whipped cream.

Northwest Cherry Chocolate
Northwest cherries, Ghirardelli chocolate.

Mocha Perk
Cold-brewed Portland Roasting coffee, Ghirardelli chocolate.

Triple Berry Blast
Three berries (marionberry, raspberry and blueberry).

Strawberry Splash
Strawberries, fresh bananas and orange juice.

Chocolate Monkey
Ghirardelli chocolate, fresh bananas and apple juice.

Ask us about our seasonal milkshake and smoothie flavor.

Exhibit 4: Food Alliance Certification

Exhibit 5: Employee Demographics

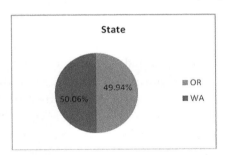

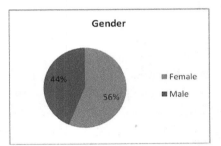

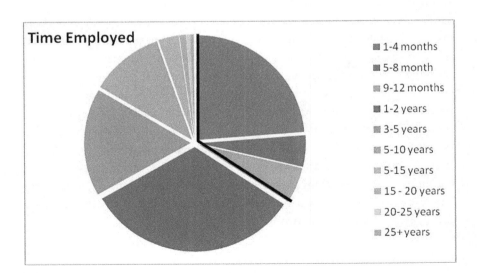

Exhibit 6: Burgerville Managers

MATT WRIGHT

Matt is a 9-year veteran of Burgerville, and is currently the manager of the Burgerville #41 located on Powell Ave. and 92nd Ave. He first came to Burgerville as a counter employee and fondly tells the story about his first day, when he was given many responsibilities after two other employees called in sick. He has worked in five different restaurants, the corporate office on the "Lean Green Team," was a team manager for three and a half years, and has been at the Powell Ave. and 92nd Ave location for two years. The "Lean Green Team" was a project to measure efficiencies in Burgerville's operations. Matt strongly believes in Burgerville's initiatives and takes pride in the company values.

PAUL RIDLON

Paul is the manager of Burgerville #42, which has traditionally ranked 6th or 7th companywide in sales. His experience in the industry is vast. He has worked throughout the East coast and South for 25 years, with Fudruckers, Longhorn Steakhouse and Macaroni Grill. He has opened, managed as well as partially owned and operated a variety of fast food and sit down restaurants. He also spent several years on the Burgerville development team working assessing potential store locations.

Paul has been at his current location for only a few months, but has been given the responsibility to implement the core values of the company in hopes that the store can get to a higher level of service and performance. His main objective is to find things that the employee is interested in, so that they can smoothly transition into a part of the restaurant's team, while educating the employee at the same time. According to Paul, approximately 10–15% of the employee's training time is used to teach them more about sustainability. A notice board in the employee break room is also updated weekly with new facts and ideas concerning sustainability in order to enhance the education process, and continue to provide employees with the data to educate customers. Most of the employees in his store have a high school education, while five or six have some college education, but only two have college degrees.

CHRIS WEGNER

Chris comes from a full-service restaurant background and manages Burgerville #40 at the Carman Drive location in Lake Oswego — Burgerville's busiest location. Chris entered the restaurant business in 1984 under the tutelage of a local restaurant owner named George. Chris spent 10 years learning from George how to prepare almost anything from scratch, how to be creative in menu innovation, and that people are the most important thing in life. In 1990 Chris started work with Shari's restaurants as a line cook, and in 1992 moved into a management position. In 2002 Chris was given the opportunity to work at Burgerville. His thoughts on joining and working for the company are shared below:

"My decision to engage the offer was based upon the company's mission and its track record of delivering the mission. I have absolutely no regrets. This has been one of the best decisions I have made in my life for 2 reasons: The first is that Burgerville inspires hope. I know we do not deliver 100% of the time but I know 1500 people are trying to. The second is that Burgerville delivers forgiveness. No, we are not able deliver 100% of the time, but our owner and our leadership team support and encourage every individual in our company to be a contributor in each and every moment and keep moving forward even when things don't work out… I am most thankful for the investment the company has made and continues to make in me.

"At (my restaurant), Carmen Drive, I am most proud of a few things. I am proud that our community loves us, gives us consistent feedback on how to do better, and is willing to partner with us to build new relationships. I am proud that my team was the first to break through a sales goal and continue to grow. I am proud that my team takes on any challenge with creativity and energy. I am proud that we have an incredible hospitality team that reaches out and is driven by not just the management but the crew as well."

Exhibit 7: Elements and Steps of Storytelling (from Burgerville training material)

Elements of Storytelling

Environments & Opportunity

- Lobby
- Counter
- Dining Room
- Drive Thru
- In the community
- NOMAD

Development & Training

- Serve with Love: Our Missions Competencies
- Guest Service Expert Certification (Level 1)
- Storytelling Basics (Level 2)

Storytelling Tools & Collateral
- Thankful Campaign
- Our ingredients
- Storytelling Resource Guide
- Drive Thru stake signs
- Restaurant signage
- Tell Us About Us feedback

Steps of Storytelling
- The guest asks question
- Respond with the facts
- Share your experience or what is important about that for you
- Listen to the guest's response! This may lead you to sharing even more of our story

Exhibit 8: Burgerville Posters

Exhibit 8: Burgerville Posters, cont.

Exhibit 9: Sample Receipt

Bibliography

ATTRA. "Sustainable Agriculture: An Introduction." 2010. https://extensiononline.ucdavis. edu/files/1967/download?download_frd=1&verifier=Dd4sxyXM9Yy3YtIdSgNyCZfq1d-2CwWKpGHFtbXSp.

Burgerville. "The Business Case." Accessed 2010. http://burgerville.com/sustainable-business/ the-business-case/.

Burgerville. "People Report, April 2008." Internal company document.

Datamonitor. "Fast Food in the United States." 2009.

Herrington, Gregg. "Burgerville (Vancouver)." History Link. Last modified September 30, 2008. http://www.historylink.org/index.cfm?DisplayPage=output.cfm&file_id=8791.

Oregon Farmers' Markets Association. "Oregon Farmers' Markets Directory." Accessed 2010. http://oregonfarmersmarkets.org/directory/directory.html

Pokarney, Bruce. "Local Foods Find a Bigger Stage" Oregon Department of Agriculture. *The Agriculture Quarterly* 373 (2009).

RNCOS. "US Fast Food Market Outlook."2010.

United States Department of Labor. "Minimum Wage Laws in the United States." Accessed 2010. http://www.dol.gov/whd/minwage/america.htm

Wilson, Tracy. "How Fast Food Works." How Stuff Works. Accessed 2010. http://recipes. howstuffworks.com/fast-food.htm.

Worldwatch Institute. Accessed 2010. http://www.worldwatch.org/node/1489.

CLEAN WATER GROW™[40]
"Go or No Go?"

Oikos Case Writing Competition 2nd Place (Social Entrepreneurship Track), 2014

By Scott Marshall, Ph.D., and Simon Ngawhika

Clean Water Grow™ Case Study

Introduction

As Bill Gafi and Bruce Roll headed out of the boardroom and up the broad spiral staircase of Clean Water Services' Hillsboro headquarters, there was a charge of nervous excitement in the air:

"Well," said Bruce, "seeing that the board didn't shut our idea down completely, I'd say that was a success." "The pilot is going well," replied Bill, "it's helping to show us just how much we don't know."

The Clean Water Services board was fully supportive of Bill and Bruce's project: it had the potential to reduce operational costs and turn a waste stream into a revenue stream. But Bruce and his in-house team had only six months left to prove that the Clean Water Grow™ product was a financially viable venture — otherwise the board would pull the plug.

---

40   Clean Water Grow is a trademark of Clean Water Services

Background

Clean Water Services

Clean Water Services (CWS) is the public water utility for Washington County, Oregon (Exhibit 1). Through its four wastewater treatment facilities, 42 pump stations, and 1000-mile pipe network, CWS provides sewage and stormwater treatment services to more than 500,000 homes and businesses.[41] From 2007 to 2012, annual revenues from its treatment services averaged $92 million, approximately 35% of its annual funds. Capital construction projects and operating expenses over that same period accounted for between 35% and 50% of annual spending (Exhibit 2).[42]

As a public utility, CWS treats the residents and businesses it serves as both customers and owners. The company is ultimately accountable to an elected body of commissioners, which makes decisions on the rates CWS is allowed to charge in its bi-monthly utility bill.[43] The 83-mile long Tualatin River is also top of mind for CWS: it is a prominent economic and recreational feature of Washington County, and receives the County's treated wastewater. CWS has a responsibility to state regulators and to its owners to maintain the quality and health of the river.

Bill Gafi had served as CWS' General Manager since 1994, and in 2009 was also made Executive Director of the Clean Water Institute, a newly established non-profit housed within CWS to lead efforts to restore the health of the Tualatin watershed and drive innovation in treatment technology.[44] Bruce Roll, the Institute's lead for watershed management, brought a team together in 2012 to work on a project that would cultivate a direct link between CWS' wastewater treatment business and the gardening activities of Washington County residents.

The Wastewater Treatment Industry

Wastewater treatment companies purify sewage and stormwater to mandated standards and charge a fee or 'rate' to homes and businesses in their service area. In 2013, the United States wastewater treatment industry generated $43 billion in revenues, 87% of which was derived from fees for treatment services.[45]

---

41   Clean Water Services, "About Us."
42   Clean Water Services, "Annual Report 2011–12."
43   Roll, "Sustainable Integrated Watershed Management in the Tualatin Basin."
44   Clean Water Institute, "About Us."
45   IBISWorld, "Sewage Treatment Facilities in the US." Irrigation services and the sale of purified

The wastewater treatment industry is one in which capital costs are relatively high, requiring large economies of scale relative to the number of customers served. Provision of those services is therefore most efficient when concentrated in a single firm. Thus most treatment companies are structured as public utilities, enjoying a monopoly over a specific geographic region under the control of an elected body. However, the number of private wastewater treatment operators has risen since the 2007-9 recession, as municipalities look for new funding sources and higher scale economies.[46] Responsible for the treatment and management of a public good – water – these utilities are subject to regulations on the quantity and quality of water they discharge into the natural environment.[47]

How wastewater is treated

When a sink is used, a gutter drained, or a toilet flushed, this waste stream is composed of 99% water and 1% waste, by volume.[48] That 1% of waste needs to be treated using primary, secondary, and sometimes tertiary treatment steps and either repurposed or disposed of (Exhibit 3).

Primary treatment involves the separation of anything that is not dissolved in the water. Screens first block sticks, golf balls, and wedding rings before the wastewater flows into settlement tanks, where gravel and other heavy solids fall to the bottom, and greases and oils float to the top. These are removed and the wastewater enters the secondary step, where microorganisms are used in a controlled environment to digest the organic waste matter. Over an average of 20 days, this bio-digestion process converts that matter into solid, pathogen-free 'biosolids' that can be disposed of or repurposed. An example of repurposing these biosolids is using them to improve soil conditions on agricultural lands. After the bio-digester, the organic waste has been removed and the water that remains can be treated further, discharged into a river or other water body, or used to irrigate a golf course or park.[49]

Less than 2% of municipal wastewater utilities in the US have a tertiary system in place.[50] One reason to perform tertiary wastewater treatment is to remove inorganic matter such as nitrates and phosphates – elements needed for the plants we eat to grow – from the wastewater. Discharge of those nutrients into waterways is regulated in some states as they can cause harm to aquatic life.

water make up the remaining 10% and 3% of industry revenues, respectively.

46   IBISWorld, "Sewage Treatment Facilities in the US."
47   Ibid.
48   Interview with Clean Water Services, August 15, 2013
49   Regional Utilities, "Wastewater Explained."
50   Clean Water Services, "Treatment Process."

Challenges Facing the Wastewater Treatment Industry

Regulatory challenges

As regulated monopolies, wastewater utilities are subject to limits on the quality of the water they discharge, the rates they charge to customers, and the sources of funding they can access. These constraints challenge utilities to innovate to find the most cost-effective means of providing needed services, while complying with regulations.

Operational challenges

The cost of maintaining and expanding treatment infrastructure to accommodate growth is extremely high. The U.S. Environmental Protection Agency estimates that between 2004 and 2024, over $200 billion will need to be spent upgrading and expanding America's wastewater infrastructure.[51]

One significant challenge in maintaining the infrastructure is the build-up of struvite – a compound made up of magnesium, ammonium (a form of nitrogen), and phosphorus. Struvite accumulates inside the pipe networks of a wastewater facility, reducing the capacity of the pipes and forcing hydraulic systems to work longer, increasing operating and maintenance costs.[52] Struvite formation presents a common challenge in wastewater treatment systems that utilize biological treatment techniques and anaerobic bio-digestion (the secondary process noted earlier). Given that maintaining and enhancing infrastructure represents a significant portion of a water utility's operating budget, mitigating struvite-related costs is a key objective.

Environmental challenges

While not consistently regulated across the US, discharging concentrated amounts of nitrogen and phosphorus (two key nutrients used to grow food) can cause significant harm to the natural environment. For example, rivers and lakes can suffer from intense growth in algae populations, called algal blooms. Algae are short-lived, resulting in a high concentration of dead organic matter which starts to decay. As they decompose, the oxygen dissolved in the water is consumed, leading to large die-offs of animals and plants in the affected areas.[53] As an example, the 'Dead Zone' in the Gulf of Mexico is the result of nutrients

---

51   IBISWorld, "Sewage Treatment Facilities in the US."
52   Fattah, "Assessing Struvite Formation Potential at Wastewater Treatment Plants."
53   Lathrop, "Phosphorus lading reductions needed to control blue-green algal blooms in Lake Mendota.".

applied to agricultural lands flowing down the Mississippi River, causing the depletion of oxygen in the water and the significant loss of marine life.[54]

Innovative Solutions at Clean Water Services

Because a monopoly has a captured market, there is often little incentive for innovation. However, in order to overcome the numerous challenges noted earlier, CWS has initiated a range of innovative solutions in service delivery, operational efficiency, and regulatory compliance. These innovations have positioned CWS to successfully serve a growing community within a sensitive natural environment.

At the strategic level, CWS' board and management has adopted the view that CWS is a steward of the overall health of the Tualatin River. This stewardship approach enables CWS to justify expenditures that are not directly related to treating wastewater, but support core functions and ensure regulatory compliance. Examples from CWS' 2011-12 annual report include:

- Swept more than 12,000 miles of streets, cleaned 13,500 catch basins, and collected 750 dump truck loads of material to keep pollutants out of the river and streams.
- Coordinated and funded the planting of 15,000 accumulated acres of riparian buffers (streamside vegetation), which prevent sediment and agricultural nutrients from entering the river, as well as creating shade that mitigates temperature increases at waste treatment outflows.
- Provided a Clean Water Hero Program, a free service to help homeowners create a sustainable stormwater landscape that will reduce polluted runoff from their property.[55]
- Captured the methane resulting from the bio-digestion process to generate power for its treatment facilities.[56]

On the operational front, CWS worked with the Clean Water Institute to implement a groundbreaking solution to the challenge of struvite — one that also had the potential to turn a waste into a value-added consumer product.

---

54   Main, "Gulf of Mexico dead zone is the size of Connecticut6
55   Clean Water Services, "Annual Report 2011-12."
56   Clean Water Services, "Meeteing Minutes 2011-19-08."

Crystal Green®

In 2009, CWS partnered with a Canadian technology vendor to deploy an advanced technology that could remove phosphorus, magnesium and ammonium from the waste stream, before it could crystallize as struvite and clog up the pipe system (Exhibit 4). The process employed microbes to turn those nutrients into dry, odorless 'prills' or pearls (Exhibit 5). Being reconstituted nutrients that plants need to grow, these pearls represent the key ingredient of an effective, safe to handle garden fertilizer, which has been commercialized as Crystal Green®.[57] CWS was the world's first utility to implement this commercialized nutrient recovery system and has produced over 1,000 tons of Crystal Green® since the technology was implemented (Exhibit 6). In 2012 CWS grew its Crystal Green® capacity to 1,000 tons per year.

The nutrient recovery technology and the resultant Crystal Green® fertilizer poised CWS for numerous benefits:

Operational benefit

Removing the components of struvite improved throughput capacity, reduced treatment costs, and negated the need for hazardous, costly chemicals to combat struvite build-up. An internal study conducted by CWS in 2011 estimated up to $500,000 per year in saved operational costs as a result of this nutrient recovery technology.[58]

Environmental and social benefit

Environmentally, this process also had multiple benefits. It helped CWS to achieve a phosphorus concentration for its discharged water that was among the lowest of any treatment facility in the country, reducing the risk of algal blooms and loss of aquatic life. It also provided a more environmentally sound source of phosphorous. In 2012, 28 million tons of phosphate rock was mined in North America, 90% of which was used to produce fertilizer for the agricultural sector.[59] Repurposing nutrients from the waste stream reduces the reliance on phosphate rock mining as a source of fertilizer materials, substantially improving the environmental effects of the nearly $40 billion dollar U.S. home gardening market. On the social front, it had the potential to alleviate industrial supply constraints in the fertilizer market, and resulting price fluctuations that impact food prices.[60]

---

57   Crystal Green is trademarked by Ostara Inc., the Canadian technology vendor.
58   Clean Water Institute, "Green Technology for Clean Water."
59   IBISWorld, "Mineral and Phosphate Mining in the US."
60   Blodget and Wile, "A Genius Investor Thinks Billions Of People Are Going To Starve To Death —

Commercial benefit

Crucially, Crystal Green® also had commercial value as a safe, effective garden fertilizer. Since implementation at CWS in 2009, all Crystal Green® was sold back to the technology vendor, who then sold it as an ingredient to downstream fertilizer companies. This revenue stream, combined with the operational benefit, led CWS to estimate a five to seven year payback period on its investment in the nutrient recovery technology. However, there was no way for CWS to know where their Crystal Green® was going, or to tell consumers about the many public benefits it was capturing.

Clean Water Grow™

Knowing that the Crystal Green® CWS produced was essentially sourced from within Washington County, Bruce and Bill grew concerned about where it was ending up:

'We thought that they [the technology vendor] would use the struvite locally, but their interest was in building facilities and they weren't interested in local. I think it's going into turf across the United States', said Bruce. 'In fact, a year after it started up we were like "Wow, we're calling this a great, ecologically sustainable product. Shouldn't we have a product here locally?"'

When the technology vendor declined to develop a local product with CWS, Bruce wasn't fazed: 'Bill and I looked at each other and said "We're going to do it anyway."' The brand name they landed on was Clean Water Grow™ (Exhibit 7).

The Pilot Market Test

In mid-2012, the CWS Board gave Bill and Bruce the green light to produce grow, and pilot the product to test its commercial viability in the local market. There was plenty of work to do, and if the venture couldn't at least break even, it would likely be scrapped altogether. They assembled an in-house team consisting of operations, watershed management, public affairs, and science expertise to develop a marketable consumer fertilizer product.

Here's Why."

Strategic objectives

The "Grow Team" identified three objectives in selling Clean Water Grow™. The venture would prevent phosphorus, nitrogen and other nutrients from becoming pollutants in the Tualatin River, helping CWS to achieve its social and environmental mandates. The second objective was to recycle those nutrients already within the natural cycle of plants and animals, effectively creating a 'closed loop', zero waste system. Third, the Grow Team wanted to exemplify to other treatment facilities that a waste product could be turned into a useful resource that has commercial value.[61] Finally, if the product did better than break even, the extra revenue for CWS would be an additional benefit.

Product development

By weight, each bag of Grow contained 39% of CWS Crystal Green®. A third party would blend in potassium and other nutrients that help plants to grow to complete the fertilizer product. The blend formulation selected was designed for flowers, shrubs, vegetables, and herbs planted in raised garden beds, hanging baskets, and other containers. Other formulations optimal for use on lawn turf were tested but not pursued during the commercial pilot.

Production

Until the terms of the technology license were reviewed, CWS had to continue selling all of its Crystal Green® to the technology vendor. This arrangement meant that the product went through two other entities – the technology vendor and the blender – before it came back to CWS as a final product (Exhibit 8). It still needed to be packaged as Clean Water Grow™ and shipped for sale.

Packaging and promotion

With essentially no market research, the Grow team decided to conduct a trial of the product with 1.5lb bags. Although the team considered purchasing bags pre-printed with the product messaging, Bill could not justify the $7,500 cost of purchasing the minimum order quantity of 43,000 units.[62] Instead, for the pilot, CWS opted to order 5,000 unlabeled bags for $1,455. This required CWS to design, print, and attach their own labels, a process that added an extra $1.40 to the cost of each bag. The Grow Team also produced 100 20lb bags for CWS staff to test at their own homes and provide feedback on their experience with the product.

---

61   Interview with Clean Water Services, August 15, 2013
62   Olson, "Clean Water Grow Market Analysis."

To promote the product, a $3.00 discount coupon was sent to Washington County ratepayers as an insert with their bi-monthly utility bill from CWS.

Distribution channels

Two distribution channels were explored during the pilot: retail and online. Local nurseries and garden stores were a priority retail target since they were rooted in the community. In addition, larger home and garden retail chains had already finalized their inventory for the Spring 2013 growing season. Bruce attended farmers' markets, plant sales, and garden shows to raise consumer awareness and make on-the-spot sales. Bruce also developed an e-commerce portal– www. cleanwatergrow.com – to provide a direct link to consumers and potentially capture a higher margin. The wholesale distributor they partnered with for the pilot charged a service fee of $7 per wholesale order and $2.40 per retail order.[63]

Pricing

The Grow team decided to test the product at a retail price of $12.99 for the 1.5lb bag. The wholesale price they received from the distributor was $7.00 per bag.

Market Feedback

While Bruce was busy attending markets, plant sales, and nurseries on the weekends, local retailers remained skeptical about Clean Water Grow:

- 'Since the product was new, it was difficult to answer questions regarding its performance. To address this issue we worked directly with a number of garden clubs, nurseries and a local gardening education program to field-test the product.'[64]
- Discussions with these product testers found that they valued a fertilizer product that worked, was safe to use, and was locally sourced or produced. As testimonials on the product's performance trickled in, Bruce and his team were able to identify Grow's key features and benefits:
- Slow release: It won't break down too quickly and burn the roots of the plant, or wash away. As a result, the product is highly effective and fewer applications are required, reducing the total amount of fertilizer and the time or labor required.

---

63   Olson, "Clean Water Grow Market Analysis."
64   Interview with Clean Water Services. August 16, 2013

- Blended for strong root structure and bright color: Contains phosphorous for strong roots, and a 5% magnesium blend that makes colors more vibrant.
- Environmentally sound: Low solubility reduces the risk and impact of nutrient enrichment on streams, rivers, lakes and oceans.
- Made locally: Environmentally conscious, locally sourced ingredients reduce the reliance on nutrients sourced from mining and other less sustainable methods.

As the pilot progressed into 2013, Bruce faced some significant challenges in generating sales. For example, Grow retailed at $12.99 for a 1.5lb bag, while similar sized bags were priced at $6.99-10.99 (Exhibit 9), and most fertilizers offered in the home gardening market were between 3 and 4.5lbs in size. Bruce thought that the smaller 1.5lb package would suit households with a few pots and planter boxes on their balconies, but a larger property with more space to garden would require much more. Further, very few Washington County residents were aware of the discount coupon, and retailers did not promote it because the $3.00 price reduction came out of their margin.

Further Direction from the Board

By January 2013, Bruce found himself running around town getting Grow into the hands of as many gardeners, nurseries, landscapers, and retailers as possible. During this time, the CWS board invited the Grow team to give an update on the progress of the pilot. The results at that time were nothing to boast about: 642 bags sold in six months (Exhibit 10). The board was willing to continue the pilot to July, however, they wanted a business plan drawn up for Grow before they would approve continuation of the project. Walking out of that meeting, it occurred to Bill that the in-house team did not have the business skills or the staff time needed to complete an analysis of the Grow operation and the home gardening market. He approached the local business school to bring a couple of MBA students onto the team. Their role over the second half of the pilot would be to clarify the market opportunity, production and distribution options, and break-even projections. An excerpt of the student team's analysis follows:

The total market

The total U.S. lawn and garden products market generated $37.5 billion in 2011, $27.2 billion for garden products (flowers, bulbs, vegetables, herbs, etc.) and $10.3 billion for lawn products (Exhibit 11). The rate of population growth and urban development, the volume of house sales, the popularity of home and gardening-related television shows, and the affordability of food are the key drivers of sales in this market, which were on the rise again following the recession, and were expected to rise to $39.1 billion in 2013, and to $45.1 billion by 2016.[65]

Gardening is increasingly seen as a benefit to a person's health, their wallet, and their overall wellbeing. For example, the First Lady Michelle Obama established the White House Garden to promote healthy eating and lifestyles in 2009. [66] The industry has seen renewed gains since the end of the Great Recession, which saw revenues decline over 2008-9.[67]

Garden consumables segment

The packaged lawn and garden consumables market (which includes bags of fertilizer) declined by 0.1% between 2006 and 2011, due largely to the economic downturn. Fertilizer sales accounted for $2.45 billion in sales in 2011, the second most valuable product within that segment. Fertilizer is expected to see the highest growth from 2011 to 2016 (Exhibit 12).[68]

Demand for environmentally friendly, organic and/or natural garden consumables has also grown. The number of U.S. households using all-natural fertilizers, weed, or insect controls jumped from 5 million in 2004 to 12 million in 2008.[69]

The DIY (do it yourself) home garden market

Key factors in this segment are the number of single-family homes and changes in household consumer behavior toward healthier lifestyles and home improvement. Between 1998 and 2003 the DIY segment saw 25% growth, measured in constant prices.[70]

Scotts Miracle-Gro Company, one of the largest players in the DIY market, conducted a study in 2007 that identified the most salient consumer segments for this market:

People 55 years of age and older, college graduates, married households, households with annual incomes of $75,000 and over, two-person households and households with no children at home.[71]

---

65   Mintel, "Lawn and Garden Products – US."
66   Ibid.
67   Ibid.
68   Feedonia Group, "Lawn and Garden Consumables."
69   Gale Group, "Lawn and Garden Services."
70   Mintel, "Gardening – US."
71   Olson, "Clean Water Grow Market Analysis."

During 2011, U.S. consumers with small outdoor spaces (e.g. balconies, window boxes) spent on average $42 more than those with larger outdoor spaces (e.g. a yard) because they need materials that are not readily available: soil, plant containers, etc. Apartment or townhouse dwellers – both those under 35 and those over 55 – were therefore likely to spend more on garden consumables than other home or family types.[72]

The commercial lawn and garden market

In 2010, 92,000 lawn and garden services firms brought in revenues of $23.9 billion in the U.S. However, the blend of nutrients used in the piloted Grow product was not optimal for use on lawns and its slow release feature requires fewer applications, potentially reducing consumer demand for professional gardening services.

The available Washington County home garden fertilizer market

Two garden center companies provided information for the sales analysis. Both reported that the most popular weight for fertilizer sales is between 3–4.5 pound units. Interviews with the retailers provided an estimation of 2400 unit sales of fertilizer per store per year. Web searches revealed 35 garden consumable product retailers in Washington County. The Grow pilot sales data of 600 unit sales across three stores provides an estimate of 200 unit sales per store, or 8.3% of the market.

Production and Distribution

Cost structure

For the pilot, CWS produced 4,932 1.5lb units. Variable costs consisted of plastic bags, direct materials and labor, plastic scoops and cardboard boxes. Direct materials and labor cost $7,015. Boxes to pack the 4932 1.5lb bags in cost $589. Plastic scoops for 4932 bags cost $134.

Fixed costs included labor, marketing, e-commerce, overhead labor, and various consultants. Per month, these costs were approximately $7,323. The total costs sunk into R&D for the Grow venture was $57,359.

---

72   Mintel, "Lawn and Garden Products – US."

Distribution

If the technology vendor released control over the marketing and sale of CWS' Crystal Green®, CWS has options on the type of distributor with which to work. During the pilot, $2,478 was paid to hold and/or deliver 4,932 1.5lb bags. The three options analyzed were a master distributor, an independent manufacturer's representative (an IMR), and online sales.

During the pilot, distribution was handled by a wholesaler who paid CWS $7 per unit.

Bruce received interest from a local master distributor about taking over the distribution of Grow. A master distributor typically purchases the product from the producer at a discounted wholesale rate and then sells to other distributors or directly to retailers. The wholesale price CWS received would be reduced from $7 to $5 per unit. The expected payoff for that lower per unit revenue was access to a high percentage of the 35 retail garden supply outlets in Washington County.

Using an IMR would mean Bruce would no longer be needed for sales tasks, reducing fixed costs by $2,300 per month. Variable costs would increase by 5% of the retail price of every bag they sold, as the IMR's commission.

Finally, based on the pilot it was estimated that only 10% of sales would come through online sales. While the margin to CWS was higher for online deliveries, the low sales volumes preclude online sales from consideration as a distribution channel, and were excluded from break-even calculations.

Packaging

The analysis took the cost structure used during the pilot to calculate costs per pound, and used those to estimate costs for a 3.0lb bag. During the pilot, the material and labor costs to attach product labels onto plain bags added $1.40 to the per-unit cost of the product. Even though there is a minimum order quantity on the pre-printed bags, the lower per unit costs would have a significantly positive impact on the break-even point.

Pricing

It is important that, whichever distributor was selected, the retail price of Grow stayed near the average per pound price of competitors' products (Exhibit 9). The retail price is relevant for the break-even calculations due to the IMR's commission, a variable cost. The master distributor would be willing to pay $5 per bag, rather than the piloted $7.

Calculating break-even

Only the preprinted bags for the 1.5lb and 3.0lb sizes should be considered for the break-even analysis. As a result, the only per unit costs not associated with the different size was the 2.7 cents for the plastic scoop. Obviously, a decision to switch to either the master distributor or IMR would also alter the cost and price structure of the Grow value chain.

Conclusion: will it break even?

As Bruce, Bill and the rest of the Grow team looked ahead to the final July board meeting, they had a lot of questions to find answers to: Which mix of packaging and pricing, and which distributor, should they go for? How many units would they need to sell in order to break even? Was that number within reach of their locally focused base of consumers and their own production capacity? Was it possible to make this a positive revenue earner, even recoup some of the $57,000 that had been initially invested in R&D, product development, and promotional design? The third and final set of analyses was needed in order to determine whether this should be a 'Go' or 'No go.'

Exhibits

Exhibit 1: Tualatin River Basin, Washington County, and CWS Service Area

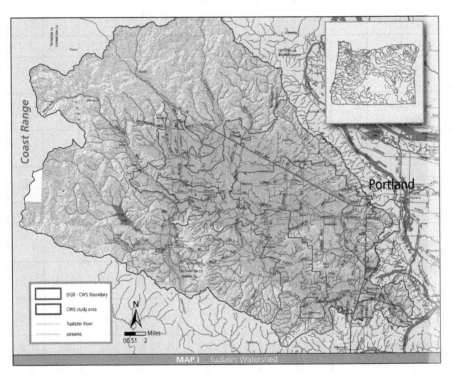

Source: Clean Water Services, "Healthy Streams Plan"

Exhibit 2: CWS sources and uses of funds 2007-2012

Sources of Funds (US$ millions)										
Year	'07–'08	%	'08–'09	%	'09–'10	%	'10–'11	%	'11–'12	%
Beginning Balances	53.3	25.6	50.7	23	93.4	32.8	176.1	60.9	156	47.2
Service Fees	80.9	38.9	86.3	39.2	93.6	32.9	98.9	34.2	101.5	30.7
Bond Sale Proceeds	55	26.5	55	25	75	26.3	0	0	54.4	16.5
Water Supply Funding	0	0	14.5	6.6	9.4	1	1	0.3	0.4	0.1
Interest & Miscellaneous	18.1	9	6.6	6.2	13.4	7	13.3	5	18	5.5
Total Funds Available	207.3	100	213.1	100	284.8	100	289.3	100	330.3	100
Uses of Funds (US$ millions)										
Year	'07–'08	%	'08–'09	%	'09–'10	%	'10–'11	%	'11–'12	%
Operating Expenses	42.6	20.5	48.1	22	50.2	18	51	18	52.4	15.9
Capital Construction	50.6	24.4	67	30	74.5	26	46.9	16	48.3	14.6
Debt Service	28.2	13.6	28.3	13	29.5	10	34.3	12	35	10.6
Ending Balances	78	37.5	69.1	31	123.1	43	156	54	194.2	58.8
Other Uses of Funds	8.4	4	7.8	4	7.7	3	1.1	0.4	0.4	0.1
Total Funds Used	207.8	100	220.3	100	285	100	289.3	100	330.3	100

Source: Clean Water Services Annual Reports, 2007-2012

Exhibit 3: Standard Wastewater Treatment Process

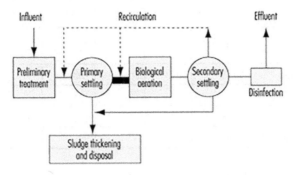

Source: International Labor Organization, "Encyclopedia of Occupational Health & Safety."

Exhibit 4: CWS' advanced treatment process

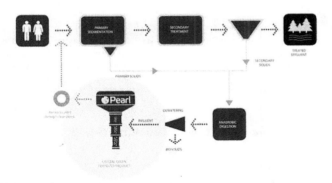

Source: Clean Water Services presentation.

Exhibit 5: Crystal Green® fertilizer pearls

Source: Clean Water Services, "Annual Report 2009–10."

Exhibit 6: Crystal Green production at CWS' Durham and Rock Creek facilities (tons)

	2009-10	2010-11	2011-12	2012-13	2013-14 (Est.)
Durham	249	243	206	203	
Rock Creek	0	0	76	115	
Total	249	243	282	318	514
Total to date	1092				

Source: Clean Water Services annual reports.

Exhibit 7: Clean Water Grow™

Time to Grow!

Clean Water Grow™ All-Purpose Plant Food is perfectly formulated for flowers, shrubs, fruits and vegetables. The slow-release formula of phosphorus, nitrogen, and magnesium (14-15-11) provides a steady supply of vital plant nutrients for up to six months. The unique slow-release blend helps to reduces fertilizer leaching and protect local waterways by gently releasing the needed nutrients as the plants use them.

Source: Clean Water Grow, "Clean Water Grow Plant Food."

Exhibit 8: Clean Water Grow™ pilot test supply chain

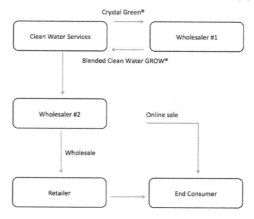

Source: Olson, "Clean Water Grow Market Analysis."

Exhibit 9: Price comparisons of environmentally friendly fertilizers

Brand	Size	Average retail price
Clean Water Grow™	1.5lb	$12.99
Dr. Earth Life Organic All Purpose Fertilizer	4lb	$8.99
EB Stone Organics-Sure Start	4lb	$8.49
Osmocote	1.25lb	$7.99
Tiger Bloom	2.25lb	$16.25

Source: Olson, "Clean Water Grow Market Analysis."

Exhibit 10: Clean Water Grow™ pilot midpoint sales

Outlet	Quantity Sold
Farmington Gardens	576
Ace Hardware	18
Jackson Bottom	45
Online	3
Total	642

Source: Olson, "Clean Water Grow Market Analysis."
Note: The Farmington Gardens figure represents the number sold to them, not the number they sold to end users.

Exhibit 11: US garden and lawn product industry revenues 2008-11 and projected 2012-16 (US$ millions)

	2008	2009	2010	2011	2012	2013	2014	2015	2016
Garden	29.2	26.3	25.8	27.2	27.2	28.8	29.7	31.4	32.5
Lawn	10.7	9.6	9.7	10.3	10.5	10.3	10.8	11.4	12.6
Total	39.9	35.9	35.5	37.5	37.7	39.1	40.5	42.8	45.1

Source: Mintel, "Lawn and Garden Products – US."

Exhibit 12: US Garden packaged consumables revenues (US$ millions)

Type	2006	2011	2016
Pesticides	2755	2585	2805
Fertilizer	2495	2455	3050
Seed	800	910	1110
Growing Media	760	810	980
Mulch	430	445	525
Other	245	245	300
Packaged Consumables	7485	7450	8770

Source: Feedonia Group, "Lawn and Garden Consumables."

Bibliography

"About Us." Clean Water Institute. http://cleanwaterservices.org/about-us/clean-water-institute/about-us/. Accessed 2013.

"About Us." Clean Water Services. https://www.cleanwaterservices.org/about-us/. Accessed 2013.

"Annual Report 2009–10." 2011. Clean Water Services.

"Annual Report 2011-12." 2013. Clean Water Services.

Blodget, Henry, and Rob Wile. "A Genius Investor Thinks Billions Of People Are Going To Starve To Death — Here's Why." Business Insider. 2012. http://www.businessinsider.com/peak-phosphorus-and-food-production-2012-12?op=1#ixzz2dTR54cMB

"Clean Water Grow Plan Food." Clean Water Grow. Accessed 2013. https://www.cleanwatergrow.com/.

Clean Water Services presentation. 2010.

"Encyclopedia of Occupational Health & Safety." 2013. International Labor Organization.

Fattah, Kazi. "Assessing Struvite Formation Potential at Wastewater Treatment Plants." *International Journal of Environmental Science and Development* 3, no. 6 (2012): 548.

"Gardening – US." Mintel. 2003.

"Green Technology for Clean Water." Clean Water Institute. 2011.

"Healthy Streams Plan." 2013. Clean Water Services.

Interview with Clean Water Services. August 15, 2013

Interview with Clean Water Services. August 16, 2013

Lathrop, Richard, et al. "Phosphorus lading reductions needed to control blue-green algal blooms in Lake Mendota." *Canadian Journal of Fisheries and Aquatic Sciences* 55 (1998): 1169–1178.

"Lawn and Garden Consumables." Feedonia Group. 2012.

"Lawn and Garden Products – US." Mintel. 2012.

"Lawn and Garden Services" Gale Group. 2013.

Main, Douglas. "Gulf of Mexico dead zone is the size of Connecticut." Last modified November 2, 2015. http://www.nbcnews.com/science/gulf-mexico-dead-zone-size-connecticut-6C10798946

"Meeting Minutes 2011-19-08." Clean Water Services. 2011. http://www.cleanwaterservices. org/content/AboutUs/CWAC/Meeting%20Minutes%2011-19-08.pdf

"Mineral and Phosphate Mining in the US." IBISWorld. 2013.

Olson "Clean Water Grow Market Analysis." 2013.

Roll, Bruce, et al. "Sustainable Integrated Watershed Management in the Tualatin Basin." 2008.

"Sewage Treatment Facilities in the US." 2013. IBISWorld.

"Treatment Process." Clean Water Services. http://www.cleanwaterservices.org/AboutUs/ WastewaterAndStormwater/TreatmentProcess.aspx. Accessed 2013.

"Wastewater Explained." Regional Utilities Water & Sewer for South Walton County. http:// regionalutilities.net/documents/Wastewater%20Explained.pdf. Accessed 2013.

COLUMBIA FOREST PRODUCTS
Pursuit of Sustainability in a Changing Market

Oikos Case Writing Competition 3rd Place (Corporate Sustainability Track), 2009

By Scott Marshall, Ph.D., Zachary Anderson, Matthew Flax, Daniel Gambetta, Jacen Greene, and Madeleine E. Pullman, Ph.D.

Columbia Forest Products Case Study

Introduction

Upon reading the latest report from the Department of Housing and Urban Affairs, Harry Demorest found his concerns confirmed – the construction of new homes had fallen yet again across the United States. Over the past month, new home starts had declined over 14% in December; this marked the end of 2007 during which housing starts were down 25% compared to the previous year and hit a low not experienced since 1993. The question was no longer "will there be a recession?" but rather "how long will the recession last?"

The fate of Columbia Forest Products, the company that Harry led for 16 years as Chairman and CEO, is tightly bound to the US housing market. CFP has over a 40% market share in hardwood plywood products, most of which go into new home construction. Further, over the past three years, CFP has embarked on a journey into sustainability. This journey is marked most profoundly by the introduction of PureBond® non-formaldehyde plywood in 2006. A first in the industry, PureBond® provides significant health benefits to CFP employees and customers by removing a known carcinogen from its products. It also has been a catalyst for CFP to pursue a more comprehensive, sustainability-inspired strategy. But in the midst of the dreadful housing market in the US, Harry and the rest of CFP executive team wondered if further pursuit of a sustainability strategy would be detrimental to their company's competitiveness.

Background

From Single Mill to National Competitor

In 1957, A.J. Honzel and a small group of business associates purchased a shuttered plywood mill in Klamath Falls, Oregon. Known as Klamath Hardwoods, the company was led by Honzel until 1962. In 1963 Columbia Plywood Corporation purchased Klamath Hardwood. The name changed one more time when, in 1976, the employees purchased the company and it became Columbia Forest Products.

Through both external and organic growth strategies, CFP grew quickly in scale and scope of operations. Between 1963 and 1989 CFP added a laminated products division in Thomasville, North Carolina, acquired two hardwood plywood plants in Chatham, Virginia, constructed a hardwood plywood mill in Old Fort, North Carolina and purchased the hardwood veneer operations of Indian Head Company in Presque Isle, Maine and Newport, Vermont.

In the 1990s, CFP continued its aggressive growth strategy. In 1991, it purchased a half-round slicing operation in New Freedom, Pennsylvania, and a hardwood veneer face manufacturing mill in Rutherglen, Ontario. The following year it built a poplar core veneer plant in Craigsville, West Virginia. In 1996 and 1997, CFP acquired five more hardwood plywood plants – three in the US Southeast and two in Canada – as well as a raised panel and door plant in Corpus Christi, Texas. The late 1990s were marked by a few plant closings, including the hardwood plywood plant in Arkansas in 1998 that had been purchased only 2 years previous as well as the slicing plant in Pennsylvania in 1999 that had been acquired in 1991.

Overall, CFP maintained a consistent and aggressive growth strategy while seeking production efficiencies through adding production capacity and closing selected operations. This strategy proved beneficial – by the late 1990s, CFP had become the largest manufacturer of hardwood plywood in the United States.

Early 2000's to Current: A Period of Growth and Restructuring

From 2000 to 2007, CFP continued its acquisition and investment strategy. These efforts built up both CFP's plywood and flooring product divisions. Operations in Arkansas, Ontario and Oregon were expanded and new operations were purchased in Arkansas, Ontario, Tennessee, West Virginia and Kentucky. However, this expansion was mixed with a series of plant closures across its portfolio of operations. Other plants in North Carolina, Kentucky and Texas were closed. The mixture of acquisitions and divestitures over this period of time were motivated primarily by a desire to maximize the value and streamline production of the plywood and flooring divisions. In 2007, CFP sold its Columbia Flooring Division to Mohawk Industries, marking an important departure from being a manufacturer to being a supplier to the hardwood flooring industry.

CFP remains the largest manufacturer of hardwood plywood and veneer products in North America and also produces laminated products and hardwood logs. It maintains a 40% market share in the hardwood plywood segment, earns approximately one billion dollars in annual revenue and employs approximately 4,500 people. All the company's employees share in the success of CFP as the company continues to operate under the employee stock ownership plan (ESOP) established in 1976.

CFP's veneer is created using Northern Appalachian hardwoods such as birch, red oak, maple, ash, poplar, cherry, hickory, pine, walnut and others. Columbia's rotary cut veneer ranges in thickness from 1/30 to 1/42 of an inch and is sold throughout the decorative plywood, furniture, cabinetry, door and profile-wrap industries. Its products are used in cabinets, architectural millwork, commercial fixtures, and assorted other applications in homes and commercial buildings. The company sells its products to original equipment manufacturers, wholesale distributors, and mass merchandisers.

To complement CFP's domestic sourcing activities, its international division began importing hardwood plywood in 1995. Since then, Columbia has grown to become the largest importer of Russian birch plywood in North America. With a wide selection of imported panel and flooring products from Indonesia, Malaysia, Taiwan, Africa and countries throughout South America and Europe, inventories are maintained regionally at strategic North American ports and CFP's plant sites.

Hardwood Plywood Industry: A Mature Industry

Plywood is made from an odd number of constructional veneers glued face to face with the grain running in alternate directions (cross bonding). The glued veneers are then placed between the shelves of a large hydraulic press where they are heated and squeezed together tightly. The heat dries the glue and adheres the veneers together. Then the plywood is trimmed and can be sanded to give a smoother finish. Exhibits 1 and 2 describe the processes of making veneer and plywood.

In 1905, the Portland Manufacturing Company was recorded as the first company in the United States to utilize plywood in commercial applications. In the following century, plywood manufacturing grew into a major domestic industry earning approximately $3.13 billion in revenue in 2006. It remains a fairly fragmented industry with 301 companies manufacturing plywood at the end of 2006. At this time, the annual revenue per company was $10.39 million and the average gross profit margin was 11.06%.

Although fragmented, the industry is highly competitive. It is characterized by relatively slow growth, a lack of product differentiation, and production overcapacity. Further, relationships in the industry — particularly along the supply chain — are by nature relationship based. Builders are loyal to suppliers because they value predictable prices and material quality.

With the competition fierce and demand slackening, major North American producers of paper and wood products, including Abitibi Consolidated Inc., Domtar Inc., Weyerhaeuser Co., and Louisiana Pacific Corp., have gone through a series of consolidations in recent years. These consolidations are primarily in the form of facility shutdowns to attempt to ameliorate the excess of supply. The changes in the structure of the industry are creating new challenges for existing competitors in the industry.

Key External Pressures

Housing Trends

Hardwood plywood and veneer is used for furniture, high-end cabinetry, and architectural millwork in homes and commercial buildings. The industry's performance, therefore, correlates directly to home building and remodeling trends. Housing starts, a measurement of initial construction of residential units each month and an indicator of overall demand for residential wood products, had risen from 2001 through 2005. This rise was fueled by favorable interest rates and steadily increasing home prices. However, starting in 2006, both housing starts as well as housing permits had begun a significant downward trend, driven by a financial crisis in the subprime mortgage markets and excesses in housing supply. This translated to a substantial decline in demand for and sales of residential wood products.

International Competition

The slumping housing market has been one of two major forces causing the US plywood industry to restructure. The second is the rise of international competition. Most US companies in the plywood and veneer industry manufacture their products within the domestic market in which labor and manufacturing costs are much higher than in many emerging markets. Between 2002 and 2006, imports of hardwood plywood to the US rose 93%, from 2.2 million to 4.4 million cubic meters. China's share of total imports increased from 10% to 54% over the same period of time, while imports from other countries declined. The entry of Chinese hardwood plywood manufacturers into the US market was sudden and aggressive. Within only a few years the US plywood market's competitive landscape was significantly altered – mostly to the detriment of US manufacturers. Due to low labor costs, tariff avoidance, and government subsidies designed to encourage export, Chinese manufacturers maintain a substantial price advantage over U.S. manufacturers. This holds true even though a large percentage of Chinese plywood exports are manufactured using raw logs imported from overseas. However, Chinese products suffer from quality and consistency issues and generally higher levels of formaldehyde emissions compared to plywood provided by US domestic manufacturers.

Domestic Survival Strategies: Specialization and Differentiation

Intense competition domestically and internationally, commodity products, and production overcapacity are all creating havoc in the US plywood industry. To survive, the US-based companies are struggling to compete on a cost basis. Recent moves by International Paper and Weyerhaeuser to concentrate on a few major businesses indicate that the forest products industry is rapidly shifting to a more specialized focus. In 2007, International Paper sold eighteen mills and closed one in North America. Weyerhaeuser recently closed six facilities in North America, sold a European sales division for Engineered Wood Products, and sold its timber rights. International Paper also purchased the Containerboard Packaging & Recycling Business from Weyerhaeuser. Across the industry, companies are searching for relatively narrow segments of the market where they can attain high market shares and better returns in a capital-intensive industry.

Although the plywood industry is affected high rivalry, fierce competition, and declining margins, it may be possible that competitive advantages can be achieved through product differentiation, product innovation, and improved supply-chain management. Implementing a 'sustainability'-based strategy that incorporates environmentally-sound policies and practices throughout a company's value chain potentially provides a viable differentiation strategy in this mature industry.

Sustainability as Differentiation

Building construction, maintenance, and demolition have a profound impact on the environment and well-being of communities. Buildings in the United States account for 65% of electricity consumption, 30% of raw materials use, and 30% of greenhouse gas emissions. Increasing population growth, resource consumption, and energy costs are creating a significant market transformation in the US building industry.

Green building — defined as the utilization of environmentally preferred building practices and materials in the design, location, construction, operation and disposal of buildings — has experienced tremendous growth, and seems to remain resilient during the housing downturn. Based on this growth in demand for green building materials, the price premium required for green building is shrinking, reducing one of the few barriers to growth and entry. However, despite this growth, green building currently represents only 2 percent of the commercial edifices and 0.3 percent of new homes in the US.

FMI, a construction management consulting firm, projected that by 2008 nearly $21.2 billion of new nonresidential construction will employ the use of green-building principles — a 58% increase. By 2010, approximately 10% of commercial construction starts are expected to be 'green', and the total value of green building construction starts is forecasted to be at $60 billion. Another market researcher, SBI, predicts that the market for green building materials, which has been growing at a rate of 23% annually through 2006, will slow slightly, to 17% in the upcoming years.

Sourcing FSC Certified Wood
According to the Food and Agriculture Organization, an additional 25 to 30% of the greenhouse gases released into the atmosphere each year — 1.6 billion

tons — are caused by deforestation. The majority of this deforestation is in the tropics, and approximately 70% of it is tied to logging and logging roads. These forests are also vitally important for other uses and ecological services such as non-timber forest products, medicinal plants, protection of biodiversity, watershed protection, production of fish and wildlife, and providing a home for indigenous people.

The Forest Stewardship Council (FSC) created the first worldwide certification system based on a set of 10 principles established for forests and forest products (See Exhibit 3A: Forest Stewardship Council Principles). This certification empowers consumers to express their demand in the market for responsible forestry by offering an independent, global and credible label for forest products. FSC involves a complex tracking system called chain of custody that allows manufacturers and traders to demonstrate that timber comes from a forest that is responsibly managed in accordance with the FSC Principles. The flow of FSC certified wood is tracked through the entire supply chain — including processing, transformation and manufacturing — all the way to the final product. Such certification generally adds a price premium of between 0.05% – 2.5% to hardwood plywood.

Building Green with LEED Certification Standards

The United States Green Building Council (USGBC) is a 501(c) (3) non-profit community of leaders working to make green buildings accessible to everyone within a generation. In 1998, the USBC established the Leadership in Energy Efficiency and Design (LEED) framework which has quickly become the dominant accrediting body for green construction.

LEED addresses all building types and emphasizes state-of-the-art strategies in five areas: sustainable site development, water savings, energy efficiency, materials and resources selection, and indoor environmental quality. The LEED system awards points for improvements in categories such as Sustainable Sites, Energy and Atmosphere, Materials and Resources, and Indoor Air Quality. Buildings may be rated silver, gold, or platinum depending on how many points they are able to achieve. Registered LEED projects grew from 5 in 2001 to over 9,800 in 2007, with another 1,280 already certified. In 2008, there were LEED projects in every state and 41 countries. Currently, LEED certification only carries bragging rights, however state and local governments are beginning to provide incentives towards attainment of such goals.

The pace of growth had also increased every year since the LEED framework was introduced. There were several contributing factors to the rapid adoption of green building:

- Awareness of green design principles and building techniques has spread quickly throughout the architecture and development community. Innovative methods and processes are becoming "best practice" for many design and building firms.
- The availability and quality of environmentally sound building materials and products has also expanded considerably as the movement has gained traction. Acceptance of new or substitute products grows as they build a track record in the industry.
- Green buildings yield significant savings in comparison with traditional construction. Energy savings, worker productivity, and public relations and marketing can benefit from building green.

By all appearances, the housing slump has not slowed the pace of LEED registration for new construction. Mandates and incentives from local governments have encouraged, and in many cases, mandated green building for new construction, and new LEED ratings systems are in pilot phase for residential, existing buildings, schools, and neighborhood development. In the first five months of 2007, more than 100 green building bills were introduced at the state level.

The Critics of FSC and LEED

However, there has been some criticism of LEED certification and Rainforest advocacy groups have maintained that LEED certification is not doing enough to protect rainforests. LEED only awards a single, optional point for selecting woods independently-certified as coming from well-managed forests (i.e., under the protocol of FSC) out of a total of 69 points that can be earned. Because a minimum of 52 points earns a rating of "platinum," and there is no specific requirement to avoid destructively-harvested rainforest woods, it is still possible to use these woods and still achieve the highest possible level of LEED certification. Exhibit 3B: Rainforest Relief Policy Draft outlines how one advocacy group, Rainforest Relief, seeks to ensure that tropical hardwood is sourced responsibly through local policy initiatives.

Columbia Forest Products' Pursuit of a Sustainability Strategy

Early Adoption of Forest Stewardship Council Standards

CFP is no stranger to the Forest Stewardship Council certification standards. CFP joined the FSC in 1999 and by 2007 sourced more than 30% of its wood from FSC-certified forests. This initiative provided CFP with the ability to offer a line of environmentally friendly decorative panels and veneered particleboard that carried the FSC certification.

Ed Woods, executive vice president of CFP, stated in regards to producing only FSC certified products, "I don't think we have enough raw materials sources to go a hundred percent. That would be a goal." There is simply not enough FSC wood being produced, but CFP continues to both encourage suppliers to be certified and search for more sources of FSC certified wood. With the explosion of the green building movement and LEED point system, Woods believes that increasing the percentage of its products that utilize certified wood could position CFP to be ready to meet the increasing demand.

Eco-Innovation in Product: The Introduction of PureBond®

In 2007 CFP unveiled PureBond® formaldehyde-free plywood adhesive. With this innovation CFP has a proprietary adhesive with greater bonding strength, better moisture resistance, and no off-gassing of formaldehyde, all without added cost to the customer.

Doctor Kaichang Li, an Assistant Professor at Oregon State University's College of Forestry, invented PureBond®. Utilizing principles of biomimicry,[73] Dr. Li developed a method to create a protein-based adhesive modeled from a mussel's innate ability to attach to shoreline rocks. Li and his team replicated this adhesive by blending protein-rich soy flour with the same amino acids used by the mussels. The resulting product provides a cost-effective alternative to formaldehyde resins. Not only did PureBond® outperform formaldehyde in terms of strength, water resistance, and toxicity, but it was soon cheaper to produce than formaldehyde-based alternatives.

At a cost of $250,000 per facility, in addition to significant costs for development of the technology, CFP converted its veneer-core hardwood plywood

---

73 The derivation of scientific advances through the study of natural processes. Popularized by Janine Benyus in her book of the same name.

plants to formaldehyde-free manufacturing. Using a patented, non-toxic, soy-based adhesive cooperatively developed in conjunction with CFP, Oregon State University, and Hercules Incorporated, CFP became the only producer in the industry with a cost neutral alternative to formaldehyde-based adhesives.

While only a component of green construction, CFP's PureBond® product line helps a building project achieve higher environmental standards with positive benefits to indoor air quality and sustainable sourced wood. Since its introduction the demand for PureBond® has been strong. Ed Woods, stated that "we've definitely noticed PureBond® being specified and folks seeking it out." Exhibit 4 shows examples of Columbia Forest Products' PureBond® and Forest Stewardship Council certified products.

Building a Brand and a Reputation — the Good and the Bad

This technological innovation had clear implications for CFP's product line and reputation. When CFP first announced its intentions to adopt formaldehyde-free resins, the plywood industry reacted with boycott threats and an extensive public relations campaign against CFP. Elizabeth Whalen, Director of Sustainability at CFP, recalls that the "advertising campaign was fairly controversial. It was incredibly effective from my viewpoint and the rest of us at Columbia, but it actually irritated the industry even more when we came out with it just because of the messaging. Their opinion implied that we were demonizing formaldehyde—which was sort of the point."

In early 2007, California Air Resources Board (CARB) enacted strict regulation focused on indoor air quality. Under the new regulations, manufacturers that continue to use formaldehyde-added resins in regulated products must obtain third-party certification that emissions standards are met. Distributors, importers, fabricators and retailers must record product purchase dates, supplier names, and evidence that they have obtained compliance documentation from the supplier to establish a product's chain of custody.

With this legislation CFP found itself in a very advantageous position for two reasons. First, it is the only hardwood plywood company in the industry with a cost-competitive alternative to formaldehyde-based products. This is a significant, albeit not indefinite, advantage, particularly in California. The second, and more subtle, advantage results from the relationships that CFP will be able to develop. It is the only company that can tell its customers not to worry about the new regulations. Price, delivery schedules, and performance will not be affected for customers of CFP when the regulations take effect. If CFP can create those relationships while competitors struggle to satisfy the CARB regulations, CFP may have an opportunity to capture and retain considerable market share.

The Future of CFP's Sustainability Strategy

After achieving success with PureBond® and incorporating FSC certified wood into its products, the questions for CFP now are "what else should it consider doing to clearly establish itself as an environmental leader?" and "what else should it actually do given the severe downturn in the US housing market?"

Existing Product Differentiation

As a forest products company, CFP is always going to be involved in a resource extraction industry. Currently, there is not enough FSC-certified wood to satisfy market demand, and new sources are expensive and take time to develop. CFP may be able to develop new substrates on which to apply hardwood veneers, but uncertainty remains around the costs and performance of the new substrates. For example, in recent years, wheat board has found some success in the marketplace as a substitute for wood in cabinetry. However, wheat board and other substrates based on renewable, rather than extractive, resources remain limited in supply, leaving CFP to confront the same constraints it has with FSC-certified wood. Further, the conversion of its mills to utilize PureBond® cost CFP millions of dollars; there is little capability to accurately forecast the costs of switching to alternative substrates.

CFP is also considering other applications for its proprietary PureBond® adhesive. Multi-dimensional fiberboard (or, MDF) and particleboard products are made by gluing sawdust and mill waste into sheets for use in cabinetry and furniture. These products are also key materials in home and commercial construction. If CFP were able to formulate PureBond® to be as effective in these products as it has in veneer core plywood, it may be able to capitalize further on the emerging green building segment.

Vertical and Horizontal Diversification

Entirely new products might offer other options for CFP's sustainability strategy. CFP is thinking about the potential extension of PureBond® into a line of wood and wall glues to be sold to both commercial and consumer markets. Given that there are very limited offerings in this segment that are non-toxic, this presents an intriguing option. Initial discussions with Hercules, the supplier of PureBond® suggest that it may be willing to sign an agreement that provides CFP the exclusive rights to market and sell related products based on the PureBond® formulation. However, CFP has never offered packaged products and the distribution channels for such products are very different from those CFP currently utilizes for its hardwood and veneer products.

With the rapid growth of the green building industry, CFP is also looking at the possibility of expanding vertically to manufacture its own line of cabinetry. Currently there are only a few companies offering hardwood cabinetry that is environmentally sound and these companies maintain a limited selection and operate at relatively small scales. CFP may be able to develop its own branded line of cabinetry that builds from the reputation it created through the introduction of PureBond®.

Making Sustainability Strategies Profitable

All of these strategies rely on demand in the marketplace. As Harry Demorest said, "…what really drives change are, in my opinion, consumers." Is there enough demand in the marketplace for green products, and if so, is that demand so great that customers will pay a premium for it? PureBond® recovered the development investments quickly because it was cost neutral to CFP's customers; they did not have to pay more for a formaldehyde-free product. The key question remained: Would there be sufficient demand in the marketplace so that CFP can recoup any investments made in future sustainability-related initiatives?

Despite the encouraging signs of growth in the green building market, it is still a very small portion of the overall construction market. In 2006 green homes made up only 0.3 percent of the housing market. Although the growth rate in the green building segment remains high during the current downturn it is not certain that the size of the market will justify significant investments.

The threat of domestic and international competition is ever present. Elizabeth Whalen is well aware that the advantage provided by PureBond® is only temporary. She estimates that CFP's domestic competition will be able to offer competitive non-formaldehyde products in 1 ½ to 2 years. It would likely take China and other overseas manufacturers another year at least to offer comparable products.

The final consideration is CFP's reputation. It has spent many years building recognition for its sustainability initiatives. By further pursuing a sustainability-based strategy, CFP invites greater public scrutiny. Given the recent criticisms of LEED and FSC, CFP needs to be clear on how it commits itself to sustainability and the reputation that it built as a result. There is always the potential that well intentioned and ambitious sustainability efforts can turn into PR disasters.

The potential disadvantages and pitfalls of pursuing sustainability strategies can be difficult to anticipate and react to effectively. CFP must be able to commit to a clear strategy and prosper in the intensely competitive hardwood plywood industry.

Exhibits

Exhibit 1: Making Veneer

The Five Basic Steps

1. Debarking: Either with sharp-toothed grinding wheels or with jets of high-pressure water the bark is removed from the log as it is slowly rotated about its long axis.

2. Sectioning: Debarked logs are cut into sections about 8 ft-4 in (2.5 m) to 8 ft-6 in (2.6 m) long, suitable for making standard 8 ft (2.4 m) long sheets. These log sections are known as peeler blocks.

3. Softening: Before the veneer can be cut, the peeler blocks must be heated and soaked to soften the wood. This process takes 12-40 hours depending on the type of wood, the diameter of the block, and other factors.

4. Peeling: The heated peeler blocks are then transported to the peeler lathe, where they are automatically aligned and fed into the lathe one at a time. As the lathe rotates the block rapidly about its long axis, a full-length knife blade peels a continuous sheet of veneer from the surface of the spinning block at a rate of 300-800 ft/min (90-240 m/min). When the diameter of the block is reduced to about 3-4 in (230-305 mm), the remaining piece of wood, known as the peeler core, is ejected from the lathe and a new peeler block is fed into place.

5. Rolling: Wet strips of veneer are wound into a roll, while an optical scanner detects any unacceptable defects in the wood. Once dried the veneer is graded and stacked.

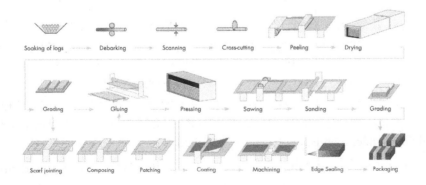

Source: WISA Plywood

Exhibit 2: Making Plywood

The Four Basic Steps:

1. Laying Up and Gluing: Appropriate sections of veneer are assembled for a particular run of plywood and the process of laying up and gluing the pieces together begins. In the simplest case of three-ply sheets, the back veneer is laid flat and is run through a glue spreader, which applies a layer of glue to the upper surface. The short sections of core veneer are then laid crossways on top of the glued back, and the whole sheet is run through the glue spreader a second time. Finally, the face veneer is laid on top of the glued core, and the sheet is stacked with other sheets waiting to go into the press.

2. Pressing: Glued sheets are loaded into a multiple-opening hot press, which can handle 20-40 sheets at a time. The press squeezes them together under a pressure of about 110-200 psi (7.6-13.8 bar), while at the same time heating them to a temperature of about 230-315° F (109.9-157.2° C).

3. Finishing: Higher grade sheets pass through a set of 4 ft (1.2 m) wide belt sanders, which sand both the face and back. Intermediate grade sheets are manually spot sanded to clean up rough areas. Some sheets are run through a set of circular saw blades, which cut shallow grooves in the face to give the plywood a textured appearance.

4. Stamping: Finished sheets are stamped with a grade-trademark that gives the buyer information about the exposure rating, grade, mill number, and other factors.

Exhibit 3A: Forest Stewardship Council Principles

PRINCIPLE #1: COMPLIANCE WITH LAWS AND FSC PRINCIPLES. Forest management shall respect all applicable laws of the country in which they occur, and international treaties and agreements to which the country is a signatory, and comply with all FSC Principles and Criteria.

PRINCIPLE #2: TENURE AND USE RIGHTS AND RESPONSIBILITIES. Long-term tenure and use rights to the land and forest resources shall be clearly defined, documented and legally established.

PRINCIPLE #3: INDIGENOUS PEOPLES' RIGHTS. The legal and customary rights of indigenous peoples to own, use and manage their lands, territories, and resources shall be recognized and respected.

PRINCIPLE #4: COMMUNITY RELATIONS AND WORKER'S RIGHTS. Forest management operations shall maintain or enhance the long-term social and economic well being of forest workers and local communities.

PRINCIPLE #5: BENEFITS FROM THE FOREST. Forest management operations shall encourage the efficient use of the forest's multiple products and services to ensure economic viability and a wide range of environmental and social benefits.

PRINCIPLE #6: ENVIRONMENTAL IMPACT. Forest management shall conserve biological diversity and its associated values, water resources, soils, and unique and fragile ecosystems and landscapes, and, by so doing, maintain the ecological functions and the integrity of the forest.

PRINCIPLE #7: MANAGEMENT PLAN. A management plan — appropriate to the scale and intensity of the operations — shall be written, implemented, and kept up to date. The long-term objectives of management, and the means of achieving them, shall be clearly stated.

PRINCIPLE #8: MONITORING AND ASSESSMENT. Monitoring shall be conducted — appropriate to the scale and intensity of forest management — to assess the condition of the forest, yields of forest products, chain of custody, management activities and their social and environmental impacts.

PRINCIPLE # 9: MAINTENANCE OF HIGH CONSERVATION VALUE FORESTS. Management activities in high conservation value forests shall maintain or enhance the attributes which define such forests. Decisions regarding high conservation value forests shall always be considered in the context of a precautionary approach.

PRINCIPLE # 10: PLANTATIONS. Plantations shall be planned and managed in accordance with Principles and Criteria 1 – 9, and Principle 10 and its Criteria. While plantations can provide an array of social and economic benefits, and can contribute to satisfying the world's needs for forest products, they should complement the management of, reduce pressures on, and promote the restoration and conservation of natural forests.

Exhibit 3B: Rain Forest Relief Policy Draft

A POLICY TO PROTECT TROPICAL AND TEMPERATE RAINFORESTS BY ELIMINATING MUNICIPAL PURCHASES OF WOOD PRODUCTS CONSISTING, IN WHOLE OR IN PART, OF TROPICAL OR TEMPERATE RAINFOREST WOODS THAT ARE NOT HARVESTED SUSTAINABLY.

WHEREAS, the rate of rainforest loss is high and accelerating;

WHEREAS, clearing and burning of rainforests is linked to atmospheric imbalance, global warming, species extinctions, loss of indigenous cultures, loss of potential medicines, and displacement of local peoples;

WHEREAS, commercial logging is currently directly responsible for 12% of tropical deforestation,

WHEREAS, according to the United Nations Food and Agriculture Organization commercial logging is indirectly responsible for up to 70% of tropical deforestation due to the access provided to shifting cultivators by logging roads;

WHEREAS, commercial logging is the greatest cause of deforestation in tropical Southeast Asia;

WHEREAS, commercial logging is the greatest cause of the loss old-growth temperate rainforests;

WHEREAS, a large portion of the wood produced from commercial logging in the tropics is exported to the United States and other industrialized nations;

WHEREAS, it is in the interest of the health, safety and welfare of all who live, work and do business in Portland, Oregon that measures be taken to reduce and stop the destruction of rainforests worldwide;

NOW, THEREFORE, BE IT RESOLVED BY THE PORTLAND CITY COUNCIL that the City of Portland, Oregon will not use, purchase, or fund the purchase of products containing, in whole or in part, wood from tropical forests, or tropical or temperate rainforests, excepting those woods that are proven to have been harvested in an environmentally sound manner in accordance with the guidelines set forth in Paragraph A

Paragraph A

Terms of this resolution will be met if it can be proven through an independent certification program accredited by the Forest Stewardship Council that the rainforest wood product has come from a forest operation that can be shown to meet the following conditions:

Local Involvement

Local communities are involved in all stages of planning and management of diverse forest products for sustainable yields.

Land Rights

Projects must not interfere with aboriginal or traditional land rights of indigenous peoples, or other current land tenants.

Ecology

Timber harvesting cannot adversely affect beneficial physical processes such as climate regulation, the surface or ground water quality or the overall watershed function.

Timber harvesting must maintain soil productivity and not increase erosion rates.

Timber harvesting must not use synthetic or other harmful pesticides or herbicides.

Timber harvesting does not diminish ecological integrity or species richness (number of species of flora and fauna, including trees) at the scale of the logging operation or the watershed in which it is located.

Exhibit 4: Columbia Forest Products' Sustainability-Based Products

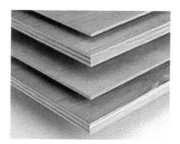

Columbia Forest Products' Forest Stewardship Council certified plywood panels.

Kitchen cabinets made by Neil Kelly Cabinets, using Columbia Forest Products'
PureBond® formaldehyde-free hardwood plywood.

COUNTRY NATURAL BEEF
A Maturing Co-op at the Crossroads

By Madeleine E. Pullman, Ph.D., Victoria Villa-Lobos, and Zhaohui Wu, Ph.D.

Country Natural Beef Case Study

Introduction

After the three-hour drive from Roaring Springs Ranch in Frenchglen, Oregon, Stacey Davies eased his pickup into the gates of Probert Ranch in Vale, Oregon near the Idaho border. He had only a couple hours to stop there and then continue west to the feedlot partner in Boardman, Oregon. As the new Marketing Internal Partner for Country Natural Beef (CNB) cooperative (co-op), Stacey had come to visit Dan and Suzy Probert. While Stacey routinely spoke to the Proberts on the phone, meeting in person was helpful in their new roles, Dan, the elected president and Stacy, the new Marketing Manager. A producer of naturally raised meat, the co-op had become a major player in the value-added beef industry as the natural product industry has experienced rapid growth in the past decade. Lately, the members were concerned with union problems at the feedlot, animal welfare issues and the stress of continued growth. In the previous summer, several ranchers had financially suffered from their cows getting sick in the feedlot and receiving treatment with antibiotics. The cows that recovered were taken out of the natural beef program while some died.

"You know," said Dan, "these economic times aren't too much different from when CNB got started." Stacey countered, 'Decommodify or die' still applies, but the world has changed. There's a lot more cowboys playing our game, the rules are tougher." Dan nodded, "We always have to be cognizant of what our customers want, address animal compassion issues and find new markets opportunities. But if this gets too complicated, we might also cause a lot of frustration for our members." Both men wondered what they could do to stay vital when sales had been flat recently after rapid growth for many years.

Cattle Ranching Industry

Industry Overview

In the commodity or generic beef market, inputs and outputs are bought and sold along a well-established transaction path where price is largely determined by cost and individual cattle weight. The beef supply chain is highly fragmented. On the one hand, approximately 750,000 operators command $500 billion in annual revenue and only 5,000 ranchers own more than 500 head (individual cows). The top fifty operators amount to under two percent of the market (Beef Cattle Ranching, 2009). On the other hand, the meat fabrication industry (i.e. slaughterers, primary and secondary processors, and distributors) is highly concentrated and earns annual revenues of $85 billion. In the slaughterer segment, the 50 largest slaughterers control 90 percent of the market, whereas the secondary processor segment is less concentrated with the top 50 companies managing 60 percent of the market. Top firms include Tyson Foods, the largest slaughterer and beef products manufacturer; Cargill Meat Solutions, a diversified meat processor and distributor; and JBS-USA, the Brazilian corporation that recently acquired two major processors—Swift & Co and Smithfield Beef Group—and the largest feedlot operation (Exhibits 1 and 2). Feeders tend to be concentrated; the larger feedlots market about 80 percent to 90 percent of the feedlot finished cattle, whereas 95 percent of feedlots have a one-time capacity of less than 1,000 head. As of 2006, the National Cattlemen's Association reported the 25 largest feed yards had a combined one-time capacity of 5.15 million head.

Cattle and Beef Supply Chain

The cattle and beef supply chain has five major players (Exhibit 3). Ranchers (cow/calf operators) raise young calves. The young calves receive mothers' milk and are weaned; the weaned calves graze on pasture and range land. Some ranchers sell the weaned calves (400-600 pounds each) to stocker operators whose role is to add more weight to the calves. Typically, the full–grown calves are fattened in feedlots before slaughter where the feedlot buys the calves from the cow/calf or stocker operators. Commodity beef is generally ranch-raised for six to nine months weighing between 600 and 800 pounds, and then sold to feedlot operators in the Midwest (Iowa and Illinois) or high plains (Texas to Nebraska). There, they are finished on high grain rations for 120 to 140 days and slaughtered by packers at 1,200 to 1,400 pounds. Typically, cattle producers sell livestock through local or remote auctions conducted over video or the internet. Live cattle prices are negotiated based on sex, weight, genetics, health, location and estimated cost to finish. Truckload quantities of stock with similar traits are purchased by feedlot operators to be delivered one to eight weeks in the future.

During the finishing phase, prior to slaughter, diet has a strong impact on final meat characteristics such as flavor, tenderness and marbling. Dietary programs are typically designed to realize three goals: 1) meat consistency across herds that are raised in various climates and with varying diets, 2) weight gain maximization, and 3) cost minimization. Diets can consist of forage (harvested or grazed herbaceous plants such as hay and alfalfa) grains, corn, or vegetables such as potatoes. Though not the industry standard, cattle can also be finished in open pastures, or large enclosed areas, sometimes called "bunkers", pens of varying sizes that are provide more space per cow than typical feedlots.

With feed as their largest direct cost, operators are concerned with feed efficiency or the rate that feed translates into gained weight and have sought to optimize production by building increasingly larger operations. Forage quality of a given range or pasture varies according to soil, terrain, rainfall and climate conditions which affect the carrying capacity of the land to support the herd size. Rancher costs rise with the need to supplement their own available ranch forage with purchased grazing rights on other's land and/or feed supplements. Large scale feed yards (100,000 to 200,000 head capacity) known as concentrated animal feeding operations (CAFO) attempt to leverage economies of scale by concentrating animals into small spaces. Issues over "factory farming" of animals extend into food safety, animal compassion and environmental arguments against the backdrop of globalization and increasing complex supply chains.

Hidden costs associated with CAFOs have drawn increasing scrutiny from animal rights activists and consumers alike. Organic contaminants like E. coli from manure "dumps" near feedlots create runoff into proximate rivers, streams and ground water. Animal welfare issues have moved mainstream in recent years. Hot topics include stressed animals confined in poor living conditions; the incompatibility of high corn diets with bovine digestion; and the trucking of cattle over long distances, all of which can translate into more sickness, antibiotics, vaccinations and premature deaths. A body of work by Temple Grandin (2008), an animal scientist at Colorado State University, includes research into bovine behavior and the effects of stress involved with farm-factory production. She details optimum methods to minimize cattle fear and insure cattle stay calm and injury-free during especially hazardous phases of transport, feedlot maneuvering and slaughter. Her animal empathic approach has gained acceptance across the industry and has been acknowledged for fostering higher yields and higher quality of meat as well as improved humane conditions. The USDA Food Safety and Inspection Service has consulted with Dr. Grandin to incorporate her objective scoring system for evaluating animal handling and stunning prior to death, into guidelines and training materials for cattle and pig operations.

Meat processors buy feeder cows through agents who cover cattle auctions, sales barns and feed yard sales, then sell finished product to across diverse marketing channels: grocery chains, hotel and restaurant chains, foodservice distributors, food brokers and other processors. Finished product can be sold as wholesale meat parts ("boxed beef") for secondary processing, ground beef, or retail "case ready" cuts prepared for grocery store display. Facing product perishability and price/quality competition, marketing activities by larger processors have been characterized by extensive distribution systems with regional warehouse and sales hubs, quick turnaround order placement and the absence of long–term contracts.

Country Natural Beef

History

The co-op began at a time that seemed to be "end of the family ranch." Many small ranchers were in dire straits under a combination of factors: mounting pressures from dieticians to "eat less red meat", a popular perception of the abuse of public land by cattle over-grazing activities, rising interest rates and wildly fluctuating commodity beef prices.

In 1986, Doc and Connie Hatfield invited 14 ranchers over to their place in Brothers, Oregon to figure out how to survive. As Connie summed up, "there has to be a better way to market cattle." After long discussions, the marketing co-op was born. They would produce higher margin product with lean, natural beef *and* would hold members to high standards of ranching practices. Country Natural Beef, originally Oregon Country Beef, would seek markets for their products as an alternative to conventional meat. The founding couples believed they should listen to folks that wanted their product. Over time CNB found that, beyond concerns with growth promotants and antibiotics in the meat products, consumers who were willing to pay more for quality aspects were becoming concerned with such issues as open land grazing, watershed management, and habitat preservation. CNB recognized that their products and the story behind the products were in alignment with the concerns of the customers. The early days were challenging. As Doc recalled, several ranchers made cold calls to potential customers in the city, delivering one or two cattle in a blizzard to a slaughter house near Portland before Christmas. The business grew gradually. Over 23 years CNB grew from a 14-family cooperative into a niche beef market leader with about 120 family ranches in Oregon, Washington, California, Arizona, Nevada, Idaho, Montana, Wyoming, and Colorado.

Co-op Strategy

Members adopted a "consumer-centric" focus for specifying the differentiating product attributes that informed the development of their operational practices. As its mission statement stipulates, "…Country Natural Beef will excel at developing markets which best utilize practical ranch cattle and at translating cost and carcass data into information which assists members in making sound management decisions." Ranchers own the product from "birth to plate" or from mother cow to calf to steer, and from their ranches to the feed yard, virtually throughout the fabrication process and into the sales channels. Beef steers are born from cows raised on member ranches, not purchased from livestock auctions, a practice that makes CNB livestock traceable to its ranch origins. Cattle are free of antibiotics, growth hormone implants and animal by-product feed additives. CNB followed a 100% vegetarian diet for cattle before mammalian protein was prohibited from ruminant feed manufacture Food and Drug Administration in 1997. When CNB first decided to stop using hormones and antibiotics in the early 90s, it was a big challenge for some ranchers because they had depended on these products for disease control. But, over-time, they learned preventative cattle and range management practices that naturally improved the immunity of the herd.

The founding ranchers were among the first to adopt Holistic Range Management principles created by Savory and Butterfield. These ideas formed the basis of CNB's Grazewell Principles to which each ranch must subscribe. And, each ranch is third-party certified for their animal, worker, and environmental practices by Food Alliance, a non-profit organization that develops sustainable agriculture and food handling standards. Third-party verification is central to the brand promise of authenticity; few natural beef brands boast the claim of outside agency audits for specific, measurable sustainability practices for naturally-raised beef. It takes two years of trial membership to make the operational changes and undertake lengthy verification with Food Alliance before ranchers become full-fledged members. Members initially pay a fee for the comprehensive onsite audit covering soil, water and wildlife habitat conservation, labor practices, pesticide reduction, animal welfare guidelines and continual improvement plan. The certification also requires a signed affidavit and audit renewal every three years. The presence of a certification procedure has discouraged some ranchers from joining particularly those who did not welcome outside interference. But, it has clearly raised the management standard across every stage of supply chain from animal handling to feedlot operations.

Governance and Decision-making

As shown in Exhibit 5, CNB has a cooperative structure. It is a "brickless" organization in the sense that they hold no assets except ear tags and some office equipment. CNB closely controls its product; it does not transfer the product title and relinquish ownership until cattle have been processed and the meat is ready for distribution. Although the meat processing company AB Foods purchases animal carcass from CNB, it sells back the end product to CNB, who then makes payment to the co-op members. Exhibit 6 illustrates key players of CNB's supply chain.

Every ranching family in CNB is considered a board of director, exercises one vote, and has veto power in decision making. Decisions are made based on consensus, meaning that everyone comments on major issues and eventually gives a "yes" vote. Years ago Connie Hatfield had insisted that the women take equal part in the organization which has broken down gender barriers and added a broader perspective to the group.

As CNB grew in size, the inefficiency of slow consensus-based decision-making at meetings became more apparent. CNB created the management team, who is responsible for effective communications, insuring transparency, and providing decisions are made in a timely fashion. The co-op is composed of team leaders and internal partners. Four team leaders are elected by the board to three-year terms and oversee all business affairs of the cooperative. Newly elected team leaders designate the chairman/president who directs the entire management team and is accountable directly to the board. Other officers include vice-chairman, secretary and treasurer. The Management Team (MT) decides by consensus and can formulate subcommittees to address evolving issues such as environmental and private label programs.

Members work tirelessly on solutions that everyone can live with. The bi-annual board meetings open in a "Full Circle," a ritual where members sit in a circle, introduce themselves and mention what issue concerns or pleases them most. Agenda items are brought up in the beginning of the meeting. They are hashed out over sessions of smaller group meetings. As members argue and negotiate, those who chair sessions routinely remind attendees to "speak and listen with respect." Emotions often run high in the group with traditions of equanimity and transparency. Solutions from the breakout groups are proposed for a vote on the final day in another round of Full Circle.

Delivery Scheduling and Pricing
Each family ranch is a production unit and operates independently, acquiring and managing its own means of production, including land, labor, equipment, and livestock. Families commit to "place" calves at the feedlot during specific monthly slots on the calendar each year. These delivery time slots are allocated based on a family's tenure in the co-op. Each year, the production team uses demand forecasts to develop placement slots which are announced at the meeting and ranchers promise to deliver based on their production schedule with consideration of the breeding cows, weaning calves, and securing grazing capacity, etc.

The co-op uses data from two dozen ranches of different sizes to determine the cost of production each year and a cost–plus method to determine the product price. The entire carcass is pre-sold to committed buyers based on forecast numbers worked out with customers a year ahead. The price does not change over the year during this time period. This fixed price removes the traditional price fluctuations and secures the ranchers a steady and predictable cash flow. While the price is fixed, the production office managers and the customers constantly monitor meats sales data to adjust the sales price between meat cuts (ground beef versus New York steaks) to balance demand and supply.

CBN aims for leaner beef than premium types of commodity beef. Instead of the adopting and rewarding the usual USDA grading system (i.e. Prime-highest price, Choice, Select and Standard-lowest prices), CNB rewards are tied to "target" and "bullseye" goals based on a combination of lean characteristics (similar to Choice and Select grades) and size of the rib-eye steak cuts. The ranchers are paid three checks: animal placement fee (the fee is higher for winter than summer months), the basic price per pound along with a bonus for meeting the target meat specification, and finally a bonus for meeting the "bullseye" requirement: additional reward for meeting a narrower specification of lean and rib-eye size. The co-op members also pay fees for their marketing organization, cost of feedlot (feed cost per day and veterinarian care) and insurance for the out-of-program cattle on a per-head basis.

Internal Partners

Internal partners take on different traditional business functions (marketing, production, and finance) as shown in Exhibit 6 and detailed below.

Marketing

For many years Connie and Doc had led the marketing team with an emphasis on maintaining critical relationships with retail customers. The Hatfield's personal touch nurtured the relationship with the western region buyer at Whole Foods before all buying was centralized in the Texas headquarters. The CNB team receives weekly customer orders, manages boxed inventory, delivers forecasts 18 months in advance, oversees marketing communications, and coordinates rancher in-store events with retail customers at various grocer outlets. Ranchers are required to spend two days a year doing in-store demonstrations, wearing their cowboy hats, boots, and aprons, and engaging shoppers with free meat samples, recipes and information (Exhibit 7). They also build relationships with meat managers in the stores. These in-store events help to build a direct relationship with the customers. One rancher remarked, "marketing events represent a loss of time and money to members for whom ranching is full time job. I drove 200 miles yesterday, spent six hours at one store, got up this morning to do it again here and I'll drive home tonight. But when it's all said and done, it's important each one of us get to know our customers, share stories, and let 'em know what goes into the product…what their choice in selecting our beef means to ranchers and the land." After each in-store event, the ranchers submit a detailed report intended to capture changes in customer attitudes, perceptions and preferences that are published by Production in a newsletter.

By the end of the spring 2009 meeting, the marketing co-op had entered a new era when leadership transitioned from the Hatfields to Stacey Davies. Discussion on the transition had been heated. For one, Doc and Connie Hatfield had been the leaders of the co-op since the beginning. As charismatic leaders, their presence had strongly affected the culture of the co-op and played a critical role in establishing close relationships with the key customers of the co-op over the years. The transition was emotional for both Doc and Connie and the co-op members. Second, the transition signified an important milestone for CNB. It took place when CNB had evolved into a key player in the natural beef industry and considered changes its marketing and business processes. The management styles of Stacy Davis and Doc and Connie Hatfield differed. Portraying the public face of the co–op, Doc and Connie have worked closely with key customers since the beginning and were well-regarded by the customers with whom they have built personal friendships. Stacey was more goal-oriented with an eye for market development and cost control. Some ranchers were uneasy with the sudden call for change, expecting the transition to take place over years. Others worried that Stacy's results-oriented focus might inhibit group synergy. In the end of the meeting, Stacy was inducted at the new Internal Marketing Partner in a room with few dry eyes. Whether Stacey's leadership style or his strategy would sustain the culture of the co-op and insure returns to ranchers or that members would value his business sense enough to give him a fair shake, remained to be seen, but it was clear there were more pressing concerns.

Production

After Dan Probert was elected President, Ryan Steele was named Production Team leader, responsible for scheduling calf placements entering the Beef Northwest feedlot. Ryan's team worked closely with Marketing to make the necessary adjustments for cattle flowing into the feedlot and out to the slaughter site, all at the correct weight and time that corresponded to customer demand. Balancing the demand and supply required innate understanding of the cattle, markets, and partners. They worked closely with the customers to coordinate promotions to ensure all products were sold at maximal level of profit.

Accounting

Mary Forman led a small team that handled all the enterprise's finances from banking and accounting, to demand projections and risk management. The team members were wives of several ranch families who lived close by the Foreman ranch in Antelope, Oregon, where the accounting office is located. The team manages carcass and profitability data, interfaces with other partners, and reports to the board. They worked on various projects to provide accounting information to support the co-op decisions processes. For instance, the team came up with a standard method to track individual operational costs, which were then aggregated into a production model reflecting overall cost production and the minimum profit required.

External Partners

There are three essential external partners who form the rest of the CNB value chain: the feeder, the processor and the distributor.

Feeder

CNB members sent cattle to Beef Northwest (BNW) in Boardman, Oregon, when a calf is 14 to 16 months old (roughly 800 pounds). After 90 days on a mixed ration of cooked potatoes (50%)[74] and an alfalfa and corn mix (50%), cattle are slaughtered at an average weight of 1,150 pounds. The shorter stay is designed to reduce the time that animals are subject to the more stressful conditions of the feedlot. The goal is to produce the smaller cuts of lean beef that customers want. About one third of BNW operation is dedicated to CNB cattle, the rest to commodity production. Although corn or grain finishing is scorned by some for unnecessary roughness on bovine digestive systems naturally suited to forage or possible contribution to E. coli problems, and BNW cannot guarantee their corn comes from non-genetically modified sources, the feed yard operator is regarded by some as more progressive in the industry. Working in its favor is its moderate size (40,000 head capacity) and location in a temperate, dry climate which helps mitigate the effects of mud and heat stress. Managers have developed facilities design, staff training programs, and handling practices in conjunction with CNB ranchers and expert advice from Drs. Temple Grandin and Tom Nofsinger. Careful record keeping, special care and separation from generic herds are needed at this phase to maintain the integrity of CNB standards. The feeder also contracts nutrition and veterinary services for improved animal health performance. Sick CNB cattle are treated with vitamins and sulfa drugs and moved to antibiotics only as a last resort.

Prior to harvest, cattle are observed for the kind of weight gain that ameliorates tenderness and consistency attributes. CNB cattle are pasture fed longer than generic beef but shorter than purely pasture-fed beef sold as "grass-fed." Different pasture grasses across many ranches causes flavor profile variation, something BNW tries to even out with a standardized diet applied to incoming herds of various breeds and weights. The goal is for 90 percent of cattle to meet target specifications and over 60 percent to meet tighter bulls eye specifications.

Slaughter & Processing

---

74 The Boardman facility uses potato byproducts from a nearby potato processing plants that furnishes fries to fast food chains.

AB Foods receives the cattle trucked from BNW bearing identifying ear tags that trace the animal back to rancher origins. Keeping animals (and eventually the end product) separate from the commodity beef, AB Foods kills the animals following humane criteria set by CNB. The rest of the process includes removing non-edible parts, trimming waste, and packaging the salable meat into large sections. AB Foods also sells animal byproduct (hide, hooves, innards, etc. for the automotive, garment and sporting goods industries), and any surplus boxed inventory or out-of-program cows. The processor furnishes carcass analysis data covering grade, yield, size and quality metrics directly to the ranchers. AB Foods is third party audited by Steritech for humane handling and sanitation practices.

Distribution

Secondary processor and specialty meat distributor, Fulton Provisions Company receives boxed inventory from AB Foods, grinds select parts into ground beef, and distributes to grocery, restaurant and industrial buyers. Fulton was acquired by food service giant, Sysco, in 2000, yet retains independent operations in Portland, Oregon with 100 employees and 1000 customers. Influential customers, Burgerville and Whole Foods, pressured Fulton into improving internal standards and in 2008, Fulton became third-party certified by Food Alliance for sustainable business practices. The audit encompassed waste management, worker conditions, water and energy conservation and transportation. Fulton took steps such as converting trucks to biodiesel, recycling packaging materials, salvaging wood pallets, installing a water recirculation system, replacing processing chemicals with non-residue forming ones and upgrading old machines with energy efficient models. Vice President of Sales and Marketing, Tom Semke, admits that the program "increases costs but in the long run it'll save us money." As a consequence of the Food Alliance certification, Fulton managers rewrote their own internal standard processing procedures that verify the integrity of all meat products beyond what the USDA requires.

Fulton supplies many high-end institutional meat buyers such as Sodexho and Bon Appétit Management Company (BAMC), which provides food service to corporations and campuses, and boasts a commitment to good food and sustainability. Regional Vice President, Mark Swenson comments, "We have to work very closely with our partner suppliers to achieve both those ends. It means something when a partner like Fulton is willing to take that extra step and get Food Alliance certified."

Customers

New Seasons — *"The friendliest store in town"*

CNB had long-term partnership with Brian Rohter, CEO of New Seasons grocery stores. New Seasons is a privately held, regional natural grocery chain of nine stores in the metropolitan area of Portland, Oregon. Their annual beef sales were around 570,000 pounds. Positioned as a "neighborhood store" with easy shopping and wide aisles where "you can find Frosted Flakes as well as free range chicken," their SKU mix was roughly 75 percent natural and 25 percent conventional items.

CNB supplied all of New Seasons private label and branded case beef. Fitting well with a "Home Grown" labeling program to identify products from California, Oregon and Washington, the chain has introduced a store brand under the Pacific Village label. Other lines included organic butter, organic milk, natural pork, free-range chicken, natural beef and organic buffalo. "We're actually increasing the number of acres farmed in Oregon, Washington and Northern California," according to New Seasons President, Lisa Sedlar. CNB tested a pilot program for "pasture finished" natural beef under the Pacific Village label in 2008. Pasture or grass–fed beef is less tender, but leaner than grain fed and needs more grazing time to increase weight. With the current program, the CNB grass-fed group supplied around twelve head a week during a nine–month season (non-winter). New Seasons found that end-users were willing to pay about a $1 per pound premium over the regular natural product, but processing and transportation costs were limiting the store's margins.

The CNB marketing team relayed cut, quantity and timing details, giving New Seasons buyers an option to forward purchase when conditions have led to an abundance of specific meat selections. New Seasons often accepted these surpluses and makes merchandising decisions about how to move the product; for example by seasoning/marinating less popular non-steak cuts, creating recipes and providing and wine pairing suggestions.

Burgerville — *"Fresh. Local. Sustainable."*

Burgerville is a Pacific Northwest fast food chain which stressed local products. The ground beef supplier, Fulton's, relationship with Burgerville went back 47 years. Tom Semke credits the chain of healthy quick food with influencing Fulton to become Food Alliance certified adding "we've grown because of people like Burgerville." Since doors opened in 1961, Burgerville has concentrated on local and fresh. When Tom Mears became Burgerville's CEO, he required ingredient suppliers to practice sustainable agriculture. Centralized purchasing for the 39 restaurants in Washington and Oregon is done from a long list of direct farmer/suppliers. The most popular sandwich is by far the hamburger, and Burgerville buys all its patties, up to 40,000 pounds a week from CNB.

Burgerville had not always been the volume purchaser that it is today. Initially, CNB was unable to supply the quantity of beef patties when the chain decided to switch from frozen commodity to fresh natural beef. Burgerville executives decided to hold back the launch until the co-op could catch up. CNB eventually had sufficient supply for Burgerville as its overall production increased. In fact, the two companies have a symbiotic relationship; without Burgerville taking all the ground beef, it is not possible for CNB to sell the appropriate volume of higher end beef cuts to the other customers because they need to sell all parts of the animal. The co-op became a major part of Burgerville's vision and the restaurant became CNB's primary restaurant customer. Jack Graves, Chief Cultural Officer and 32–year veteran of the company, explained how CNB internal marketing partners facilitate carcass sales, "Norm Birch is the guy that sits down at his computer and gets all the orders from Whole Foods and all of the other groceries. He figures out how each head of cattle needs to be cut so that the processor knows how to break down the cattle for the different cuts of meat for all these different stores. And so that's a very scientific process…they just count on us to be able to take most of the hamburger."

Supply Chain Director, Alison Denis, believes that an ability to create a desirable food taste and "doing business in the neighbourhood" drives Burgerville purchasing and focuses their sustainability practices on "where there is a strong business opportunity." Their operational improvements towards sustainability include: providing used cooking grease as an input to biodiesel makers, purchasing wind power credits equal to their total electricity consumption, and diverting 85 percent of their restaurant waste to composting and recycling with annual removal cost savings of $100,000. They also subsidize affordable medical/dental/vision coverage to employees working at least 20 hours a week. Burgerville picks up 90 percent of the cost for qualifying employees and their dependents. Alison adds, "We have amazingly low attrition rates among staff than you would find in our industry as standard."

Whole Foods Market — *"Selling the highest quality natural & organic products."*

With 275 stores in the US, Canada and the UK, the Austin, Texas firm earns revenues in excess of $7.95 billion,[75] and has become world's largest natural

---

75   For FY ending September 2008.

foods corporation. John Mackey forged the natural supermarket format in 1980 and has grown it steadily through acquisition and diversification. In stores, the emphasis is on perishable products, which account for roughly two-thirds of sales. Notwithstanding poor sales and stock results for 2008, the company affirmed plans for new store openings alongside an ever-increasing portfolio of assets: a coffee company, a supplement manufacturer, a magazine, a lifestyle furnishings store, a seafood processing and distribution operation, and four private label lines carrying 2,300 items across food, personal care, supplements, clothing, household products and toys categories. By the end of 2009, Whole Foods aimed to bring all store brand products using crop sources (i.e., oils, corn syrup, corn starch and soy lecithin) under the Non-GMO Project's compliance seal. In 2005, the retailer launched the Animal Compassion Foundation, a non-profit organization formed to research the compassionate treatment of livestock. Undaunted by recent economic conditions and competition from supermarkets and Wal-Mart, officials had announced a target of $12 billion in sales by 2010.

CNB supplies all the natural, non-grass–fed beef to western Whole Foods stores and Panorama, supplies all of the organic, grass-fed beef—which runs about $1 per pound higher than the CNB product. Panorama slaughters livestock at 14-16 months. Their production agreement involves a partnership with an Arapaho Tribe in Wyoming and their certified organic reservation rangelands. The council-run operation receives $1,400 a head at harvest time and supplies 25 western stores. The retailer had begun holding sit-down dinners at certain locations where customer meet the different ranchers and hear about their practices.

Whole Foods is CNB's only national retail partner, accounting for roughly 70 percent of total annual sales. They initially sourced CNB product through their western regional office. The Marketing Team of CNB led by Doc and Connie cultivated close interpersonal relationships with key managers at the regional office and grew with the expanding retailer to supply 22 western stores. When Whole Foods consolidated its purchasing function in its Texas headquarters, those relationships were strained as the new Texas managers did not have the shared history with the co-op.

In 2006, one incident made the co-op to reassess its relationship with its biggest customer. In the fall of 2006, the United Farm Workers Union (UFW) tried to persuade workers at Beef Northwest to unionize. A drawn-out controversy followed, calling into question BNW's tolerance for unions. In a campaign for public support, the union enlisted consumer groups to question the labor practices at the feedlot.[76] Members of the Organic Consumers Association organized demonstrations at western Whole Foods stores calling for "no sweatshop beef!"[477] Aided by the union, a delegation of BNW workers personally submitted a petition to senior management at Whole Foods calling for the retailer to pressure BNW into negotiating with the union. In May 2008, Whole Foods officially requested CNB to stop sending cattle to BNW and announced they would halt purchases from CNB. Quickly, customers who have bought CNB products for years petitioned, requesting Whole Foods to rescind the decision. CNB and BNW issued public statements stressing their desire for workers to decide for themselves rather than union bosses; the union-orchestrated vote calling for union representation was neither conducted by secret ballot nor overseen by a neutral third party. After meeting with CNB ranchers in June, Whole Foods reversed its decision, announcing "we have not stopped selling their beef." The co-op convinced Whole Foods that it would be difficult to find another feedlot with the equipment, personnel, expertise and willingness to separate and finish their cattle according to the humane requirements and in a hormone and antibiotic-free environment.

CNB held in-store events in Portland Whole Foods locations, aimed at reconnecting with those store customers and organized a private ballot election to be monitored by a neutral third party. In November 2008, the dispute ended without an election, but "mutually agreed upon a process by which 80 feedlot employees … [of Beef Northwest] would decide if they want union representation."[578] CNB attributes their long history of in-stores, personal connections with retail customers, and experience in consensus-building as factors that helped them with conflict resolution at the feedlot and Whole Foods.

The union issue and centralized purchasing continued to concern CNB because of the growing physical and interpersonal distance and inherent complexities of dealing with a large growing corporation.

PCC Natural Markets — *"Our passion is food"*
What began with 15 families purchasing food together in 1953 had become a large consumer-owned natural food cooperative that rang up over $133 million in sales for 2008. The nine-store chain is held by 40,000 members in Puget Sound area of Washington who realized dividends in excess of $2.6 million in 2008—a year-over increase of 18 percent. "Our shareholders are our customers. Our profits are turned back to the members in proportion to the amount

---

76 "Union Targets Oregon Feedlot."
77 "Tell Whole Foods: No Sweatshop 'Natural' Beef!"
78 "Beef Northwest, United Farmworkers Reach Agreement on Election."

of business they do here [...] Co-ops are a way of providing local control over where you do your business," says former trustee Trudy Bialac. PCC works through an affiliated nonprofit, Farmland Trust, to assist organic farmland through loan repayment and land purchase programs. The grocer recently banned all products containing ingredients from cloned animals. Organic beef is sold under branded programs from Damar Farms (Wisconsin) and Eel River Organic Farms (Northern California), while grass fed beef is sourced from Thundering Hooves (Washington), and natural beef from CNB.

OTHER CUSTOMERS. A few local restaurants purchase smaller quantities of inventory (meat products) through Fulton Provision along with food chains and institutions that are usually represented by third party management companies. A provider of onsite eateries at 400 locations at universities, corporations and entertainment venues, Bon Appétit Management Company is CNB's largest foodservice account, followed by Sodexo and Aramark. Co-founder and CEO of Bon Appétit, Fedele Bauccio, remarked, "once we learned that livestock operations produce 18 percent of all worldwide greenhouse gas emissions, exceeding even transportation, we committed to reducing our meat consumption. We moved away from industrially raised meat to natural-beef burgers that have less water. We found that a 4-ounce natural beef patty tastes better and cooks to the same size as a conventional 5-ounce patty. If you can convince customers about the importance of what you're doing, tell a story, and offer great-tasting food, you will get higher sales that will cover a couple of percentage points in higher costs."

Economic Outlook

With rising unemployment and household budget cuts, red meat becomes more difficult to market to consumers who increasingly view the pricey protein as a luxury item. Beef consumption has trended downward since the 1970's. Recent consumption of animal protein has remained flat (Exhibit 14) and the outlook for future beef sales appears weak. The degree to which recessionary pressures come into play in niche segments is uncertain, given that continued growth is anticipated for natural, organic and grass-fed. According to FreshLook Marketing and The Beef Checkoff, natural/organic beef grew 27 percent and sales by weight increased by 22 percent from Q3 2007 to Q3 2008.

Competitors

CNB faces a variety of competitors. Regional grass-fed beef ranches had begun selling beef at near wholesale prices online direct to consumers. They are marketed to the environmental and health conscious consumers and chefs who prefer to avoid feedlot programs, particularly corn-fed animals. Estimates of domestic grass-fed beef production indicate 65,000 head sold in 2006 and 100,000 in 2007; demand is expected to reach 250,000 to 400,000 head by 2010.

Perhaps the more immediate threat comes from the proliferation of natural beef being sold through traditional grocery stores, and the growing number of "artisanal" beef products that also qualify as USDA natural beef. Coleman Natural Foods was the first USDA-certified 'natural' beef producer and is a leading national processor, marketer and distributor of processed natural meat products. Wary of private label competition, Mel Coleman Jr. noted, "Retailers could start bidding on beef and purchase the cheapest brand instead of trying to develop a product line that will allow ranchers…to make a fair margin." Whole Foods radically changed its supplier requirements and meat receiving procedures *and* its relationship with Coleman due to ground beef E. coli contamination in its eastern stores, which occurred after Coleman temporarily switched to Nebraska Beef for processing without informing Whole Foods. In 2008, Coleman sold its beef business to Meyer Natural Angus, and continues to sell packaged poultry and pork to Whole Foods, Kroger, and Costco.

After purchasing Laura's Lean Beef in 2007 and Coleman Natural Beef in 2008, Meyer Natural Angus is now a leading national producer and marketer of natural beef. Its beef comes from its own 43,000-acre ranch in Montana and 200 contracted Red Angus cattle ranchers across the U.S. They fabricate approximately 10,000 head of cattle a month and sell fresh and frozen product nationwide in foodservice and direct-to-consumer channels as well as grocery and restaurant chains, including Whole Foods, Wegmans and Chipotle Mexican Grill. Between 2005 and 2008, the company grew from $10 million to $150 million in sales, and recently announced plans to double office space in order to grow their internet sales. Their corn-finished, USDA Prime grade product is sold under specific process claims including humane certification by Farm Animal Care, and "verified origins" of the cattle to specific ranches.

Laura's Lean Beef recruits independent producers across the U.S. for their natural beef program: cow/calf operators, finishers, and slaughter.[79] The

---

79   See http://www.laurasleanbeef.com for cattle specifications, bonus programs, and affidavit forms.

company gives bonuses for increased weights, hitting lean targets and rewards retained ownership. Incentives for finishers are free trucking, carcass data and ear tagging. Signed affidavits are required to ensure that no antibiotics or hormones were administered and that good animal husbandry practices were followed. Branded portion-packed products (fresh beef, cooked entrees, and frozen ground beef patties) are sold in 6,500 stores in 47 states, including Kroger, Albertsons and Lucky supermarkets.

Niman Ranch is another competitor. Some say Bill Niman pioneered standards for humane animal husbandry methods and hormone and antibiotic-free practices when he started small in 1970. He left Niman Ranch at its $85 million-a-year pinnacle in 2007 after accepting outside investors and having run-ins with the new management, headed by Jeff Swain, formerly of Coleman Natural Beef. Bill was against selling off assets (their own custom butchering plant and feedlots) only to buy finished cattle from other feedlots. Transport distances became another issue; Bill thought transporting animals to slaughter over 500 miles was inhumane, while Swain maintained that a 24–hour rest period could remedy travel stress. Swain criticized Bill's management of the beef program, "Any change to Bill's business model, he didn't like…we needed to make the company financially sustainable." Bill is now in the natural goat business. The Niman brand fresh and prepared beef, pork and lamb products are distributed through foodservice, specialty retailers, chain restaurants such as Chipotle Mexican Grill and Big Bowl, and its web site. The company sources meat from about 650 contracted ranchers and processes about 400 cattle a week. Their website mentions "Third Party Verification" in reference to humane and sustainable practices and mentions an affiliation with Temple Grandin, but does not cite the verifying agency or protocols.

Another diversified national niche meat player is Maverick Ranch Natural Meats, offering fresh and ready-to-eat natural pork, lamb, buffalo, beef, and free-range chicken to over 2,000 grocers. Due to soft sales in recessionary conditions, Maverick recently announced staff layoffs, a plant closure and a joint venture—licensing the Maverick brand to Heritage Acres Foods.

Another Pacific Northwestern competitor, Painted Hills Corporation, was started by seven small ranchers from coastal Oregon in 1997. As a rancher-owned and operated group, it sells packaged and fresh beef products to small grocery chains and foodservice accounts. Natural beef attributes and cattle source verification is handled by rancher-signed affidavits. Cattle are corn-finished 150 days at Simplot Feeders in Pasco, Washington to produce a higher marbled USDA Choice grade. Roughly 350 to 550 head per week are processed at the adjacent Tyson meat packing operation. By walking the cattle to slaughter, the corporation saves from $10 to $15 a head in transportation costs and greater yield. According to Painted Hills, Tyson works with Temple Grandin and follows a set of "tough standards to ensure animal are properly handled. Tyson also offer Painted Hills an integrated marketing program to grocery and restaurant customers, including consumer education, pricing guidance, point-of-purchase materials and co-op advertising reimbursements.

Challenges Ahead

Animal Welfare Concerns

Whole Foods commissioned a survey in 2006 that revealed that besides flavor, consumers were concerned with safety and the humane treatment of animals when choosing quality meat. "Whole Foods had required basic animal welfare in what we sold—no antibiotics or hormones—but we felt we needed to do more," explained Margaret Wittenberg, Global VP of Quality and Public Affairs last summer. The former member of the USDA National Organic Standards Board, Wittenberg has been at the helm of meat standards development at Whole Foods for eight years. Whole Foods invited animal-welfare groups and scientists to join them at the table with producers to tackle all the species. After five years, the company settled on a system that recognizes that there can be variation as well as continuous improvement. By spring 2008, the Global Animal Partnership (GAP) standard was created to improve the way farm animals are cared for from birth to slaughter. GAP authored compassionate farm animal treatment standards with graduated levels. The USDA Food Safety and Inspection Service (FSIS) has approved Whole Foods Market's *5-Step TM Animal Welfare Rating System*. At the store level, the program features a labeling system as a shoppers' guide to identify progressively higher standards of animal treatment through production.

At the CNB spring 2009 board meeting, it became clear that Whole Foods was eager to have CNB onboard as the first supplier. Some ranchers voiced strong concerns of the practicality of the standard and potential impact of the adoption to the brand equity of CNB products. CNB considered drafting its own animal compassion standard with help from Dr. Temple Grandin, whose work influenced the GAP and other standards.

OP Issues and Feedlot

Recent challenges at Beef Northwest have impacted the bottom line for several ranch families. There was a surge of sick cows resulting in many going out-of-program (OP). When a cow gets sick and receives antibiotics, it gets tagged, pulled out of the natural beef category and sold in the commodity market. The OP condition is believed to more frequently occur with newer, less experienced ranchers and those ranchers who have to transport animals over long distances to get to the feedlot. Another theory was that newer members generally have to place their cattle in the feedlot during winter when it is trickier to achieve efficient weights and severe temperature swings over trucking routes put more stress on the cattle. Yet there is no clear consensus on the reasons for the OP surge. The ranchers also wondered what could happen at the feedlot when cattle from different ranches mingle. OP designations can cause tremendous financial losses for smaller ranches. After hours of discussion, an "OP insurance" plan was approved where ranchers and BNW paid premiums into the program which would reimburse ranchers who encountered an above average level of OP cows.

Some ranchers felt consumer pressure to move away from corn feed; others thought that CNB should prepare for a growing market of grass–fed beef. Another emerging hot button for consumers appeared to be humane animal treatment at feedlots. Currently, there were two auditing agencies for feed lots: one reviews standard operating procedures and the other, animal handling practices. While Beef Northwest was not "humane certified" they were "animal compassion tested." Dan Probert wondered if it didn't make sense to add another feedlot just for Whole Foods cattle, one that could be setup with all the specifications from the get-go and be more centrally located. He remembered Charlotte Reid, CNB's environmental program director, telling him, "Transportation to the feedlot for ranchers further out increases direct costs and it's at odds with our aim to lower carbon footprint wherever possible."

Another issue was the traceability of ranch origin from feedlot through to processing into specific cuts so that the packaged product can be branded as "local" in various retail locations. Some customer purchasing programs call for verifiable information indicating where and how far their food has come, but according to BNW, separating out meat cuts (hamburger or steak) by-ranch was not currently feasible.

Moving Forward

Dan and Stacey had covered a lot of ground that morning, figuratively and literally. There were several strategies to be considered, and they both knew they had to carefully pick the next steps. In terms of working with their largest customer, Whole Foods, if CNB forged ahead with an independent animal welfare standard, would it be accepted by Whole Foods and its customers? What was the value proposition of a CNB standard to Whole Foods or other customers? Also, in light of progressive commoditization of naturally-raised beef and blurred distinctions between niche beef categories in the marketplace, what could CNB do to differentiate itself in various market segments? Would a move into grass fed be feasible for CNB's relatively large–scale cattle operation and would it garner more business from Whole Foods and other potential customers in new markets? Dan mentioned their time-tested skills in consensus-building and conflict resolution and wondered how they could leverage such skills to build consensus within CNB and major retail customers.

As Stacy Davis left the Probert Ranch, he suggested to Dan that they needed to schedule a meeting with Whole Foods in Austin before Thanksgiving to discuss next year's sales and contract. Of course, animal compassion will be an important issue for both sides to discuss. As Stacy prepared for the long drive to the Beef Northwest feedlot, he thought about the issues there. He would need to talk to the managers and vet to get an update on their investigation of last year's OP issues and remedial measures. The lower-than-expected sales will give the feedlot and CNB some breathing room to address these issues. Stacy looked at his PDA and realized that he needed to make phone calls and touch base with several team leaders who were working on the small-scale grass-fed beef project. Another group of members were working with local universities on ranching and feed lot carbon-footprint calculations; he was curious to see if any progress is made there since the in-store demonstration feedback to ranchers had indicated that this topic was a major concern. Finally, he needed to determine how the co-op should respond to increasing reports of meat supply chain's contribution to global warming.

Exhibits

Exhibit 1: National and Regional Feedlot Players

Name	Location-Hdqtrs.	Ownership	Capacity	No. of Feedlots
Five Rivers Cattle Feeding	Loveland, CO	JBS—USA	811,000	10
Cactus Feeders, Inc.	Amarillo, TX	Engler Family & ESOP	510,000	9
Cargill Cattle Feeders LLC	Wichita, KS	Cargill	330,000	4
Friona Industries LP	Amarillo, TX	Private—limited partnership	275,000	4
AxTx Cattle Co.	Hereford, TX	private—Jossarand Family	242,000	5
J.R. Simplot Co.	Boise, ID	private—Simplot Family	230,000	2
Four States Feedyard LP	Lamar, CO	Privately held	195,000	6
Heritage Feeders LP	Oklahoma City, OK	private—Tom L. Ward	189,000	5
AgriBeef Co.	Boise, ID	private—Rebholtz Famliy	180,000	3
Pinal Feeding Co.	Laveen, AZ	private—Petznick Family	175,000	1

Exhibit 2: Pacific Northwest Region Feedlots with Capacity over 10,000

Name	Location	Capacity
Simplot	Grandview, ID	150,000
Simplot	Pasco, WA	90,000
Agri Beef—Oro Cattle Feeders	Moses Lake, WA	60,000
Van de Graaf Ranches, Inc.	Sunnyside, WA	50,000
Beef Northwest Feeders	Boardman, OR	40,000
Beef Northwest Feeders	Nyssa, OR	30,000
Agri Beef—Snake River Cattle Feeders	American Falls, ID	25,000
Agri Beef—Boise Valley Feeders	Parma, ID	25,000
Intermountian Beef	Eden, ID	15,000
Beef Northwest Feeders	Quincy, WA	26,000

Source: "Industry Perspectives Feedlot"

Exhibit 3: Beef Supply Chain

Supply Chain Member	Traditional Beef Characteristics	Traditional Ownership	CNB Beef Characteristics	CNB Ownership
Cow/Calf Operator	Cattle graze on ranch for 12 months	Rancher	Cattle graze on ranch for 12 to 18 months	Rancher
Stocker Operator	Cattle graze or feed for 12 to 20 months	Operator		Rancher
Feedlot	Cattle feed for 180 days on corn & grain (500 lb average gain)	Feedlot	Cattle feed for 90 days on potato waste; small amounts grain and corn (300 lb gain)	Rancher
Packer	Heavy cows and high fat marbling, unknown history	Packer	Lighter cows, lean meat, individual history on ear ID tag	Rancher
Retailer	Different quality characteristics desired depending on final retailer	Retailer	Healthy, natural beef with consistently lean characteristics	Rancher & Retailer Partnership

Exhibit 4: Country Natural Beef Annual Production

Annual Production by Head Fabricated

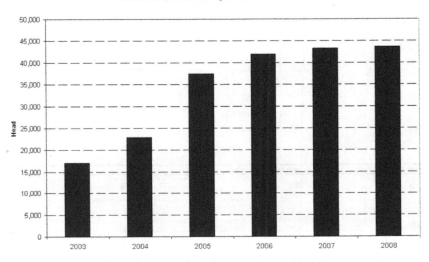

Exhibit 5: Country Natural Beef Organization Chart

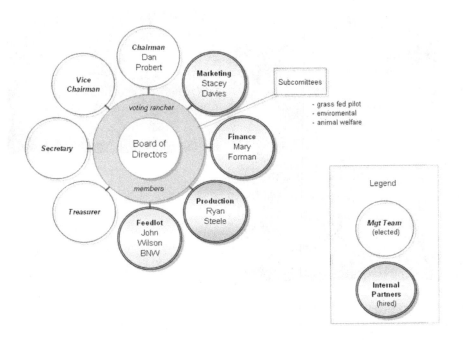

Exhibit 6: Country Natural Beef Value Chain

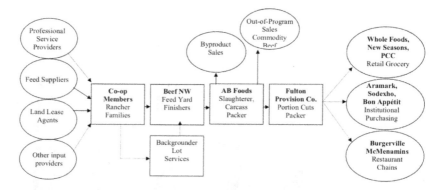

Value Chain	Cow/calf	Background lot	Feedlot	Packer	Retailer
Unit	Ranch	Ranch	Beef NW	AB Foods & Fulton Foods (burger)	Retail Distributor:
CNB	Graze-well Principles & quality guidelines	Rules for In & Out of Program Cattle	Negotiates with Feedlot for financing.	Marketing negotiates with Processor based on CNB cost models Finance receives final product data and compensation for beef.	Marketing negotiates contract with retail distributors, monitors transparency of credibility attributes
Rancher	Cow/calf timing, ranch management	Negotiates for feed cost and provides CNB criteria	Responsible for feedlot costs	Receives revenues from beef (commodity & placement)	Product demonstrations, interaction with customers
Verification	Food Alliance Cert	Food Alliance Certification	Feed Lot Audit	Food Alliance Cert.	

Exhibit 7: Marketing Beef Display, Doc, and Another Rancher at In-store Demonstration

Exhibit 8: US Unemployment Rate, Seasonally Adjusted, September 2009

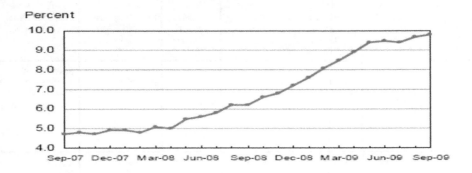

Source: Bureau of Labor Statistics, US Department of Labor

Exhibit 9: Beef Consumption Trends

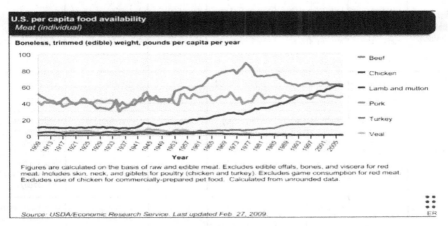

Source: Mintel "Red Meat 2008" Report

Exhibit 10: Animal Welfare Standards: A Comparison of Industry Guidelines and Independent Labels

Practice	Industry Guideline (Individual industry trade associations)	American Humane Certified (American Humane Association)	Certified Humane Program (Humane Farm Animal Care)	Animal Welfare Approved (A Greener World)	Global Animal Partnership 5-Step Animal Welfare Rating Program (GAP)	Certified Organic (USDA Agricultural Marketing Service)
Use of growth hormones	Growth promotants, including ractopamine, are allowed	Must not be given growth promoter (M7, M11)	Must not be fed or implanted with any growth promoter (FW4)	Growth hormones or the use of any substance promoting weight gain are prohibited (3.1.3)	Growth hormones are prohibited (3.1.2) at all Steps	Growth hormones are prohibited (§ 205.238(c)(3))
Pain relief for castration	Recommended that it be performed under 3 months: pain relief not required or recommended	Castration must be performed surgically by vet with pain relief after 2 months; no pain relief required under 2 months (M48)	Pain relief must be used when performed before 6 months; after 6 months, must be performed by vet using pain relief (H10(a)(3))	Castration may be performed up to 2 months; pain relief not required (4.7.4)	May be performed up to 6 months for Step 1, and 3 months of age for Steps 2–4; no pain relief required; prohibited for Steps 5–5+ (5.5.1)	To be performed as needed to promote welfare and in a manner that minimizes pain and stress (§ 205.238(a)(5)); pain relief not explicitly required
Pain relief for dehorning or disbudding	Recommended that it be performed under 4 months: pain relief not required or reocmmended	Approved disbudding methods (M48) include cautery paste up to 7 days old and hot iron with pain relief up to 30 days old; after 30 days must be done by vet with pain relief	Approved disbudding methods include cautery paste and hot iron, both with bain relief; horn removal after 2 months also requires pain relief (H10(a)(2))	Dehorning is prohibited (4.8.2); disbudding allowed up to 2 months of age, pain relief required (4.8.5)	Disbudding must be performed before 6 weeks of age for Steps 1–4, pain relief required for us of hot iron; disbudding prohibited for Steps 5–5+ (5.6.1)	(See above)
Tail docking	Tail docking is not recommended	Not specified	Prohibited (H10(a)(4))	Prohibited (4.8.1)	Not specified	(See above)
Confinement of beef cattle to feedlots	Feedlots allowed (the use of shades should be considered if natural shade is insufficient)	Feedlots allowed but windbreaks (E40) and sunshades (E39) required in some instances	Feedlots allowed but windbreaks (E16(and sunshades (E17) required in some instances	Confinement to feedlots is prohibited	Feedlots allowed for Steps 1–2 (7.1.2)	Feedlots may be used for finish feeding ruminants; finishing period shall not exceed 1/5 of animal's life or 120 days, whichever is shorter (§ 205.239(d))
Access to pasture	Access to the outdoors and to pasture not required	Access to pasture not required; access to the outdoors not clear (E19)	Must have year-round access to the outdoors, but not to pasture (E1)	Continuous outdoor pasture access is required for all animals (7.0.1)	For Steps 1–2, must spend at least 2/3 of their lives on range or pasture; at Step 4, must spend at least 3/4 of their lives on range or pasture, for Steps 5–5+, must live continuously on range or pasture (7.1.1)	All ruminants must have daily access to pasture during the grazing season (including in the finishing period (§ 205.239(a)(1) and (2), § 205.239(d))
Maximum length of transport	Stress is to be minimized in transport (no time limits)	Transport is to be accomplished in the shortest time possible, with no specific time limit given (T8)	Traveling and waiting times should be minimized (no specific time limit given (T7)	Transport must not exceed 8 hours (13.1.8)	Limits are 25 hours for Step 1, 16 hours for Steps 2–4, and 8 hours for Step 5; transport prohibited for Step 5+ (10.4.1)	Animals must go no longer than 28 consecutive hours before being unloaded for food, water, and rest (federal 28 Hour Law)

Source: Animal Welfare Institute, "Animal Welfare Standards Comparison" (standards for beef cattle)

Bibliography

AB Foods. "Double R Ranch Brand beef." Accessed July 28, 2009. http://www.abfoodsusa. com/ABFoods/.

Agriculture and Agri-Food Trade Service of Canada. "Natural beef in the United States." December, 2005. http://www.ats.agr.gc.ca/us/4100_e.htm.

Agriculture of the Middle. "Food Alliance." Accessed 2009. http://www.agofthemiddle.org/ pubs/alliance_case.pdf.

All Business. "Whole Foods survey shows 'strong demand' for natural meats." *Progressive Grocer* May 10, 2006. http://www.allbusiness.com/retail-trade/food-stores/4261075-1.html.

American Grassfed Association. "Grassfed ruminant standards." Last modified January, 2009. http://www.americangrassfed.org/wp-content/uploads/2009/ 02/aga_grassfed_stan-dards_1_091.pdf.

Beef NW. "Environment" Accessed July 17, 2009. http://www.beefnw.com/environment.php.

Bennyhoff, Steve. "Impressed with Whole Foods." Wordpress, January 21, 2009. http://steve-bennyhoffsblog.blogspot.com/2009/08/impressed-with-whole-foods.html.

Bernard, Jeff. "Beef co-op prospers in Oregon." *KGW*, September 19, 2005. http://www.kgw. com/business/stories/kgw_091905_biz_oregon_beef.71dfd5e7.html.

Bonné, Jon. "Tales of the $100 steak: ultrapremium Wagyu beef gets better — and pricier." *MSNBC*, September 13, 2004. http://www.msnbc.msn.com/id/5963343.

Campbell, Dan. "The Natural: brickless marketing co-op helps ranchers tap growing market for lean, natural beef." *Rural Cooperatives* 4, no. 9 (2006).

Cattle Network. "Jolly: Five minutes with Ron Rowan, Beef Northwest." October 24, 2008. http://www.cattlenetwork.com/Cattle_Features_Content.asp? ContentID=263259.

Clause, R. and S. Clarahan. "Natural beef profile." Agricultural Marketing Resource Center. 2007. http://www.agmrc.org/commodities__products/livestock/beef/ natural_beef_pro-file.cfm.

Cooney, E. "E. coli cases traced to Whole Foods beef." The Boston Globe, August 8, 2008. http://www.boston.com/news/health/blog/2008/08/seventh_e_coli.html.

Country Natural Beef. "Country Natural Beef." Accessed 2009. http://www.countrynatural-beef.com.

Country Natural Beef. "The Omnivore's Dilemma and Country Natural Beef." June 12, 2006. http://countrynaturalbeef.com/index.php?option=com_content&task=view&id=40 &Itemid=64

Food Alliance. "Farm and ranch certification." Accessed July 30, 2008. http://www.foodalli-ance.org/certification/farm-ranch/.

Fussell, Betty. "Raising Steaks: The life and times of American beef." Orlando: Houghton Mifflin Harcourt, 2008.

Gale Group. "Beef Cattle Feedlots." *Encyclopedia of American Industries*. Online Edition. Reproduced in *Business and Company Resource Center*. Farmington Hills: Gale Group, 2009. http://galenet.galegroup.com.proxy.lib.pdx.edu/servlet/BCRC

Gordon, Kindra. "Trends to track." *Beef-mag* May, 2006.

Grandin, Temple. *Humane Livestock Handling: Understanding Livestock Behavior and Building Facilities for Healthier Animals*. North Adams: Storey Publishing, 2008.

Gwin, Lauren, and Shermain Hardesty. "Northern California Niche Meat Market Demand Study." University of California Cooperative Extension. March, 2008. http://www.sfc.uc-davis.edu/animal/hardesty_niche_meat_marketing_2008.pdf.

Hoovers Online. "Beef Cattle Ranching." 2009.

Hoover's Online. "Meat Products Manufacture." 2009.

Ishmael, Wes. "Matching consumer to rancher." *Beef Magazine* August, 2008. http://beefmagazine.com/markets/marketing/0801-matching-consumer-rancher.

"Loveland natural beef company expands." *The Associated Press State and Local Wire*, August 29, 2009.

Major, Meg. "Stampede!" *Progressive Grocer* 85, vol. 10 (2006).

Mintert, James, Glynn Tonsor, and Ted Schroeder. "U.S. beef demand drivers and enhancement opportunities: a research summary." Beef Board, January, 2009. http://www.beef-board.org/news/files/factsheets/Beef_Demand_ Drivers_January_2009.pdf.

"Natural News." *National Provisioner* 221, vol. 3.

New Seasons. "Country Natural Beef, Brothers Oregon." Accessed May 9, 2007. http://www.newseasonsmarket.com/dynamicContent.aspx?loc =973&subloc=1>.

Oliver, Gordon. "Beef Northwest, United Farm Workers reach agreement on election." *Oregonlive* November 6, 2006. http://www.oregonlive.com/business/index.ssf/2008/11/beef_northwest-united/farm-wor.html.

Organic Consumers. "Tell Whole Foods: No Sweatshop 'Natural' Beef!" *Mobilize* September 24, 2008. http: www.organicconsumers.org/bytes/ob145.cfm.

The Pig Site. "Oregon Meat Co First to Gain Sustainable Certificate." March 20, 2008. http://www.thepigsite.com/ swinenews/17364/oregon-meat-co-first-to-gain-sustainable-certificate.

Peck, Clint. "From niche to norm." *BEEF* 41, vol. 12 (2005).

Provisioner Online. "Maverick Ranch Natural Meats announces new strategic partner." April 13, 2009. http://www.provisioneronline.com/Articles/Suppliers_Marketplace_BNP_GUID_9-5-2006_A_1000000000000541861.

Quaid, Libby. "Ranchers decry grass-fed beef rule plan." *The Washington Post* September 3, 2006. http://www.washingtonpost.com/wp-dyn/ content/article/2006/09/03/AR2006090300382.html.

Sam, Sarpy. "Mandatory is back." March 6, 2008. Message posted to http://www.noanimalid.com

Savory, Allan. and Jody Butterfield. *Holistic Management: A New Framework for Decision Making.* Washington, D.C.: Island Press, 1998.

Severson, Kim. "With goat, a rancher breaks away from the herd." *The New York Times* October 14, 2008. http://www.nytimes.com/2008/10/15/dining/15goat.html.

Shah, Anup. "Creating Mass Consumption of Beef." Global Issues. Accessed May 30, 2007. http://www.globalissues.org/article/240/beef#Creatingmassconsumptionofbeef.

Southworth, Jack. "Graze well." Managing Wholes. Accessed April 18, 2007. http://managingwholes.com/graze-well.htm.

"Union Targets Oregon Feedlot; Whole Foods Caves." *Beef Magazine* June 6, 2008. http://beefmagazine.com/cowcalfweekly/union-targets-oregon-feedlot.

United States Food and Drug Administration. "Bovine Spongiform Encephalopathy." Accessed 2009. http://www.fda.gov/AnimalVeterinary/GuidanceComplianceEnforcement/ComplianceEnforcement/BovineSpongiform Encephalopathy/default.htm.

Whole Foods. "United States Securities and Exchange Commission Form 10K." September 28, 2008. http://www.wholefoodsmarket.com/company/pdfs/2008_10K.pdf.

Animal Ag Alliance. "USDA issues humane handling materials for small plants." March 6, 2009. http://www.animalagalliance.org/current/home.cfm?Category=Current_Issues&Section=20090306_USDA.

United States Department of Agriculture Agricultural Marketing Service. "11-07 Agenda 5-Step Introduction." Accessed 2009. http://www.ams.usda.gov/AMSv1.0/getfile?dDocName=STELPRDC5066283.

United States Department of Agriculture Agricultural Marketing Service. "United States Standards for livestock and meat marketing claims, naturally raised claim for livestock and the meat and meat products derived from such livestock." *The Federal Register*, January 21, 2009. http://www.thefederalregister.com/d.p/2009-01-21-E9-1007.

Western Region SARE. "SARE 2000 Conference proceedings: farming and ranching for profit, stewardship and community." Utah State University 2000. http://wsare.usu.edu/pub/sare2000/084.htm.

Wise Geek. "What is a CAFO?" Accessed July 20, 2009. http://www.wisegeek.com/what-is-a-cafo.htm.

FRIENDS OF THE CHILDREN
Strategies for Scaling Impact

Oikos Case Writing Competition 2nd Place (Social
Entrepreneurship Track), 2016

By Jacen Greene, Nicki Yechin Lee, and Eric Nelsen

Friends of the Children Case Study

Introduction

Terri Sorensen, president of Friends of the Children's (FOTC) national organization, reviewed their new business plan for scaling the nonprofit's impact.
The plan had recently won the prestigious Social Impact Exchange Business
Plan Competition, and would now form the basis of a $25 million.[80] ask to
fund the scaling strategy—a massive increase from the original $3 million fore-
cast need.[81] However, the scale of the problem they faced was equally daunting. FOTC identified the most at-risk children in poverty and paired them
with a paid mentor for the entire 12 years of their schooling, greatly reducing
the risk of teen pregnancy or incarceration, boosting graduation rates, and

---

80   "Copy of Scaling Strategies."
81   "Friends of the Children Business Plan 2015-2017."

ultimately helping break generational cycles of poverty. They reached 1400 youth,[82] but in the United States alone, 2.25 million children under the age of 5 lived in extreme poverty.[83]

The model, first launched in Portland, Oregon, had proven successful in social return on investment calculations and preliminary results from a longitudinal, randomized control trial. Now, FOTC hoped to take those results to potential funders as proof the model should be scaled nationally. However, to successfully grow from a few initial chapters and affiliates into a national organization, FOTC planned to radically rethink their funding model and organizational framework, incorporating even more of the business methods that Sorensen and FOTC's founder, retired entrepreneur Duncan Campbell, were known for. Although still a nonprofit, FOTC was focusing more and more on a social entrepreneurship approach of earned revenue and, potentially, funding from investors in addition to grants from foundations and donors.

The long-term success of FOTC relied on Sorensen's ability to navigate this difficult transformation, secure new funding sources, and successfully implement their model in new areas and with new partners. It wasn't merely a question of scaling their impact; two of their early chapters had been forced to close when they ran out of money during the recession. Sorensen was proud of her background as an accountant and manager in the private sector, and of the business acumen she brought to the role, but there were associated risks. Could she successfully incorporate more of a social entrepreneurship approach into FOTC's model in a way that ensured financial sustainability without compromising the nonprofit's mission and values?

History

When Duncan Campbell, founder of Friends of the Children, was three years old, he woke up in the middle of the night to discover that his parents were gone. With the help of a police officer, he eventually found them at a local bar. His childhood was marked with such episodes of neglect by his alcoholic parents, including a father who spent time in prison. Against all odds, Campbell graduated from high school, then college, working three jobs to put himself through. He earned a CPA, then a law degree, and later started one of the first timber investment funds in the nation. After he sold it in 1990, Campbell

---

82   Ibid.
83   "Child Poverty in America 2014: National Analysis."

turned from business innovation to social innovation: he wanted to find a way to help children who grew up in households like his to escape generational cycles of poverty.[84]

When Campbell surveyed the various resources available to Oregon's at-risk children, he saw a gap in long-term support from existing charities, which focused predominately on meeting day-to-day needs. In his own research and in discussions with a child psychologist,[85] it became clear that long-term, personalized engagement with at-risk children was necessary to help them escape poverty. To realize his vision of changing the trajectory of children's futures, a new type of organization was needed, and Campbell would have to build it from scratch. He believed that by applying his business experience and acumen to the nonprofit world, he could realize the same success, but this time as a "social entrepreneur."

In 1993, Campbell donated $1.5 million to found nonprofit Friends of the Children (FOTC) in Portland, Oregon with three paid mentors (called "Friends") and 24 children.[86] Each Friend received a salary and specialized training to provide a long-term, stable, and supportive relationship with several children. When a child reached high school, they would transition to a new Friend, enabling the Friends to specialize in different age groups and giving children a model for a positive transition in adult support, rather than one catalyzed by poverty, addiction, or incarceration. The model was closely based on Campbell's own research and the advice he had received from child psychologists and educators.

The program's unique perspective—that an organization can counter societal impacts and influences by providing a permanent role model throughout a child's life—showed promising results, and interest grew. By 2014, Friends of the Children had expanded domestically to locations including Seattle, New York, Boston, and Klamath Falls, added an affiliate partner in Tampa Bay, and launched internationally with a presence in Cornwall, UK.[87] At that time, over 148 Friends worked with an estimated 1,400 youth.[88]

---

84   The information in this paragraph came from the following source: Caroline Fairchild.
85   Duncan Campbell.
86   "NEXT: How Duncan Campbell went from forests to friends."
87   "Locations."
88   "Expansion Fund."

Model

Our vision is that one day all children will have a long-term, consistent relationship with a caring adult who believes in them. We want to change the way the world views and treats our most vulnerable children.

— Friends of the Children Vision Statement[89]

FOTC's mission was to build a more caring, loving, and safer world for children.[90] It targeted the highest-risk children living in the highest-risk conditions. These children weathered a storm of unrelenting risk factors that ranged from the generational (such as incarcerated parents and family poverty), to the environmental (including neglect or abuse), to those in the community (failing schools, high crime, or violence) (Exhibit 1). Taken together, these risk factors greatly increased a child's odds of dropping out of school, becoming a teen parent, or becoming incarcerated.

FOTC sought to intervene early in a child's life—by age 6—before negative behaviors were deeply imprinted and to guide that child to successful high school graduation. Children with the highest risk factors were identified with the help of teachers and school staff using National Institutes for Health guidelines, and then paired with a Friend as they entered elementary school. Friends spent 16 hours a month with each child, providing positive interactions and supporting progress towards specific developmental goals personalized by age and individual circumstance (Exhibit 2).[91] Mentored children remained in the program for a total of 12 years, even if they changed schools or moved within the service area.[92]

Friends underwent a rigorous selection process including four rounds of interviews, a supervised trial outing with a child, first aid certification, a background check, and drug testing. As FOTC President Terri Sorensen put it, "We are slow to hire and quick to fire." Once hired, Friends made a three-year commitment, although the average tenure was seven years. Friends received 12 hours of training in their first year and participated in monthly meetings with supervisors to review the progress of youth clients. Each friend was assigned no more than eight children in grades K through 5, or 14 adolescents in grades 6 through 12.[93]

---

89   "Business Plan."
90   "Finding Great Friends."
91   Information in this paragraph comes from the following source: "Business Plan."
92   "Network Program Fidelity Agreement."
93   Information in this paragraph comes from the following source: "Business Plan."

FOTC was organized around a network model, with a national organization, local chapters, and affiliate organizations. The national organization was in charge of research, marketing, and strategy, while chapters and affiliates focused on fundraising and program delivery. Chapters operated in Portland, Seattle, Harlem, Boston, and Klamath Falls; two others in San Francisco and Cincinnati had closed due to a lack funding during the recession. Local chapter boards were responsible for raising startup and operating funds, but were eligible for development loans, technical assistance, and marketing support from the national organization. In exchange, each chapter shared revenue with the national organization, which was also supported by a $10 million endowment, corporate and foundation grants, and individual donations. Affiliate organizations, including Trelya in the UK and Eckerd in the US, embedded the FOTC model into existing programs.[94]

Outcomes and Impact

FOTC used three different types of analysis to demonstrate the outcomes and impacts of their model: third-party evaluations; a longitudinal study; and a Social Return on Investment (SROI) calculation. Third-party evaluations conducted annually by NPC Research showed that 83% of FOTC youth clients obtained a high school diploma or GED, 93% avoided incarceration through age 18, and 98% avoided becoming a teen parent.[95] Among a comparison group, only 57% received a diploma or equivalent, 69% had avoided incarceration by age 18, and only 33% had not become a teen parent.[96]

FOTC client success rates were much higher than in comparable populations, but to definitively prove the effectiveness of the model, FOTC participated in a longitudinal, randomized control trial beginning in 2007. By comparing FOTC clients randomly selected from among eligible youth to similar youth who were not selected (since FOTC could not serve them all), the study was intended to prove or disprove impact over time. Early results showed that FOTC clients significantly outperformed similarly situated children, and began to more closely resemble those in the general population with respect to high school graduation, incarceration, and teen parenting rates.[97]

An SROI calculation performed by Harvard Business School Association of

94   Ibid.
95   Ibid.
96   "Return on Investment Model for Friends of the Children."
97   Ibid.

Oregon and Benefitics LLC compared individual and societal benefits against the cost of the program itself. Program outcomes in graduation, avoided incarceration, and avoided teen pregnancy were compared to those of demographically similar groups in the same area. The economic benefits of these outcomes, such as higher lifetime wages and tax contributions or lower government expenditures on criminal justice and welfare, were calculated over an individual's lifetime. These benefits amounted to roughly $840,000 for every child enrolled in an FOTC program, even after controlling for outcomes in comparable populations (Exhibit 3). This meant that every $1 invested in FOTC programs generated nearly $7 in return for their clients and society at large.[98]

Growth and Challenges

In 2014, FOTC embarked on an ambitious plan to scale the organization to serve, directly or indirectly, more than 7,500 children by 2017. They aimed to do this through three approaches: demonstrating the model's impact to secure funding for existing and new local chapters; embedding their model in affiliate organizations already poised to grow; and sharing what worked with policymakers, educational institutions, and other organizations interacting with at-risk youth (Exhibit 4). Most of the intended scale would come through the third approach, but all three required an increase in staff and other expenses, changes in the organization's operating structure, and the pursuit of new funding sources. They also introduced additional risks to the model. An initial target of $3 million was set, but then raised to $25 million when it became apparent that to avoid the risk of new chapters shutting down, FOTC's national organization had to be able to provide matching grants, loans to cover development costs, and additional financial support over a longer time period.[99]

In order to attract Friends who were well-qualified and willing to make a long-term commitment to the program and the children they served, FOTC provided a living wage and covered 100% of health benefits costs, which, along with administrative support functions, meant 86% of the organization's expenses went to staff. The remaining 14% covered operating costs for facilities, technology, third-party research, and variable costs such as travel and activities for youth served. In fiscal year 2015, FOTC expected to serve 2650 youth at a total organizational expense of $13.77 million, resulting in a yearly cost per

---

98   Ibid.
99   Ibid.

child of $5196. This cost was forecast to be only $1960 by 2018, as a result of achieving economies of scale through more effective sharing of best practices and expanded engagement with affiliates. However, this was still high when compared with similar youth-oriented organizations.[100]

Other mentor or youth development organizations, such as Big Brothers and Big Sisters of America or Head Start, also identified children at an early age and offered 1:1 relationships, but they failed to provide the mentee with a long-term commitment. Court Appointed Special Advocates addressed the needs of foster children, but used volunteers as opposed to paid professionals (Exhibit 5).[101] Government agencies that served at-risk youth were often underfunded and overwhelmed. FOTC the filled the gap left by competing organizations and governments, but to attract funders for their comparatively more expensive model, they needed to conduct additional research on the effectiveness of their long-term approach. For example, funding for the longitudinal trial had recently run out, and FTOC would need to finance completion.[102] In addition, the results of this research needed to be communicated to policymakers, funders, and the general public through an expanded marketing strategy.

FOTC had pro bono relationships with leading advertising and communication firms including Wieden+Kennedy, Interbrand, and GMMB, which enabled them to develop high-quality campaigns.[103] According to Sarah Biederman, Strategic Business Analyst at FOTC, "We are focused on: making advances in website capabilities and brand, social media engagement, and email communications. We are also making investments in building relationships with media, key influencers, and thought-leaders." FOTC's planned marketing efforts included hiring a Chief Expansion Officer to work with affiliates, becoming featured in more publications, and reaching policymakers through participation in national conferences (Exhibit 6).[104] This was key to their hope to share research on the effectiveness of their model with a wider audience. Ultimately, the goal was to shape the way other organizations interacted with at-risk youth.

Funding for new chapters, additional research, added development staff at the national level, and improved marketing was sought from several sources. FOTC already had a diversified revenue stream that included individual donations, corporate and foundation giving, government grants, and, at the

---

100   Ibid.
101   "Business Plan."
102   Terri Sorensen.
103   "Business Plan."
104   Ibid.

national level, chapter revenue sharing, affiliate fees, and training revenue.[105] Endowment funds could be used to meet gaps, but were intended to bridge lean times and reduce the chance of chapter closures. The other types of funding each had their own risks: all of them would decline during recession; government and foundation grants often had restrictive requirements for how the money could be used; revenue sharing, affiliate fees, and training revenue all depended on successfully scaling the model. A new source of funding was needed to hit the vastly increased target of $25 million.

FOTC had begun to investigate Pay-For-Success (PFS) models, including Social Impact Bonds, in which a group of investors pay a nonprofit to deliver a specific intervention. If that intervention surpassed targeted outcomes, as agreed on upfront and measured by a third party, state or country governments repaid the investors with a profit. If the intervention failed, investors lost their money, although some models mixed investments from banks and foundations, with foundations assuming most of the risk. The PFS model, pioneered in Europe, had recently been piloted in New York State, Massachusetts, Utah, Illinois, and Ohio, with varying levels of success (Exhibit 7). To be considered for such an approach, an organization typically needed a proven approach, impacts that could be measured in monetary terms, a model that reduced the cost of service delivery for government, and a willing state legislature or government leaders.[106] Friends of the Children had recently been selected by Third Sector Capital Partners, a nonprofit advisory firm, as one of the first organizations in Oregon to receive a grant from the U.S. government's Social Innovation Fund for exploring PFS models.[107] That research could help Friends of the Children determine whether PFS would be a feasible funding strategy.

Conclusion

As Sorensen completed her review of the business plan, she reflected on the challenges of their new strategy. How could they raise the $25 million needed to scale their impact? What new funding sources or models would they need to pursue, and how might the organization have to change as a result? Could they achieve the same successful outcomes as they grew, especially if they brought in more affiliate partners rather than directly managing every new

---

105   Ibid.
106   Kasturi and Chase, "The Payoff of Pay-for-Success."
107   Wang and Hernandez, "Will Private Investors Help Pay for Social Services? Oregon Projects Seek to Find Out."

implementation? For that matter, was Friends of the Children even pursuing the right pathways to scaling their impact, or were there other options that might be cheaper or more effective?

The organization had already been forced to close two chapters during the recession, and Sorensen knew that if the funding strategy was only partially successful, they might face the same outcome in the future. Their model held the promise of transforming the lives of millions of children, but only with a significant commitment of time and resources. Could Sorensen continue Duncan Campbell's entrepreneurial approach to create a national organization able to deliver on that promise, and to secure the funding and support it needed to do so?

Exhibits

Exhibit 1: Factors Contributing to Youth Risks

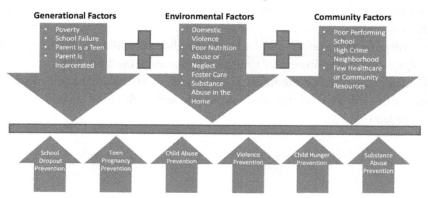

Source: "Friends of the Children Business Plan 2015-2017." Friends of the Children. 2014. Internal document.

Exhibit 2: Role of Friends

	# Children and Time	Do	Don't
Role of the Friend	Children in Grades K-5: • Minimum of 14-16 direct or indirect hours spent with each child per month • Maximum of 8 children per Friend Children in Grades 6-12: • Minimum of 14-16 direct or indirect hours per month with 4 hours of 1:1 time • Maximum of 14 adolescents per Friend	• Encourage children to use their strengths, follow dreams and accept challenges • Support children without conditions • Help children build self-esteem, self-confidence, and cultural pride • Trust the children and provide a steadfast and enduring presence • Actively connect and listen	• Take on decision making responsibilities held by a parent/guardian • Become a crutch • Break confidentiality (except in cases of potential harm to child or others) • Break promises • Expect too much or too little • Condone negative behaviors • Be inconsistent • Force children to do anything • Talk down • Cause friction

Source: "Friends of the Children Business Plan 2015-2017." Friends of the Children. 2014. Internal document.

Exhibit 3: Social Return on Investment Analysis

Friends of the Children's Social Return on Investment (SROI) analysis—a method of monetizing the individual and social benefits to society of a specific intervention—was conducted by Benefitics, LLC and the Harvard Business School Association of Oregon. The analysis focused on FOTC's three target areas of reduced youth incarceration, reduced teen pregnancy rates, and improved high school graduation rates. Each offered clear financial benefits to individuals and society as a whole, and specifically to government programs, but the SROI analysis focused on the benefits that had the most robust economic data available:

- Reduced youth incarceration (under 18 years old) resulted in lower criminal justice system costs, lower victim costs, and less lost wages/tax revenue due to incarceration
- Reduced teen pregnancy rates (under 18 years old) resulted in lower child welfare costs, less lost wages/tax revenue, and lower public healthcare costs
- Improved high school graduation rates resulted in higher wages, higher income tax revenues, and lower demand for public services.

FOTC client outcomes, and the resulting calculated benefits, for the Portland chapter were compared to those of a control group in the same area. The control group comprised 18-year-olds in Multnomah County (Portland) Oregon who were economically disadvantaged and predominately (70%) African-American, which captured a group broadly similar in demographic and economic makeup to FOTC youth clients.

For each category of benefit, the following calculation was performed:

For example, in the education category (numbers rounded):

The SROI analysis provided the following totals:

- Reduced youth incarceration: estimated lifetime benefit of $1.06 million, net lifetime benefit of $221, 747 per FOTC graduate
- Reduced teen pregnancy: estimated lifetime benefit of $409,000, net lifetime benefit of $254,846 per FOTC graduate
- Improved high school graduation rates: estimated lifetime benefit of $1.3 million, net lifetime benefit of $361,437 per FOTC graduate

This resulted in a total, net lifetime benefit for each FOTC graduate of $838,030.

The estimated cost of serving one FOTC youth client for the entire 12-year length of the program was then calculated using a pro rata share of fixed costs (facilities, technology, administrative), semi-fixed costs (supervisory and development roles), and variable costs (Friends, activities, and direct program support).

The following calculation was performed to determine the final SROI ratio (numbers rounded):

The model used fairly conservative estimates, excluding some cost savings for which economic data were not available, using data sources that precluded double counting benefits, and selecting control group participants who were often less economically disadvantaged than FOTC clients. This meant the total SROI ratio of benefits to costs was likely higher than the estimate.

Source: "Return on Investment Model for Friends of the Children." The Harvard Business School Association of Oregon. Friends of the Children internal document. 2010.

Exhibit 4: Scaling Strategies

SCALING STRATEGIES (Revised 2015)	CHILDREN SERVED & CAPITAL REQUIRED			
	2015 (Year 1)	2016 (Year 2)	2017 (Year 3)	2018 (Year 4)
SCALE THROUGH CHAPTERS • Grow national board for increased capacity in fundraising • Provide capacity building loan to hire development staff at chapter demonstration sites • Number of mentored children served at existing chapters expected to grow to 40% • Add 2 new Friends at each FOTC chapter • Hire key National staff (2 Fundraising Directors)	Children: 950 Capital: $350,000	Children: 1060 Capital: $500,000	Children: 1200 Capital: $1,650,000	Capital: $5,000,000
SCALE THROUGH AFFILIATES • Leverage current infrastructure and expertise of existing organizations (affiliates) while sharing FOTC benefits and best practices for faster expansion • Feasibility study and technology enhancements are required • Add 1-2 new affiliates • Hire Chief Expansion Officer	Children: 200 Capital: $200,000	Children: 300 Capital: $800,000	Children: 500 Capital: $4,000,000	Capital: $10,000,000
SCALE THROUGH COLLABORATIVE PARTNERSHIPS • Additional staff and infrastructure needed to support RCT study • Hire Share What Works Manager to present at conferences and publish articles about FOTC best practices • Add 1-2 new collaborative partnerships	Children: 1,500 Capital: $350,000	Children: 3,000 Capital: $550,000	Children: 5,800 Capital: $600,000	Capital: $1,000,000

Adapted from "Copy of Scaling Strategies." Friends of the Children. 2016. Internal document.

Exhibit 5: Competitive Landscape

PROGRAM MODEL	Friends of the Children	Big Brothers Big Sisters of America	Boys and Girls Clubs of America	Communities in Schools	Court Appointed Special Advocates	Head Start	Nurse Home Visit Program
Large national footprint		X	X	X	X	X	X
Long-term commitment: 12+ years	X						
Intensive: 16+ hours mentoring/month/child	X					X	
Individualized developmental plans	X			X	X	X	X
Comprehensive: Spend time with youth during school, in their homes, and in the community	X					X	
Full-time, paid, professional mentors or advocates	X						X
Individualized one-on-one relationships with each child	X	X			X	X	X
Start early: Before first grade	X	X			X	X	X
Formal selection process for highest risk children	X				X	X	X
Evidence of preventing school failure	X	X		X		X	X
Evidence of preventing early parenting	X					X	X
Evidence of preventing involvement in the criminal justice system	X					X	X

Source: *"Friends of the Children Business Plan 2015-2017." Friends of the Children. 2014. Internal document.*

Exhibit 6: Marketing Strategy

Marketing Metrics: Number of Presentations and Meetings

Approach	Affinity Sectors	Current Year	Year 1	Year 2	Year 3
Conferences	Grantmakers	1	1	2	2
	Evidence-Based Practice (EBP)	0	0	1	2
	Social Entrepreneur	1	2	4	5
	Providers	2	3	6	10
	Provider/Funder Advocacy Coalition	0	0	2	4
	University EBP and Policy Forums	0	1	2	3
Approach	**Affinity Sectors**	**Current Year**	**Year 1**	**Year 2**	**Year 3**
1:1 Meetings	Policy-Makers/Agency Leaders	8	27	40	57
	System Change/SIF Funders	3	5	6	7
	Scaling Thought leaders	0	2	4	5
	Collective Impact Convenors	1	2	3	4

Source: *"Friends of the Children Business Plan 2015-2017." Friends of the Children. 2014. Internal document.*

Exhibit 7: Recent U.S. Pay-for-Success Contracts

CONTRACT	ISSUE AREA	SIZE	TARGET	LENDERS	SUCCESS PAYMENT
New York City (2012)	Young adult recidivism	3000 young men	10% reduction in recidivism	Goldman Sachs, Bloomberg Philanthropies	$9.6 to $11.7 million
Salt Lake County, UT (2013)	Early childhood education	2600 children	Per-child payment	Goldman Sachs, J.B. Pritzker	95% of avoided costs
New York (2013)	Adult recidivism/ job training	2000 adults	8% reduction in recidivism; 5% increase in employment	Bank of America, Rockefeller Foundation	$17.5 to $21.5 million
Massachusetts (2014)	Young adult recidivism	929 young men	40% reduction in recidivism	Goldman Sachs, various foundations	$22 to $27 million
Chicago (2014)	Early childhood education	2618 children	50% increase in 3rd grade literacy	Goldman Sachs, Northern Trust, Pritzker Foundation	$25.8 to $34 million
Cuyahoga County, OH (2014)	Foster care / homelessness	135 families	25% reduction in foster care	Reinvestment Fund, various foundations	$4.1 to $5 million
Massachusetts (2014)	Homelessness	800 adults	85% occupancy	Santander Bank, United Way, Corporation for Supportive Housing	$3.5 to $6 million

Source: Rangan, V. Kasturi, and Lisa A. Chase. "The Payoff of Pay-for-Success." *Stanford Social Innovation Review, Fall 2015.*

Bibliography

"Copy of Scaling Strategies." Friends of the Children, 2016. Internal document.

"Friends of the Children Business Plan 2015-2017." Friends of the Children, 2014. Internal document.

"Child Poverty in America 2014: National Analysis." 2015. Children's Defense Fund, 9 Sep. 2015. Web. 25 Nov. 2015. http://www.childrensdefense.org/child-research-data-publications/data/child-poverty-in-america-2012.pdf

Fairchild, Caroline. "NEXT: How Duncan Campbell went from forests to friends." *Fortune*, April 14, 2014. http://fortune.com/2014/04/04/next-how-duncan-campbell-went-from-forests-to-friends/

Campbell, Duncan. Personal interview. September 25, 2015.

"Locations." Friends of the Children. Accessed November 30, 2015. http://friendsofthechildren.org/locations

"Expansion Fund." Friends of the Children, 2015. Internal document.

"Business Plan." Friends of the Children, 2014. Internal document.

"Finding Great Friends." Friends of the Children, 2015. Internal document.

"Network Program Fidelity Agreement." Friends of the Children. Revised July 31, 2015. Internal document.

Sorensen, Terri. Personal interview. September 23, 2015.

"Return on Investment Model for Friends of the Children." Harvard Business Association of Oregon, 2010. Internal document.

Biederman, Sarah. Message to the authors. October 7, 2015. Email.

Rangan, V. Kasturi, and Lisa A. Chase. "The Payoff of Pay-for-Success." *Stanford Social Innovation Review*, Fall 2015. http://ssir.org/up_for_debate/article/the_payoff_of_pay_for_success

Wang, Amy, and Tony Hernandez. "Will Private Investors Help Pay for Social Services? Oregon Projects Seek to Find Out." *The Oregonian*, March 12, 2015. http://www.oregonlive.com/portland/index.ssf/2015/03/pay_for_prevention.htm

HOPWORKS URBAN BREWERY
A Case of Sustainable Beer

Oikos Case Writing Competition 1st Place (Corporate Sustainability Track), 2015

By Madeleine E. Pullman, Ph.D., Jacen Greene, Devin Liebmann, Nga Ho, and Xan Pedisich

Hopworks Case Study

Introduction

"Use the brewery as the means to change the world."
— Christian Ettinger, Founder, Hopworks Urban Brewery

On a windy fall day, Hopworks Urban Brewery's Founder and Brewmaster, Christian Ettinger, sat in a lofted conference room overlooking brewery operations and listened to a local company pitch new brewery management software, but his mind was elsewhere. It was lunchtime, and beneath the meeting room, the brewpub restaurant was full, packed with families thanks to a no-school day. Children of all ages covered the play area and spilled out from under booths. The kitchen was working hard to keep Hopworks' 200 dining customers happy, however young or old. Ettinger knew he needed the software being pitched to him. It seemed almost unbelievable to him that in seven short years, Hopworks had grown to the point where it now needed that type of technical infrastructure. On his mind, aside from details like software, was the new 5-year plan Hopworks was implementing that called for tripling three categories: revenue, locations, and brewing capacity. Ettinger knew these were inextricably tied together; 70% of Hopworks' revenue came from on-premise sales, while wholesale accounted for only 30%. However, the profit margins on these two distinct areas of their business were wildly different; the restaurant's margin was 5%, compared to the brewery's 25%. What did this mean for their hope to expand, and how could they do so sustainably?

Hopworks valued sustainability for its environmental benefits, but Ettinger knew firsthand that economic and social sustainability were also a key part of the equation. If you go out of business, you can't continue doing good in your community, and your environmental impact is irrelevant. He was committed to sustainable growth in both senses of the word. How could Hopworks keep its commitment to produce the best, most sustainable beer? They were at a turning point, facing intense pressure from Portland's 83 other craft breweries[108], and needed to expand operations to increase revenue and maintain their leadership position. But what was the best path forward in line with their values? Ettinger reflected on what it was like when he was starting Hopworks over seven years ago, and tried to channel that younger, perhaps more idealistic, brewer for guidance. But how would he know what was right for Hopworks today?[109] More specifically, some of his major decisions included:

- What kind of equipment or software was needed to continue to grow and run as sustainably yet profitably as possible?
- Should he pursue two new brewpub locations?
- Could they distribute their wholesale products more widely without increasing their carbon footprint significantly?
- Should they replace or augment their organic certification with other certifications like Salmon Safe?

Overall, how could Hopworks balance their ideals with a continued commitment to making the best beer, while staying economically sustainable as well?

Company History

Ettinger founded Hopworks Urban Brewery (HUB) in 2007 with sustainability

---

108   Oregon Craft Beer, "Economic Impact."
109   The information in this section came from the following sources: Christian Ettinger, personal interview.

as its core mission and differentiation strategy from the beginning. His vision was to produce world class, organic beer with fresh, local ingredients in an eco-friendly, sustainable building that would serve as a gathering point for the community. Seven years later, his dream flourished in the original brewpub in southeast Portland and the Hopworks BikeBar in northeast Portland. Portland is well known as the U.S. city with the most microbreweries per capita: 84 total within the metro area, according to the Oregon Brewer's Guild.[110] By 2013, Hopworks was the 11th largest producer in Oregon[111] out of more than 170 craft breweries in the state.[112]

Ettinger's passion for brewing started well before the recent explosion of the craft beer market in the United States. The son of a German architect and a mother who worked at a local private university, Ettinger was allowed to sip from the keg while conversing in German with professors visiting as part of German exchange programs. In college, Ettinger spent a year in Cologne, Germany, home of Kölsch beer, as part of a business degree, and says that immersion in Germany's rich brewing culture "changed [him] forever."[113] After attending brewing school at the American Brewers Guild, he started out washing kegs and brewing beer at other local breweries, before going on to help launch Laurelwood Brewing Company in Portland in 2000.[114]

Hopworks' brewery started production in 2007 as Ettinger and crew refurbished an old building to house a brewpub on the premises. The 16,800 square foot building, constructed in 1948 as a showroom for Caterpillar bulldozers and then repurposed as Sunshine Fuel headquarters, was a concrete shell filled with cubicles and drop ceilings when Hopworks acquired it. While full demolition would have been cheaper, with his background in construction, Ettinger decided instead to deconstruct the old building to serve as a sustainability showcase. In this way, Hopworks' foundation is both literally and metaphorically sustainable, a key demonstration of their commitment to sustainability from the beginning.[115]

Yet to Hopworks, sustainability was more than making ecologically responsible decisions. They modeled an ethos of "do what you can" in actions big and small, from employees turning the lights off when they left a room, to energy-saving thermostat settings, to selling kegged local wine instead of

---

110   Ibid.
111   John Bell, "Christian Ettinger Revolutionizes Craft Brew Scene ... Again."
112   "Economic Impact."
113   Christian Ettinger.
114   "Christian Ettinger Revolutionizes Craft Brew Scene ... Again."
115   The information in this paragraph came from the source: Hopworks, "Building Green."

bottled wine. In every interview, potential employees were asked what sustainability means to them, and Nate Young, Director of Sustainability, reported that company awareness of sustainable practices was high enough that he'd discussed them with nearly everyone, including a 17-year-old busboy with an after-school job at the brewpub. This culture earned them an accolade as one of the 100 Best Green Employers in the State of Oregon for 2013[116], as well as the Governor's Oregon Sustainability Grand Champion Award.[117]

Social sustainability was also important set of values for the company. Some might argue that alcohol itself has negative consequences for society related to alcoholism, addiction, and anti-social behavior. Others would claim that the pub has always been an important social place in many communities. In that respect, community was a cornerstone of Hopworks' values. When naming the brewery Hopworks Urban Brewery, or HUB, Ettinger thought of the "most important mechanical invention of the modern world — the wheel — with the middle of that being the most important part of the wheel. Then the metaphors are a mile deep: pizza, cycles of carbon, oxygen and water; the way the spokes radiate from the middle, of which the middle is the heart or the town hall, the social center, etc."[118] Hopworks strove to produce the best, most sustainable beer, but also to do the most good in the community. Their brewpubs were designed to be a central meeting spot for the neighborhood, the sought-after "third place" between work and home, featuring a children's play area and a free, bi-weekly story time for toddlers.

In an effort to keep their beer as fresh as possible and minimize carbon emissions from transport, Hopworks only distributed beer by truck in the Pacific Northwest, and used rail to ship farther afield. This effectively ruled out export markets and parts of the U.S. not connected by a hub-and-spoke system that could easily move containers from train to truck. Sticking to local distribution harkened back to a time when all beer in America was craft beer, brewed locally.

Craft Brewing History

Before the age of mass production and refrigerated delivery trucks, all of the

116   Oregon Business, "100 Best Green Companies to Work for in Oregon 2013."
117   Nate Young, "2013 Sustainability Report."
118   Warren Willis, "At Hopworks Urban Brewery, Christian Ettinger's Strategy for Success Revolves Around Sustainability." >

beer brewed in America was, technically, craft beer.[119] American craft brewing enjoys a storied, colorful past, and Ettinger loved to share facts about the history of brewing with anyone willing to listen. He contended the Mayflower landed when and where it did only because ship was running low on beer, the only safe liquid to drink at sea. According to Mayflower Brewing, "Men, women and children drank beer daily, and sailors aboard the Mayflower received a daily ration of a gallon."[120] Regardless of the veracity of this beer folktale, Ettinger and many other craft brewers reveled in the history and traditions surrounding America's brewing heritage.

America boasted a pre-prohibition total of some 4,000 craft breweries, which consolidated as the industry modernized.[121] By 1976, there were only two craft breweries in all of North America.[122] However, the pendulum soon swung in the opposite direction, with 1,370 craft breweries in the United States alone by the late 1990s.[123] A major catalyst of this revival can be found in the 1978 passage into law of House Resolution (H.R.) 1337 by President Jimmy Carter. The legislation made home brewing legal in the United States, creating room for small brewers.[124] "As a result of this new freedom, successful home brewers ramped up their production and eventually formed the beginnings of what is now considered the modern craft beer industry."[125]

Yakima Brewing and Malting Co. became the first brewpub in the U.S. in 1982[126] (a *brewpub* is defined as a restaurant/brewery that serves its own food and its own beer on premises). The first generation of Portland craft breweries, Bridgeport, Widmer, McMenamins, and Portland Brewing, were able to open for business after an Oregon law permitted brewing and retail sales on the same premises.[127] As of 2014, there were 84 breweries operating in Portland, the most breweries of any city in the world.[128]

Breweries in the Pacific Northwest were advantageously located in close proximity to some of their most important suppliers. Ettinger pointed out that the region produced about 23% of the world's hops, helping drive the quality-focused (and very hoppy) craft brewing movement in Portland.

119   "Craft Beer," Encyclopedia of Emerging Industries.
120   "About Mayflower Brewing Company." Mayflower Brewing Company — Craft Beer Microbrewery.
121   "Craft Beer."
122   Ibid.
123   Ibid.
124   Gary Glass, "Statutes."
125   Davis Brown, "MetaCraft Cultural Drive Behind Craft Brewing."
126   Dale P. Van Wieren, American breweries II, 2nd ed.
127   Woodward and Bennett, "Oregon Beer History."
128   "Economic Impact."

The Northwest produced nearly all commercially used hops in the United States: approximately 30,600 acres in Washington, 6,400 acres in Oregon, and 3,900 acres in Idaho. The region was also a major producer of barley, with roughly 900,000 acres in Montana, 570,000 acres in Idaho, and 235,000 acres in Washington.[129] Other inputs were readily available: pure water from Portland's Bull Run watershed, malted barley from Great Western Maltin in Vancouver, Washington, and yeast strains supplied by local labs such as Wyeast Laboratories.

The West Coast dominated the U.S. craft brewing market, with nearly one third of all craft brewing establishments. The three states with the largest share of craft breweries were California at 13.5%, Washington at 7.1%, and Oregon at 6.4%, even though Oregon and Washington combined only represented 3.4% of the total U.S. population.[130] Ettinger credited consumers in the Pacific Northwest as being early adopters, having a sophisticated palate, and making lifestyle choices to support local businesses. Connecting these three important components of the supply chain together — ingredients, processors, and consumers — is what made it all work.

Market and Competition

According to Hopworks Director of Sustainability Nate Young, the national trend had been toward an ever-increasing number of craft breweries selling both on premises and through retail channels (see Appendix E).[131] Although craft beer was still treated as a premium product, making up only 7.8% of beer sales by volume in the United States (but over 18% in Oregon), the "Craft Beer Production industry [had] emerged as the fastest-growing alcoholic beverage industry in the United States."[132] Consumption of craft beer was on the rise, with 19% annual revenue growth in the five years leading up to 2014, slowing to 7.4% forecast annual growth over the following five years.[133] For the first time in modern history, craft beer sales by volume had recently eclipsed sales of Budweiser.[134]

Capitalizing on the growth in demand, the number of craft breweries in

129   Mellie Pullman, "Green Brewing Part Two."
130   Nick Petrillo, "Craft Beer Production — Products and Markets."
131   Nate Young, personal interview.
132   "Craft Beer Production — Products and Markets."
133   Ibid.
134   Tripp Mickle, "Budweiser Crowded Out by Craft Beer Craze."

the U.S. had surged. During the five years leading up to 2014, "the total number of [craft brewing] industry enterprises increased by a 9.6% annualized rate to 2,619," generating an estimated $4.2 billion in revenue.[135] By mid-2014 the number of active brewery permits topped 4,500,[136] including small breweries with hardly any distribution. Market share concentration in the industry was also low, "with the top four players accounting for about 34.3% of total industry revenue in 2014."[137]

With such a large number of small players, the industry was ripe for consolidation. "Merger and acquisition activity [had] begun to occur within the industry, notably with the foundation of the North American Breweries parent corporation and its acquisition of Pyramid Breweries and Magic Hat Brewing Company in 2012."[138] Anheuser-Busch Inbev's 2014 purchase of 10 Barrel Brewing in Bend had the brought the acquisition trend home to Oregon.[139] Ettinger felt this had been driven by 10 Barrel's alleged 25% year-over-year growth rate, which he believed might lead to challenging production economies and lower quality. Because brewery capacity is typically purchased in large increments, the full production capacity needs to be utilized, and that sometimes necessitated reducing prices (or input costs) to move more beer. Otherwise, a brewery would need a capital infusion to expand marketing and distribution.

Acquisitions were not the only way that major beer brands capitalized on the craft brewing craze. In an effort to fight back and cash in, they started marketing their own craft beer lookalikes. MillerCoors produced Blue Moon, a wheat beer, and Anheuser-Busch Inbev was the maker of Shock Top Belgian White, although the producer's name was intentionally left off of the label.[140] In response, craft brewers had to work harder to set themselves apart from corporate brands. "Branding and packaging, including logo design and labeling, are essential to convey the uniqueness of craft beer."[141]

Competition was likewise fierce between craft breweries. During a tour of the Hopworks facility, Young commented that it seemed like a new craft brewery opened up almost every week, competing directly with Hopworks for valuable retail shelf space.[142] To mitigate competitive pressure in retail channels,

135   Ibid.
136   Lester Jones, "Brewery Permits Top 4,500 for First Six Months of 2014."
137   "Craft Beer Production — Products and Markets."
138   Ibid.
139   Mason Walker, "Bend's 10 Barrel Brewing bought by world's largest beer company."
140   Brad Tuttle, "That Craft Beer You're Drinking Isn't Craft Beer. Do You Care?" >
141   Ibid.
142   Nate Young.

Hopworks effectively leveraged on-premise sales. While on-premise sales had lower margins, it avoided the three-tiered distribution system required by law in most states for off-premise sales. These three tiers, a holdover of early post-prohibition laws, were the brewery, distributor, and retailer. Brewers were allowed a small amount of self-distribution below a certain level of production. Beyond that, all sales had to occur through a distributor, and then through a retailer, before reaching the end consumer.[143] Some larger craft breweries, in order to increase geographic reach and lower distribution costs, had recently opened brewing operations on the other side of the country. New Belgium Brewing of Fort Collins, Colorado, and Sierra Nevada of Chico, California had both opened new breweries in Ashland, North Carolina to serve the eastern US market.[144]

Between craft brew lookalikes offered by major brands, a rapidly expanding number of local craft breweries, and economies of scale that favored large-scale production, national distribution, and the need for investment to fuel both, Ettinger's focus on local, sustainable beer seemed under fire from all sides. However, there was a countervailing force among consumers of craft beer: most preferred to drink from local breweries. [145] In addition, more than 38% of American consumers said they purchased green products regularly or almost always, an increase of six percentage points over 2012.[146] Clearly, Hopworks' focus on sustainable, local beer fit emerging consumer trends.

Sustainability in Craft Brewing

Craft brewers by definition are smaller brewers, and they need to survive and thrive in the face of capital constraints. With less capital to invest, brewers have been forced to look for innovative and progressive ways to increase efficiencies and cut costs while maintaining the integrity and quality of their craft brews. Resource use is one key focus area for achieving both cost reductions and competitive differentiation.

Beer Brewing Process

The process starts with malted barley; this barley has been soaked in water to allow partial germination and then kiln dried and roasted to stop the

---

143   Ken Weaver, "Distributors in the Three Tier System."
144   Emily Badger, "Asheville: The New Craft Beer Capital of America?"
145   "Craft Beer Production — Products and Markets."
146   Mintel, "Marketing to the Green Consumer."

germination. In that process, enzymes are developed that will later help convert the grain's starch into sugar. In the brewery, malted barley is milled or crushed into small pieces and then mixed with warm water to steep for an hour or so in a mash tun. After all the starch has converted to sugar, the liquid "wort" is drained into a brew kettle where hops are added as the wort boils to add the aromatic and bitter flavors (the leftover grain from the mash tun is now a by-product of the process). After boiling for an hour, the liquid is cooled and transferred into a fermenter where yeast is added. The yeast gets to work converting the sugary liquid to alcohol and carbon dioxide. When fermentation is complete (a week or more depending on the style), the beer is typically filtered and transferred to a "brite" or conditioning tank where the beer sits until ready to serve. At that point, the beer can be either be served directly to the pub or packaged into kegs, bottles or cans (See Exhibit 1: Brewing Process).

Energy Use

Breweries use electrical energy to power equipment and for refrigeration, while thermal energy, in the form of natural gas, is consumed for brewing. On average, thermal energy accounted for 70% of a brewery's energy use, but only 30% of the energy cost.[147] This usage/cost breakdown indicated reducing electrical energy consumption was a major area of opportunity to reduce costs. Reducing electrical energy also had the added benefit of reducing greenhouse gas emissions.

Industry practices to reduce energy usage varied from low cost options like use of CFL or LED lamps, to moderate cost options like the purchase of ENERGY STAR equipment, to major cost options that could take more than 3 years for payback, such as installation of a refrigeration chiller (See Exhibit 2: Estimated Equipment Costs).

Water Usage

Water is a vital component of beer production, and use and disposal of water can be a large expense for craft brewers. Beer is made up of 90% water, and with the cost of municipal wastewater treatment rising in many areas,[148] breweries increasingly sought ways to improve water efficiency and reduce wastewater. Inefficient operations could consume up to 20 gallons of water per gallon of beer produced.[149] At the opposite end of the spectrum, Full Sail Brewery,

---

147   Brewers Association, "Energy Usage, GHG Reduction, Efficiency and Load Management Manual."
148   Brewers Association, "Water and Wastewater: Treatment/Volume Reduction Manual."
149   "Green Brewing Part Two."

often recognized for its comprehensive and innovative sustainability policies, used as little as 3.45 gallons of water per gallon of beer produced.

One method for reducing wastewater was through the use of anaerobic digestion systems or aerobic treatment. Aerobic treatment removed organic content through separation and composting, while anaerobic digestion produced methane in an oxygen-free environment. Sierra Nevada and New Belgium benefited from incorporating these systems into their production, with the methane produced as a by-product recaptured to power boilers.[150]

Gas Recovery

Although CO_2 is a naturally occurring gas generated during the brewing process, most breweries make no attempt to recapture it, but instead purchase tanks of CO_2 to carbonate, bottle, or keg beer. In 1998, Alaskan Brewing Company in Juneau was one of the first breweries in the U.S. to install a CO_2 reclamation system. The system captured greenhouse gases produced during fermentation and re-distributed it in other production functions. According to Alaskan Brewing, "this system saves approximately 800,000 pounds of CO_2 from being released into the atmosphere each year."[151]

Solid Waste

Spent grains, a byproduct of the mashing process, are the largest source of waste for most brewery operations. Although considered 'waste' at this point, spent grains are still rich in protein and fiber, and were commonly donated or sold as animal feed. Consolidation of cattle to select geographic regions, however, was a limiting factor for some craft brewers given the potential for spoilage in transporting these grains long distances.[152]

A common waste Key Performance Indicator (KPI) referred to the overall waste that was diverted from a landfill, called a Diversion Rate. However, brewing involved such a high volume of spent grain and yeast that it could mask the diversion of other materials. Because of this, craft brewers established a separate diversion rate that excluded spent grain and yeast.[153]

---

150   Mellie Pullman, "Green Brewing Part One.".
151   Ibid.
152   Brewers Association, "Solid Waste Reduction Manual."
153   Ibid.

Hopworks' Decision-making Process[154]

Hopworks' 20-barrel brewery[155] was operating at maximum capacity during their busiest time of year. The average craft brewery produces about 700 barrels per year, and Hopworks was up to 12,500 barrels.[156] Hopworks had done all of this while maintaining not only a level of quality that gained them prestigious awards such as two gold medals at the Great American Brewers festival, but also a commitment to being the most sustainable brewery possible. Their beer was certified organic, no small feat considering the hefty price premium and availability constraints of organic hops. They had set a goal to become zero-waste and in 2013 managed to divert 98.6% of their total waste, including spent grains. The brewery was completely carbon-neutral. Hopworks considered the impact of every decision they made, down to the sourcing of local, cage-free chicken. Their decision process of sustainability investments had evolved over time as shown next.

"Good, Better, Best"

When Hopworks first started, they were confronted with a variety of sustainability options, from good, to better, to the best that money could buy. The company carefully assessed which option would generate the best environmental or social outcomes, would provide the best payback on investment, and was most affordable at the time. Ettinger knew that overspending on these initiatives could put the brewery out of business. "The low hanging fruit," he said, "is what we shoot for out of the gate... and anything that pays for itself in 12 months is pretty rare, but we jump on that pretty quickly."[157]

From "Gut" to "Pro Forma"

Making decisions informed by a balance of reason and analysis came from a lesson the company learned early on, when they made a "gut" decision to use biodiesel to heat their water boiler. As a cleaner fuel alternative, there were clear benefits to sustainability, and the company could tout the approach in its marketing. However, Hopworks quickly learned this cleaner fuel was too expensive, and the brewery was forced to discontinue use of biodiesel altogether.

---

154 The information in this section came from the source: Nate Young, personal interview.
155 One Barrel = 31 Gallons = 1.17 Hectoliters; 20-barrel brew house is the batch size
156 PSU's Center for Executive and Professional Education, "Interview with Christian Ettinger at Hopworks Urban Brewing on Sustainability."
157 Ibid.

Breakeven Analysis

The financial metrics that Hopworks used to evaluate projects were typical of many small businesses. A simple payback period was calculated, and any project providing less than a seven-year payback would be considered. If a project could not surpass the payback hurdle rate, then Hopworks would look at associated brand benefits or try to calculate indirect labor cost savings. For example, when LED lighting was considered for the bar, the project couldn't hit a seven-year simple payback hurdle until indirect labor costs were included. Because LEDs last so much longer than other types of lighting, less of the manager's time would be spent changing light bulbs — a cost savings that helped push the project over the hurdle.

Hopworks does not use other, more sophisticated financial metrics such as Net Present Value (NPV), Internal Rate of Return (IRR), or Modified Internal Rate of Return (MIRR) to evaluate projects unless a bank requires their use as part of a loan. As with any small business, most employees fill many different roles at the company and there is a limited amount of time for financial analysis.

Water and Energy Use

Hopworks' water, electricity, and gas usage per unit of production for 2011–2012 are graphed in Exhibits 3-5. Averaging 7.6 gallons of total water used on site per gallon of beer produced, Hopworks was on a slight, yet encouraging, downward trend for water usage (Exhibit 3). Electricity and natural gas usage per barrel produced followed similar downward trends even as production ramped up 16% year-over-year (Exhibits 4 & 5). Managing the cost of water and energy was an important part of Young's job as Director of Sustainability. Increased operating efficiency was the result of continuous energy improvement practices, and if left unattended, costs could spiral out of control. Lacking the scale necessary to support larger infrastructure projects, such as bio-digesters, Hopworks had to maintain focus on the most cost-effective solutions for their current production levels.

Brand Benefits

Internal research showed that one third of Hopworks' customers selected the brand because of the company's commitment to sustainability. This was an important element of Hopworks' competitive differentiation, and the company aimed to make daily decisions about sustainability and to talk about these practices publicly. For example, Ettinger encouraged other brewers to brew at least one certified organic beer to drive market adoption of organics in general and to expand the supply base of raw organic ingredients.

As a counterexample to sustainability-led branding, Young pointed to Sierra Nevada, widely considered one of the most sustainable breweries in the United States. However, sustainability was not a major part of their marketing message. This would seemingly reduce the number of customers selecting the brand based on a perception of sustainability, and therefore the add-on brand benefits of sustainability investments. For a small craft brewery like Hopworks, those brand benefits, and the accompanying increase in sales and customer willingness to pay a premium, could often mean the difference between making and forgoing a sustainability investment.

Hopworks Sustainability Initiatives[158]

Remodeling

Deconstruction and remodeling of the flagship brewpub was the first major sustainability decision the company faced. The new building was re-built using as many reclaimed materials as possible, a painstaking process that required sorting every piece of material by hand, from plumbing to old wood. With help from locally based Lovett Deconstruction, the majority of site materials were reclaimed and reconstructed. Old kegs served as flower planters surrounding the outdoor patio. Inside, the arched wooden ceiling was restored and left exposed, old growler bottles were used as light fixtures, and old beer bottles on the walls served as decorations. One-third of the framing, as well as the restaurant booths, trim, and the bar itself, were made from repurposed material.[159]

Carbon Neutral and Energy Efficient

The brewery purchased renewable energy credits (RECs) to cover 100% of its usage, and purchased additional carbon credits to offset 100% of its scope 1, 2 and 3 emissions (covering direct, indirect from purchased energy, and other indirect sources). Energy efficient equipment was installed throughout the building: L5/L8 Fluorescent light bulbs (lighting), cool-Fit pre-insulated glycol pipes (cooling), weatherization for windows and doors (insulation), and air economizers (HVAC).

---

158   The information in this section came from the source: "2013 Sustainability Report."
159   "Building Green."

Organic Certification

Hopworks is the only brewery in Oregon fully committed to organic brewing. The brewery was certified organic by Oregon Tilth, which is overseen by the United States Department of Agriculture (USDA). This certification is an internationally recognized symbol of organic integrity, requiring food producers to adhere to strict production standards that include being free of Genetically Modified Organisms (GMO).

Employee Culture & Incentives

Hopworks encouraged its employees to practice sustainability, and offered rewards to incentivize these activities. Approximately 67% of all employees used sustainable commuting methods: bike, public transportation, carpool, or foot. Quarterly raffles were offered for employees who used "active transportation," getting to and from work through physical activity like walking, bicycling, or even skateboarding. All full-time employees were offered health insurance and earned sick leave. Although leave was required by the City of Portland, Hopworks employees could convert sick leave to paid time off, encouraging personal wellbeing.

Water Consumption

Due to committed efforts by restaurant staff and brewers, along with reconfiguration of their taps, Hopworks lowered their water use to 3.01 gallons of water per gallon of beer produced, very low by industry standards. In the brewpubs, water was served only by request, and total consumption by all operations amounted to just over "4 swimming pools' worth" of water, offset by purchasing credits from the Bonneville Environmental Foundation.

Glycol Cooling System

In 2012, the brewery installed a glycol system used to maintain cooler temperature during fermentation (72 degrees for ales, 40 degrees for lagers) and to chill finished beers for packaging. Installation of the cooling system reduced the brewery's monthly electricity bill by 8%.

Zero-Waste

Hopworks aimed to achieve zero waste. Excluding spent grains, the brewery diverted 89% of their waste from landfills through compost and recycling. Each year, 700 tons of spent brewing grain was sent to a rancher in the Willamette Valley to be used as cattle feed. Including spent grain, their total diversion rate was 98.6%.

Bike Bar

This bicycle-friendly extension of Hopworks was housed in an eco-friendly building on one of Portland's "bike highways." Bike-friendly features included a bike frame canopy, 75 bicycle parking spaces, bike tools for use, and bicycle take-out specials. Patrons also had access to Plug-Out exercycles, stationary bicycles that generated energy when in use. The building was designed to meet "NetZero" energy standards, and was constructed using reclaimed materials from Portland's Rebuilding Center. The Bike Bar itself was an incandescent bulb free zone.

Recyclable Paktech Handles

Paktech handles are made from 96% recycled HDPE plastic, and produced in Eugene, Oregon. Hopworks used the handles on their four-packs of cans, and offered incentives for customers who brought back the handles. For every Hopworks handle returned, they gave a wooden nickel worth a quarter ($0.25) towards a pint of beer, up to the price of a pint, or 19 handles in a single visit.

Challenges and Opportunities

The pressure to expand came from multiple related activities. As mentioned previously, the market for craft beer was growing more competitive daily. Large brands were launching copycat beers or acquiring other craft breweries, and the number of competing craft brewers in the region was exploding. As a result, shelf space in retail store was getting severely constrained. Getting a major chain store account was a major coup for a brewery but brought with it expectations to fill multiple stores with several of the brewery's packaged styles. One major chain account could double or triple production demand. Other breweries of similar size to Hopworks were expanding into the Northwest from California or Colorado. Other Oregon breweries were aggressively trying to grab Hopwork's existing accounts. Thus, the brewery could not maintain their current position without pushing back, maintaining relevancy and expanding in other territories. Throughout this, Hopworks had been able to reduce costs, build better connections to sustainability-minded local consumers, and reduce their impacts through consistent investment in sustainability and a focus on brewpub sales. Ettinger was proud of the recognition they had received both for beer quality and for their sustainability initiatives (see Appendix A). Yet considering the market pressures Hopworks faced, and the fact that their original brewpub was at maximum capacity, Ettinger knew the company had to make changes, both to continue their growth and their positive environmental and community impact. Otherwise, they might be completely squeezed out by their competitors.

The brewery needed to implement cost reduction strategies to become more competitive at a larger scale, especially if they moved into areas where consumers were unwilling to pay a sustainability premium. But how could they do that without compromising their mission? Hopworks had a number of options, each of which came with its own set of tradeoffs.

Ettinger had begun exploring Salmon Safe certification for Hopworks' hops. The Salmon Safe program had become one of the nation's premier eco-labels, working to preserve watersheds for salmon spawning on the West Coast from British Columbia down through California, and had a positive impact on 600,000 acres of farmland.[160] Purchasing hops from farmers that were Salmon Safe certified but not certified organic would allow Hopworks to expand their environmental impact, and encourage and promote sustainable farming practices on a greater scale. It would also lower the cost of Hopworks' raw ingredients.[161] Buying certified organic hops was one of their biggest expenditures after real estate and labor; the cost premium of producing certified organic beer was about $0.08 per pint, or up to $248,000 per year at their current rate of production.[162] At $12 to $18 per pound, organic hops were at least twice as expensive as conventional hops.[163] Although organic hops were increasing in supply — production went from 0.25% of total U.S. hops production in 2009 to 1.12% in 2012 — they were still not as easy to obtain as conventional hops, despite Hopworks' ideal location near the majority of hops grown in America.[164]

Would the addition of, or change to, Salmon Safe hops be perceived by their loyal customers as expanding their sustainable practices, or withdrawing on their promise to support organic agriculture? How could they balance different certifications, and would they be in line with Hopworks' values? Salmon Safe hops were more readily available, but large local competitors already used them in beer and marketed this as a sustainable practice.[165]

Ettinger also considered investing in new equipment to lower costs and reduce waste. Hopworks had about $100,000 in free cash flow available each quarter to invest, but it wasn't always clear where that should go first. The

160   Salmon Safe, "About: Salmon-Safe."
161   Christian Ettinger.
162   Nate Young.
163   Deena Shanker, "Organic Beer: Here to Stay, or Barley There?"
164   Ibid.
165   Jennifer Anderson, "Farmers Go Out on Limb to Grow Organic Hops."

brewery management software? A centrifuge to help reduce waste, resulting in about 5% more beer per batch? What about investing in an automated brewing system, one that could both improve energy efficiency and cut labor costs — but would it be an expensive, top-line German system or one fabricated locally? A locally sourced system was much cheaper, about 20% less than the cost of German automation, and would support another local business. However, it wouldn't be nearly as efficient, so even if they broke even on the capital expenditure sooner, the long-term benefits were not the same.

Then there was the question of finding a new brewpub space. Undeniably, brewpubs made fiscal sense, bypassing expensive distribution and enabling the type of direct customer engagement that allowed Hopworks to trumpet its sustainability practices — something hard to fit on the label of a beer bottle. However, the local real estate market was heating up and Hopworks had not been able to secure the space they wanted in suburban Portland. Should they delay their next opening or compromise on a less desirable location?

If Hopworks had trouble tripling its locations, what about expanding their reach via wider distribution? Like many artisan beer producers, Hopworks started as and remained a brewpub, selling most of its product on site. The Brewer's Association classified a brewpub as a restaurant-brewery that sells 25% or more of its beer on premises. In contrast, a microbrewery focused on distribution, with 75% or more of its beer being sold off site, but with production under 15,000 barrels per year. The next tier of production was a regional brewery, with production between 15,000 and 6 million barrels per year, but Hopworks was not planning to reach that scale. Due to their focus on sustainable community, the brewpub model had always made sense for Hopworks. Plus, distribution was an expense, and one that added to their carbon footprint. Ettinger had always felt that by definition, craft brewers focused on freshness and flavor, and you can't achieve top quality if your beer is sitting in cans in a truck and then a supermarket shelf.

However, Ettinger now wondered if there were sustainable routes of distribution that wouldn't compromise the quality of Hopworks' beer or their values. Could they find an ecologically sound way to distribute? Was it economically viable? Currently wholesale only brought in 30% of their revenue, but the profit margin was higher at 25%. How would expanding distribution affect their bottom line? Beyond that, would quality and freshness be affected as he suspected it might? Distribution also meant a marketing plan for cities the Hopworks team wasn't familiar with, and fighting for shelf space at local stores was hard enough.

The final question on Ettinger's mind was related to another of their top expenses, labor. Since sustainability was always core to Hopworks' ethos, when they were able to hire Director of Sustainability Nate Young in 2012, Ettinger was thrilled. Young completed a full audit of Hopworks' utility costs, measured the impact of new energy-saving equipment, and gave expert advice on the feasibility of new initiatives. He also produced their first-ever sustainability report in 2012, followed by a 2013 report that included their improved impacts (See Appendices B & C). But when Ettinger considered his new organizational chart and Hopworks' labor overhead, where did Young fit in now? Young had started as part-time and transitioned to full-time in 2013. However, Hopworks had recently hired a much-needed new Controller, and this role took over some of what Young had been doing.

Did a small craft brewery need a full-time Director of Sustainability, especially if they had already achieved a culture of sustainability, utilized most of their potential investments in sustainability, and fully engaged customers with that mindset? This particular question was difficult, as cutting Young's position directly affected a person key to the Hopworks community, and this in turn could impact morale or give the appearance that their focus on sustainability had waned.

Conclusion

As Ettinger's afternoon meeting drew to a close, he knew that the decisions he was faced with now would shape the future of Hopworks far beyond the scope of their five-year plan. He was certain that Hopworks needed to expand, but it wasn't completely clear how, and what sustainability initiatives might be possible — or what compromises they might have to make. Investing in equipment or software seemed minor compared to the major step of pursuing two new brewpub locations, or moving to distribute their wholesale products more widely. Hopworks was proud to be an organic brewery, but what if they could expand their sustainable impact by including other certifications like Salmon Safe? It came down to a question of their core identity, and how this evolved over time. Could Hopworks balance their ideals with a continued commitment to making the best beer, while staying economically sustainable as well?

Even if the path forward wasn't obvious, Ettinger felt lucky to be in a position where he could make a living brewing beer. He had already grown Hopworks to a company of 125 employees and was deeply committed to expanding the local impact of his business. However Hopworks' five-year plan played out, Ettinger knew that he would succeed in his mission to use the brewery to change the world, one pint at a time.

Exhibits

Exhibit 1: Beer Production

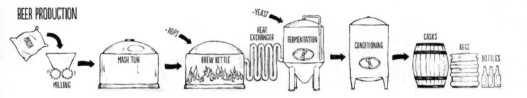

Exhibit 2: Estimated Equipment Costs

Equipment	Estimated Costs with Description
CFL or LED lightbulbs	Estimated Cost Per LED Bulb: $9.97 - $99.85 Estimated Cost Per CFL Bulb: $6.97 - $29.88 Cost dependent upon variations to design, functionality and wattage 40-100W Dimmable/Non-dimmable
Photovoltaic System (solar panels)	Estimated Cost: $3.34 per watt or 20 cents per kWh (on a 20-year levelized basis) Estimated costs are an average calculated from the following factors: size of system, system location, system efficiency, solar panel cost, system design, cost of physical installations, permitting andapplication costs, and many other factors.
Energy Star-certified Water Heater	(a) Estimated Cost: $2,232 Model: Eternal GU195S Condensing Hybrid Water Heater Up to 19.5 Gallons per Minute (GPM) Ultra low emissions (1ppm CO) Fuel Type: Natural Gas (b) Estimated Cost: $1,130 Model: Rinnai R98LSeN Tankless Water Heater Up to 9.8 Gallons Per Minute (GPM) Fuel Type: Natural Gas
Glycol Chiller	Installed Cost: $75,000 Cost includes $45,000 for unit and $30,000 for installation Estimate based on a 12,500 bbl/year production
Anaerobic digestors	Installed Cost: $700,000 - $1,200,000 Smallest entry level size: 50 kl UASB system Equivalent to a brewery size of btween 118,000-236,000 bbl per year production
Aerobic treatment system	Installed Cost: $400,000 - $900,000 Smallest entry level: sized to treat 37,854 lpd Equivalent to a brewery size of btween 235,000-470,000 bbl per year production

Source: Nate Young.

Exhibit 3: Water (gallons) usage per gallon of beer produced 2011 – 2012

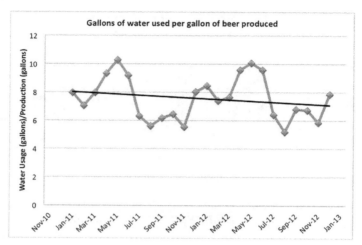

(1 Barrel = 31 U.S. Gallons = 1.17 Hectoliter)
Source: Nate Young.

Exhibit 4: Electricity usage (kWh) per barrel of beer produced 2011 – 2012

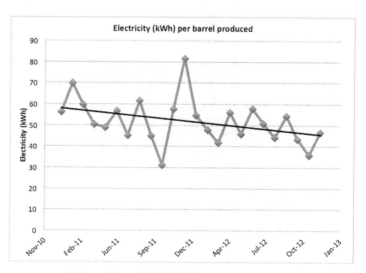

(1 Barrel = 31 U.S. Gallons = 1.17 Hectoliter)
Source: Nate Young.

Exhibit 5: Gas usage (therms x 10) per barrel of beer produced 2011 – 2012

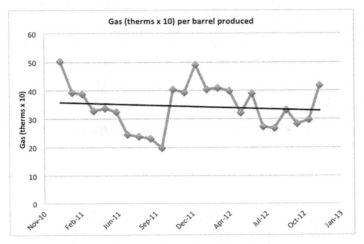

(1 Barrel = 31 U.S. Gallons = 1.17 Hectoliter)
Source: Nate Young.

Appendices

Appendix A: Hopworks Awards and Certifications

Best 100 Green Places to Work (#37), Oregon Business Journal (2013)

Grand Champion, State of Oregon Sustainability Awards (2012)

Gold Seal, Good Food Awards (2012)

Gold Medal, City of Portland Sustainability at Work (2012)

Gold Status, Travel Oregon Forever (2012)

100 Best Green Places to Work, Oregon Business Magazine (2012)

Bronze Medal for "Organic Hopworks Kellerbier": Great American Beer Festival — Kellerbier or Zwickelbier category (2012)

Gary Sheppard Memorial Trophy for Best New Exhibitor, Australian International Beer Awards (2011)

Silver Medal for *Hopworks Organic IPA*; Australian International Beer Awards, Ale Packaged – India Pale Ale category (2011)

Silver Medal for *Hopworks Organic Velvet ESB*; Australian International Beer Awards, Ale Packaged – British Style Pale Ale category (2011)

Silver Medal for *Organic Secession CDA*; Australian International Beer Awards, Ale Packaged – Other category (2011)

Bronze Medal for *HUB Organic Lager*; Australian International Beer Awards, Lager Packaged – Pilsner category (2011)

Silver Medal for *Hopworks Organic Velvet ESB*; World Beer Cup, Extra Special Bitter or Strong Bitter category (2010)

Gold Medal for *Organic Ace of Spades Imperial IPA*; Great American Beer Festival, Imperial India Pale Ale category (2009)

Gold Medal for *Organic Rise Up Red*; Great American Beer Festival, American Style Amber/Red Ale categoryn (2009)

Bronze Medal for *Hopworks Organic IPA*; Great American Beer Festival, American-Style Strong Pale Ale category (2008)

Gold Medal for *Hopworks Organic IPA*; World Beer Cup, American-Style Strong Pale Ale category (2008)

Silver Medal for *HUB Organic Lager*; World Beer Cup, Bohemian-Style Pilsner category (2008)

Certification: Certified Organic by Oregon Tilth

Source: Hopworks.com

Appendix B: Progress in Numbers (2013 Sustainability Report)

DIVERSION FROM LANDFILL

We continue to focus on our zero-waste goals stated last year: We hope to divert >90% of our non-grain waste from the landfill. We didn't quite make it this year, ending up at 85% diversion. We also sent an estimated 650 tons of spent grain to some very happy cows on an Organic Valley Coop farm—whose organic milk we serve in the restaurant—which makes for a total diversion rate of 98.6%. Not too bad!

LANDFILL 10 T
RECYCLE 22 T
COMPOST 34 T
GRAIN TO CATTLE 650 T

CERTIFIED CARBON NEUTRAL

GAS CONSUMED, HUB VEHICLES 17.65
EMPLOYEE COMMUTING 52.02
MERCHANDISE SUPPLY CHAIN 65.18
OTHER 27.60
HOPWORKS AIR TRAVEL 18.04
ELECTRICITY 198.12
NATURAL GAS 190.37
RESTAURANT SUPPLY CHAIN 293.10
BREWERY SUPPLY CHAIN 742.23

BEER IS LIQUID LOVE

Building on our previous work, and with serious efforts from our brewers and restaurant staff, our water consumption went down in both intensity and total gallons.

We reconfigured our taps so a comparison to last year's 4.23 gallons of water per gallon of beer isn't quite perfect but in 2013 we used 3.01 gallons to produce each gallon of beer, and consumed just over 4 swimming pools worth of water between the restaurants and brewery. As before, we purchased water offsets from Bonneville Environmental Foundation equivalent to more than our annual consumption.

OUR CARBON FOOTPRINT

You'll notice our carbon footprint is measurably higher compared to last year at 1827.5 metric tons CO2e equivalents (MT CO2e) gross. After we purchased renewable energy credits from our utilities and banked some offsets from waste diversion, our net footprint was 1639.5 MT CO2e.

As we grow, our footprint may grow as well, though we will strive to be more efficient and keep our emissions stable by continuing to reduce per barrel emissions going forward.

2013 BY THE NUMBERS

2,538,026
pints of great organic beer produced and sold throughout the region

120
pounds of PakTech 4-pack handles returned to Denton Plastics where they'll be melted down and remade into new plastic items here in the Pacific NW

30,855
shift meals given to our employees. We also offer health insurance to full-time employees and have over complied with Portland's sick-leave regulations by giving that time as PTO in the event that our workers stay healthy

10,371
growler fills sold at Hopworks on Powell and BikeBar—fewer than last year because cans are the new darling to-go package

88.4%
of our grains arrived to the brewery in bulk

135
community organizations supported with donations and profit-share events ranging from Cleveland High across the street to the World Affairs Council of Oregon

3,283
wine bottles no longer consumed each year thanks to our new kegged wine system at Powell—coming soon to BikeBar as well!

134,630
estimated miles Hopworks' employees commuted by foot, bike, skateboard, bus and light rail—that's 55% of all commuting miles and 67% of trips

HUB SUSTAINABILITY REPORT 2013

Source: Nate Young, "HUB Sustainability Report 2013."

BEER IS MADE OF WATER!

We take great pride and responsibility in preserving and protecting our water system. To keep tabs on our water use, we measure gallons of water used to produce a gallon of beer. In 2012 we hit 4.23 gal / gal, and improvement from 4.67 in 2011. With the industry average closer to 8 gal / gal, we are doing well, but look forward to improving for 2013.

Finally, to help offset our water consumption, we purchase water offsets from Bonneville Environmental Foundation for 2.5 million gallons, as much as we used for the brewery and both pubs combined.

WASTE NOT WANT NOT

Excluding the nearly 600 tons of spent grains and other organic brewery material we sent to an organic Willamette Valley dairy farm we created just under 50 tons of "waste" last year. Of that, 30 tons went to compost, 14 tons was recycled, and 6 tons went to landfill—true waste. Our goal for next year is first to reduce the total, and second to increase our diversion rate from 88.1% to great than 90%. Check back to see how we are doing!

OUR CARBON FOOTPRINT

In 2012, our greenhouse gas emissions totaled 1,140.49 Metric Tons CO2 equivalent (MT CO2e) partially offset by green electricity purchases and other strategies for a net footprint of 925.16 MT CO2e. This includes both internal and external emissions (scopes 1, 2, and partial scope 3.) We purchased offsets for our entire footprint up to the point where the beer leaves our doors.

THESE OFFSETS ARE THE EQUIVALENT OF REMOVING 193 PASSENGER CARS FROM THE ROAD IN A YEAR.

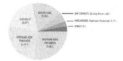

OUR PROGRESS IN NUMBERS

47,086
hamburger patties and chicken breasts from Painted Hills Natural Beef and Draper Valley Farms respectively. We strongly support local and natural producers.

2,317,213
pints of HUB beer produced and sold in 2012, a 16% increase from 2011!

133
pounds of bottle caps, corks, and other items donated to SCRAP, a local non-profit literally turning trash into treasure while teaching environmentally responsible behavior.

124,933
Miles HUB employees commuted by foot, bike, skateboard, bus, train, or carpool. We incentivize non-auto commuting and are proud that active transportation was 68.6% of all trips to work!

87%
of our grain is delivered in bulk. This greatly reduces our waste and ensures shipping efficiency since we only receive full trucks.

27,225
employee meals provided—one per shift. We also offer health insurance to full-time employees, as well as above-market wage rates. Our employees deserve nothing less!

7
awards earned for our beer or sustainable actions. Find out more on the next page

13,538
growler refills sold at Hopworks Urban Brewery and BikeBar. We love growlers because you get fresh beer at home with no waste created in the process.

78
profit-share or other community support events. Because providing beer and shopping local isn't the only way to support our communities.

Source: Nate Young, "2012: Sustainability Report."

Appendix D: Energy Practices for Breweries

Top 10 Energy Best Practices; Breweries and Brewpubs/Restaurants

ITEM	TOP 10 BREWERY RELATED ENERGY BEST PRACTICES
(1)	Turn off equipment when not in use
(2)	Engage employees on how to conserve and use energy more efficiently
(3)	Replace air filters on air handlers, HVAC units etc. on regular intervals
(4)	Identify and repair compressed air, steam and water leaks
(5)	Repair or Replace damaged or missing insulation
(6)	Eliminate the use of compressed air for cleaning, cooling or other applications
(7)	Review all energy set points on a regular basis
(8)	Upgrade incandescent, T-12 Fluorescent to more efficient lighting types
(9)	Collect steam condensate
(10)	Purchase and install energy efficient equipment

Energy Consumption In Breweries (All Sizes)

Data from the U.S. Environmental Protection Agency (EPA) show that refrigeration, packaging and compressed aire consume 70% of U.S. breweries' electricity use (A), whereas the brewhouse dominates natural gas and coal use at 45 percent (B).

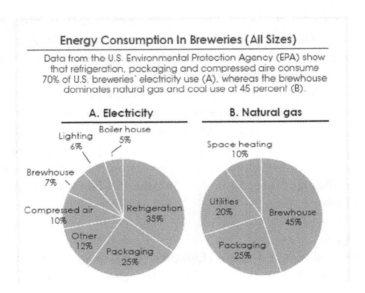

Source: Brewers Association, "Energy Usage, GHG Reduction, Efficiency and Load Management Manual."

Appendix E: U.S. Craft Brewery Competitors

Boston Beer Company

Boston Beer Company, famous for its Sam Adams line of beers, was the 800-pound gorilla in the craft beer market. Topping the charts of the largest craft brewers in the U.S., Boston Beer had twice the production (2.125 million barrels) of the next largest brewer, Sierra Nevada (at just under 1 million barrels per year).[166]

Sierra Nevada

The second largest craft brewer in the U.S. was based in Chico, California. Maintaining a strong focus on sustainability as a key part of operations, Sierra Nevada aimed to contain operating costs. However, this sustainability bent did not make its way into customer-facing marketing.[167] For a number of companies, including Sierra Nevada, where their customers might not necessarily care about sustainability, or might not be willing to pay more for sustainability, the company may not be able to use their operating practices as a marketing tool.

New Belgium

Based in Ft. Collins, Colorado, New Belgium rose to prominence on the success of its Fat Tire Amber Ale. An employee owned enterprise and certified B Corporation, New Belgium prominently displayed their sustainability credentials on their website alongside their beer.[168] Sustainability at New Belgium covered everything from buying their employees bicycles[169], in order to encourage them to bike to work, to continuous improvement and constant monitoring of their energy usage. Maintaining transparency in the supply chain so that carbon emissions could be tracked was another feature of their commitment to reducing environmental impact. In order to reduce distribution costs, New Belgium opened a brewery in Asheville, North Carolina to serve the East Coast.[170]

Fort George

Similar in production volume to Hopworks, Fort George Brewery in Astoria, Oregon distributed only in the northwest. Fort George did not bottle any of

---

166   "Top Craft Beer Makers, 2012," New York Times.
167   Sierra Nevada, "Sustainability."
168   New Belgium Brewing, "Sustainability Stories."
169   New Belgium Brewing, "Benefits."
170   "Asheville: The New Craft Beer Capital of America?"

its beer, selling only in cans and kegs. Canning seven regular beers and six seasonals, Fort George limited the number of beers distributed in cans, keeping the rest of their lineup in kegs. Operating the brewpub in Astoria in the same building as the brewery, Fort George hosted a lecture series every Thursday to draw people to the brewpub and educate people about beer.[171]

Boneyard Beer

Boneyard Beer in Bend, Oregon was started with used brewing equipment that owner Tony Lawrence collected from 13 different breweries, hence the name "Boneyard." With a 15,000 barrel production capacity, Boneyard had a similar capacity to Hopworks, but only operated a single tasting room.[172] At the time of this case, none of Boneyard's beers were available in bottles or cans.

Bridgeport

Originally founded by Dick and Nora Ponzi in 1984, Bridgeport was purchased by Gambrinus, the makers of Shiner Beer in San Antonio Texas.[173] Bridgeport is Oregon's oldest microbrewery.[174] Operating brewpubs around Portland as well as distributing bottles across a wide geographic region, Bridgeport maintained its status among the old guard of United States craft brewers.

171   Fort George Brewery, "Fort George Brewery and Public House."
172   Boneyard Beer, "About."
173   John Foyston, "A BridgePort Timeline."
174   A. Jones, "Craft Brewing Defines Oregon as U.S. "Beer Capital."

Bibliography

Anderson, Jennifer. "Farmers Go Out on Limb to Grow Organic Hops." *Portland Tribune*, September 11, 2014. http://pamplinmedia.com/sl/233297-97889-farmers-go-out-on-limb-to-grow-organic-hops.

Badger, Emily. "Asheville: The New Craft Beer Capital of America?" *Fast Company*, September 5, 2012. http://www.fastcompany.com/3000850/asheville-new-craft-beer-capital-america.

Bell, John. "Christian Ettinger Revolutionizes Craft Brew Scene... Again." *Drive the District*. May 5, 2014.

Boneyard Beer. "About." 2014. http://boneyardbeer.com/about/.

Brewers Association. "Energy Usage, GHG Reduction, Efficiency and Load Management Manual." Antea Group, 2012.

Brewers Association. "Solid Waste Reduction Manual." Antea Group, 2012. http://www.brewersassociation.org/attachments/0001/1529/Sustainability_Manual_Solid_waste.pdf.

Brewers Association. "Water and Wastewater: Treatment/Volume Reduction Manual." Antea Group, 2013. https://www.brewersassociation.org/attachments/0001/1517/Sustainability_-_Water_Wastewater.pdf.

Brown, Davis. "MetaCraft Cultural Drive Behind Craft Brewing." MetaCraft, Inc. September 2, 2014. http://www.metacraftcorp.com/?p=471.

"Craft Beer." *Encyclopedia of Emerging Industries*. Business Insights, 2000.

Ettinger, Christian. Personal Interview. November 11, 2014

Fort George Brewery and Public House. "Fort George Brewery." 2014. http://www.fortgeorgebrewery.com

Foyston, John. "A BridgePort Timeline." *The Oregonian*, August 11, 2009. http://blog.oregonlive.com/thebeerhere/2009/08/a_bridgeport_timeline.html

Glass, Gary. "Statutes." American Homebrewer's Association, 2014. http://www.homebrewersassociation.org/homebrewing-rights/statutes/.

Hopworks Urban Brewery, "Building Green." 2008. http://hopworksbeer.com/green-culture/building-green.

Jones, A. "Craft Brewing Defines Oregon as U.S. 'Beer Capital.'" National Geographic, August 10, 2001. http://news.nationalgeographic.com/news/2001/08/0808_oregonbrewing_2.html.

Jones, Lester. "Brewery Permits Top 4,500 for First Six Months of 2014." *NBWA*, July, 2014. http://www.nbwa.org/resources/brewery-permits-top-4500-first-six-months-2014.

Mayflower Brewing Company. "About Mayflower Brewing Company." 2014. http://mayflowerbrewing.com/about.php.

Mickle, Tripp. "Budweiser Crowded Out by Craft Beer Craze." *Wall Street Journal*, November 23, 2014.

Mintel. "Marketing to the Green Consumer." Mintel Group. Mintel.com, 2014. Web. 16 Mar. 2015.

New Belgium Brewing. "Benefits." 2013. http://www.newbelgium.com/Brewery/company/benefits.aspx.

New Belgium Brewing. "Sustainability Stories." 2014. http://www.newbelgium.com/Sustainability/Stories.aspx.

Oregon Business. "100 Best Green Companies to Work for in Oregon 2013." May 27, 2013. http://www.oregonbusiness.com/articles/131-june-2013/10210-100-best-green-companies-to-work-for-in-oregon-2013.

Oregon Craft Beer. "Economic Impact." Oregon Brewers Guild, 2013.

Petrillo, Nick. "Craft Beer Production — Products and Markets." *IBISWorld*, September 2014.

Pullman, Mellie. "Green Brewing Part One." *BEERnorthwest*, 2009.

Pullman, Mellie. "Green Brewing Part Two." *BEERnorthwest*, 2010.

PSU's Center for Executive and Professional Education. "Interview with Christian Ettinger at Hopworks Urban Brewing on Sustainability." YouTube, October 27, 2013. Video, 11:40. http://youtu.be/kNuPsN-PK8I.

Salmon Safe. "About." 2014. https://salmonsafe.org/about/.

Shanker, Deena. "Organic Beer: Here to Stay, or Barley There?" *Grist*, May 28, 2013. http://grist.org/food/organic-beer-here-to-stay-or-barley-there/.

Sierra Nevada Brewing Co. "Sustainability." 2014. http://www.sierranevada.com/brewery/about-us/sustainability.

"Top Craft Beer Makers, 2012." *New York Times*, October 1, 2013.

Tuttle, Brad. "That Craft Beer You're Drinking Isn't Craft Beer. Do You Care?" *Time Magazine*, August 13, 2013.

Van Wieren, Dale P. *American breweries II. 2nd ed.* North Wales: Eastern Coast Breweriana Association, 1995.

Walker, Mason. "Bend's 10 Barrel Brewing bought by world's largest beer company." *Portland Business Journal*, November 5, 2014. http://www.bizjournals.com/portland/blog/2014/11/bends-10-barrel-brewing-bought-by-worlds-largest.html.

Weaver, Ken. "Distributors in the Three Tier System." *All About Beer Magazine*, November 1, 2012. http://allaboutbeer.com/article/craft-beer-distributors/.

Willis, Warren. "At Hopworks Urban Brewery, Christian Ettinger's Strategy for Success Revolves Around Sustainability." *The Latest Just About Everything We Think Matters*. American Craft Beer. August 14, 2013. http://americancraftbeer.com/item/at-hopworks-urban-brewery-christian-ettinger-s-strategy-for-success-revolves-around-sustainability.html.

Woodward, Bob, and Laurel Bennett. "Oregon Beer History." *1859 Oregon Magazine*, January 1, 2010. http://1859oregonmagazine.com/oregon-beer-history.

Young, Nate. "2013 Sustainability Report." Hopworks Urban Brewery, 2014.

Young, Nate. Personal Interview. 6 Oct. 2014.

Young, Nate. "Sustainability Report: 2012." Hopworks Urban Brewery, 2013.

PORTLAND ROASTING COMPANY
Farm Friendly Direct

Oikos Case Competition 1st Place (Corporate
Sustainability Track), 2010

*By Madeleine E. Pullman, Ph.D., Brandon Arends, Mark Langston,
Greg Price, and Greg Stokes*

Portland Roasting Case Study

*"Coffee is now about not only finding great coffee but showcasing who you're buy-
ing from. It's about sustainability. What's driving the industry is people think of
coffee as a commodity that's picked by hand. There's a lot of work involved in it.
There are people behind this coffee bean and that's the cutting-edge stuff right now."*
— Mark Stell, Managing Partner, Portland Roasting Company

Introduction

As Mark Stell waited to board the plane to Bujumbura, the capital city of
Burundi in Africa, he contemplated an exciting market opportunity for his
specialty coffee roasting company. Within a few short weeks, Stell and his management team were pitching Fred Meyer, a major regional grocery retailer. This

account would provide access to a large retail distribution channel and represented a significant business opportunity for Portland Roasting Company (PRC). Not only would this account help PRC achieve growth goals, potentially boosting revenue by as much as 25%, it would give PRC unprecedented exposure to retail consumers. As a wholesale coffee company, PRC relied heavily on retailers to promote its brand directly to consumers. Fred Meyer would feature PRC coffee and promotional material in grocery stores throughout the Pacific Northwest. Ultimately, this was an opportunity to build the PRC brand. Last year, Stell had made significant investments in new roasting and packaging equipment and he knew he had the capacity and infrastructure to supply a large account. PRC would also promote the virtues of the Farm Friendly Direct (FFD) program and the company's long-term commitment to sustainability.

From the beginning, PRC had developed trade relationships with individual coffee growers, paid premium prices, and invested additional funds in local projects that directly benefited the lives of coffee farmers and their communities. The FFD program is featured on the company website, in marketing materials and on product packaging (Exhibit 1). In 2005, PRC was awarded the prestigious Sustainability Award by the Specialty Coffee Association of America (SCAA). Yet despite the merits of the FFD program, "Farm Friendly Direct" was relatively unknown compared to Fair Trade, Organic and Rainforest Alliance certified coffees. PRC would have to convince Fred Meyers that "Farm Friendly Direct" coffee was superior to conventional third-party certifications and competitor's direct trade programs. Stell also realized that the FFD program alone would not be sufficient to secure the account. Grocery retailers were also concerned about price, order fulfillment, brand strength, marketing support, product quality and customer service in addition to the sustainability attributes of a product.

As the last boarding call rang out over the loudspeaker, Stell picked up his laptop bag and headed for the departure gate. Stell was always searching for high quality coffee and made frequent international trips to source from different growing regions. Despite his focus on the upcoming pitch to Fred Meyer, he couldn't help reflecting on the long-term outlook for the coffee industry and the challenges facing coffee growers around the world. With global temperatures continuing to rise, the area of land around the equator capable of growing coffee was shrinking fast. Stell was eager to spend time with his new supplier from Sogestal Kayanza, in North Burundi. He was planning to spend a week getting to know the farmer and working to improve product quality. Stell hoped to establish a direct trade relationship with this farmer and negotiate an FFD project that would most effectively address local needs. Yet doing so took time, the results of such projects were difficult to measure, and the positive impacts on sustainability were not easily communicated to customers in the US. Despite these challenges, Stell believed the direct trade model was superior to conventional certification, but would it gain enough momentum in the coffee industry to ensure the long-term viability of growing regions? Stell was motivated to grow his company and extend the positive impacts of FFD, but how could PRC convince customers like Fred Meyers to base their coffee purchase decisions on the relative merits of FFD? Stell pondered these questions and continued to work on his pitch during the long flight.

Company Profile

Portland Roasting Company was headquartered in the bustling central eastside industrial district of Portland, Oregon. The 20,000-square-foot facility contained roasting equipment, warehouse space, a coffee tasting facility and offices for 27 employees. PRC's core business was sourcing, roasting and distributing high-quality coffees to wholesale customers including retail coffee shops, restaurants, businesses, food merchants and institutions. Consumers could purchase PRC coffees directly through the company website. The company sold coffee equipment and associated supplies including a line of flavored syrups. Coffees were sourced from more than 20 different countries (Exhibit 2) and Farm Friendly Direct relationships existed with farmers and cooperatives in Guatemala, Costa Rica, El Salvador, Ethiopia, India, Papua New Guinea, Sumatra and Tanzania (Exhibit 3). Working with Stell on the management team were Paul Gilles (VP of Operations) and Marie Franklin (National Sales Manager). Gilles' duties were to oversee production, customer service, human resources, risk management, international business development and general administration (Exhibit 4). Franklin led a team of sales, marketing and communications professionals. All PRC employees were encouraged to write blogs about coffee on the company website and most had already visited coffee farms that supplied the company's coffee beans in order to better understand the supply chain and farmer relationships.

Stell had participated in the United Nations Conference on Sustainable Development in 1992 in Rio de Janeiro, and as a member of a student delegation, helped to publish the "Youth Action Guide on Sustainable Development." His experience in Brazil exposed Stell to the export side of the industry and inspired him to learn more about the coffee business. After a brief apprenticeship with a local roaster in Portland, Stell opened a retail coffee shop called Abruzzi Coffee Roasters in 1993. Three years later he sold the business and opened PRC with business partner Todd Plummer, choosing to focus exclusively on the wholesale coffee business. Stell described his original vision for the company, "What we saw was a niche for small quality coffee roasters that had creative marketing, creative design and upscale packaging. We wanted to be synonymous with Portland and we wanted to buy sustainable products, and my involvement with the Earth Summit in '92 was kind of the driving factor to help us steer our direction. We wanted to be as sustainable as possible and that has always been our motivation."

In the first year of operation PRC sold 40,000 pounds of coffee. Since then PRC achieved an average of 20% annual growth and in 2007 the company sold 600,000 pounds of coffee, yielding approximately $5 million in revenues (Exhibit 5). In 2006, 2007 and 2008, PRC was a finalist for Roast Magazine's Roaster of The Year awards, and since 2005, PRC has made the Portland Business Journal's list of 100 fastest growing local businesses. After learning the pitfalls of having one customer represent 40% of total sales, PRC subsequently diversified across market segments with the largest customer representing no more than 20% of total sales. In anticipation of continued growth through targeting hotels, mass grocers, universities and other institutional accounts, PRC invested in new roasting and packaging equipment in 2008.

Coffee Production and Trade

Coffee is produced in more than 50 tropical countries generally around 23.5 degrees north or south of the equator, with approximately 63% produced in Latin America, 22% in SE Asia and 14% in Africa.[175] Similar to wine, coffee beans from different regions have distinct characteristics displayed in aroma, body, acidity and nuances of flavor. These variations are dependent not only on the appellation, or geographical location, but also the varietal grown and the manner in which the coffee is produced. The first flowers appear on coffee plants during the third year, but production is only profitable after the fifth year. Coffee cherries typically ripen around eight to 10 months after flowering and in most countries there is only one major harvest each year. Shade grown coffee often results in berries ripening more slowly, producing lower yields

---

175   International Coffee Association, "Total production of exporting countries, Crop years 2003/04 to 2008/09."

but with a higher quality and flavor. Ripened coffee cherries are typically harvested by hand, which is very labor intensive. Some coffee crops are picked all at once, but for better quality coffees only the ripe cherries are picked and for this reason harvesting may be undertaken as many as five times during a season. The ripe berries have higher aromatic oils and lower organic acid content, lending to a more fragrant and smooth flavor. Because of this, the timing of coffee picking is one of the chief determinants of the end product.

After coffee is picked, it must be processed quickly to avoid spoilage. Each coffee cherry usually contains two coffee beans, covered by a silvery skin, a layer of parchment, a pectin layer, a pulp layer and finally the outer skin (Exhibit 6). These outer layers must be removed in one of two processing methods. The dry processing method is used in arid countries where water is scarce and humidity is low. Freshly picked cherries are simply spread out on large surfaces to dry in the sun. In order to prevent the cherries from spoiling, they are raked and turned throughout the day then covered at night. When the moisture content of the cherries drops to 11%, the dried cherries are moved to warehouses where they are stored. In wet processing, the freshly harvested cherries are passed through a pulping machine where the skin and pulp is separated from the bean. The beans are then transported to large, water-filled fermentation tanks for 12-48 hours where naturally occurring enzymes dissolve the pectin layer. The beans are then removed from the tank and dried. Eduardo Ambrocio, who works for the Guatemalan National Coffee Association as a master cupper and quality control expert, believed the riskiest process in the industry is wet milling. "You need to manage the fermentation process while the cherries are in the tank, and you need to carefully control the drying process. Everything is a chain of different times and events that need to be precisely controlled." With so many variables involved in wet milling there is ample opportunity for error, but wet processing can enhance the brightness and floral acidity of coffees.

In order to compete against the larger estates, many small growers[176] have formed cooperatives to help negotiate better prices and increase access to markets. Most growers dry the coffee themselves and then sell the unprocessed coffee to intermediaries for milling. This involves a mechanical hulling process that removes the parchment layer from wet processed coffee or removes the entire dried husk from dry processed coffee cherries. The coffee beans are then graded and sorted by size and weight. The intermediaries often make a

---

176   Many coffee producers are small, family-owned farms covering two hectares or less, while larger coffee estates may be upwards of several thousand hectares.

larger profit since small growers may not have direct access to buyers, and are thus forced to accept whatever price the intermediary offers. From the intermediary, the coffee is then sold to exporters or brokers who buy and sell coffee on commission, before passing it onto importers. Importers then sell the beans to roasters who roast, package and market the coffee to distributors and retailers. Roasting is generally performed in the importing country because coffee freshness diminishes rapidly after roasting. This way the roasted beans reach the consumer as quickly as possible to ensure quality.

Large coffee importers and roasters purchase coffee futures and options traded on the Intercontinental Exchange (ICE). The ICE Futures U.S. Coffee "C" contract is the benchmark for world coffee prices. The price of coffee has fluctuated dramatically, falling as low as USD $0.415/pound in 2001 and having reached as high as $3.148/pound in 1997 (Exhibit 7). These price fluctuations are due to market influences such as natural disasters, supply surplus, transportation costs, political stability in producing countries and investor speculation. For example, a frost in Brazil in 1975 and a drought in 1985 led to a sharp drop in coffee production and significant increases in coffee prices. This price volatility is problematic for both farmers and commercial roasters, directly impacting profit margins and production costs. Just one year of low market prices can potentially put a small farmer out of business. Coffee revenue is also a significant portion of the GDP for many equatorial countries. Burundi, Uganda and Ethiopia earn more than half of their export revenues from coffee alone. The economic disparity between producing and consuming countries, and the determination of a fair price, has long been the subject of active debate within the coffee industry.

The Farmers Perspective

Many of the countries with an appropriate climate for producing coffee are in the developing world. This creates a unique set of challenges and opportunities for the coffee industry. Many of the tools, techniques, resources and technologies that farmers in the developed world use are either not affordable or not available to the vast majority of coffee farmers in developing countries. Unfortunately, there is an inverse relationship between the quality of a coffee bean and the volume of coffee that the plant can produce. Plants that produce high-quality coffee generally do not produce high quantities of coffee beans. Generally, the higher the quality of the coffee the more expensive it is to produce. In addition to processing, handling and delivery, specialty coffee requires more resources, time and attention in order to achieve the highest level of quality. The beans mature at different times on the plant and must be hand picked only when they are ripe.

Ambrocio noted, "Coffee is a lot like grapes and many other fruits. We have varieties that probably give you a good yield at times of production, but low quality. As a farmer, you are going to focus on either high quantity or high quality." Don Jorge, owner of Rancho Carmela, which is located in a region of Guatemala where PRC purchases coffee, has been producing high-quality coffee for decades. Don Jorge said that he spends anywhere from USD $0.70-0.85/lb to harvest his specialty coffee depending on the climate, labor rate and other extenuating circumstances. Jorge states that in selling to exporters, "In a good year I can get almost a dollar per pound for my best beans, but sometimes I have to settle for 80 cents." Dona Miguelina, owner of El Paternal, one of the oldest coffee farms in Nicaragua, and supplier of specialty coffee for PRC, confessed, "This has been a very dry year. If we don't get some rain soon we will not have a very good harvest this year. There is a lot that I can do to ensure a quality harvest, but if it doesn't rain, what can I do?" Dona has implemented a number of different water-saving measures, but most coffee farms must rely on rainwater for irrigation, and without it, their yields and their profits suffer.

Unfortunately for many farmers the harvest season is long, averaging two to four months. It then takes time to process the beans, and get the finished product ready to ship. From the first cherry picked to the time the bean arrives at its final destination can take up to six months. For most farmers, this is a long time to wait for payment, particularly when all of their costs for goods sold are incurred up front. This can create a heavy financial burden on coffee farms of all sizes, especially the smaller farms and premium producers who typically have higher costs of production. Historically, this is where the exporters have added value in the supply chain. Exporters will often finance the crop once it is ready to ship, or sometimes before the crop is harvested depending on the needs of the farmer. Arnoldo Leiva, General Manager of The Coffee Source, Inc., and a coffee broker for PRC, said that the role of the exporter has been changing over the last decade. Leiva, who operates out of San Jose, Costa Rica but works with coffee farmers and purchases coffee from all over the world, stated, "One of the services we provide for both the producers and the roasters is financing, because we pay the farmer up front and the roaster gets credit upon arrival. In essence it is a 90-day loan, or port-to-port plus net 30 from arrival." Such arrangements allow farmers to pay for the labor and processing before the crop has been harvested and for the roasters to purchase coffee beans as they need them versus trying to buy all they need for the season. This helps roasters maintain more stable cash flow, and in some cases eliminates the need for expensive storage and warehousing. Leiva continues by saying, "We provide a hedging for both the farmer and the roaster. That way, both can fix their price at any given time, but not necessarily at the same time."

According to Dona Miguelina, the most significant change in the industry for coffee farmers since the time of her grandfather has been the increase in market information. Just over a generation ago, many farmers had no knowledge of the value of coffee in foreign markets, but now it is as easy as looking up current prices on the internet. Ambrocio stated that access to information is really benefiting the farmer and, "They now know more about markets, prices, promotion, and perhaps most importantly, the value of consistent quality. Everything is based upon quality and that is the first thing that people need to be convinced of." Access to information has also led to a growing trend in direct relationships between farmers and roasters. By reducing the number of middlemen, both roaster and grower enjoy higher profits and roasters like PRC can add value to consumers by marketing the additional value they create for farmers. According to Leiva, "The long-term relationships that farmers are developing with buyers, like the one we have with PRC, act as a safety net for them and allows them to forecast their cash flow for more than one year. They know the markets are going to come back since the roasters tend to be more loyal and less price sensitive, since they're more focused on quality." Jorge and Miguelina agree that mutually beneficial long-term relationships with buyers, especially buyers willing to pay a premium price, is one of the most valuable assets for a coffee farmer.

In addition to fluctuating coffee prices, farmers contend with many other challenges. The rising value of land for real estate development in many Central American countries, as well as competing crops, has pushed thousands of acres out of coffee production. In addition, the average age of coffee farmers is rising and the younger generation is often not interested in following in the footsteps of their predecessors. In Leiva's home country of Costa Rica this problem is growing, "Coffee has been great for the family and allowed farmers to send their kids to school and even university. But now that they have degrees, they want to go and work for Intel, not in the fields." Meanwhile, labor rates are also growing at an alarming rate, driving coffee production costs even higher. In Central America, the expansion of the Panama Canal is expected to drive up labor costs throughout the entire continent. It is hard to imagine that this one seemingly unrelated event will likely increase the cost of a cup a coffee for consumers all around the world.

History of the US Coffee Industry

America's demand for coffee grew exponentially following the War of 1812, when Britain cut off access to tea imports. By the turn of the 19th century, a small number of entrepreneurial coffee roasting companies achieved multi-state distribution facilitated by innovations in production technology, transportation and mass media. In 1864, the early pioneer John Arbuckle installed the newly patented Jabez Burns roasting machine in his Pittsburgh plant and later added automated packaging equipment. Arbuckle began selling one-pound packages of coffee in thin paper bags, under the brand name *Ariosa*. Sales and distribution on the East Coast soared and in 1913 the Arbuckle family launched the Yuban brand. Other brands gained regional and national prominence during this period including Folgers, Hills Brothers, MJB, Chase & Sanborn and Maxwell House. The larger of these companies were able to distribute nationally, maintaining freshness by shipping their coffee in vacuum-sealed cans. Consumers steadily moved away from purchasing coffee in bulk to buying branded coffee in small packages. By the 1950s the major US coffee producers were competing aggressively for market share and invested heavily in national radio and television advertising. American consumers favored convenience over quality, driving growth in the instant coffee market. To defend against increasing competition, the growing popularity of instant coffee and rising production costs, roasters began lowering prices and substituting lower quality Robusta beans in their blends. Meanwhile, a younger generation of consumers was choosing soft drinks over coffee. These industry forces were the catalyst for significant industry consolidation during the 1960s. The downward spiral of price-cutting and erosion of quality continued for decades and by the late 1970s, the stage was set for a new generation of coffee entrepreneurs.[177]

The US Specialty Coffee Movement

Alfred Peet, an emigrant from The Netherlands, recognized the lack of quality coffee in the US and opened his first coffee house in Berkley in 1966. By using quality beans and roasting in small batches, Peet offered high quality coffee to local consumers and success followed. Peet's early success inspired three college friends, Jerry Baldwin, Gordon Bowker and Zev Siegl, to open a coffee shop

---

177   Pendergrast, Uncommon Grounds: The History of Coffee & How it Transformed Our World.

in Seattle's Pike Place Market in 1971 selling whole beans and supplies. They named the store Starbucks. Many more entrepreneurs began to recognize the market opportunity for roasting and selling wholesale specialty coffees to gourmet grocers and serving premium beans and fresh brewed coffee in retail coffee houses. During the 1970s a small yet steadily increasing number of specialty coffee merchants opened businesses in cities along the East and West coasts and began making inroads into supermarket channels. The fledgling SCAA was formed in 1982 by 42 original charter members, at a time when specialty coffee accounted for less than 1% of total US coffee sales.

During a business trip to Milan, Starbucks Director of Marketing, Howard Schulz, observed the popularity of espresso bars and visualized bringing the Italian café experience to America using premium coffee. In 1984 Schulz convinced Starbucks' owners to add an espresso bar inside an existing store and the venture became an instant hit. Schulz left Starbucks the following year to open his own coffee shop, Il Giornale. With the backing of local investors, Il Giornale acquired Starbucks in 1987 and as CEO, Schulz immediately embarked on an aggressive growth strategy driven by new store openings in major US cities. Starbucks went public in 1992 and the IPO provided capital for rapid expansion both domestically and internationally (Exhibit 8). Other large regional specialty coffee brands including Gloria Jean's, Brothers Gourmet Coffee, The Coffee Connection, Seattle's Best, Caribou Coffee and Coffee People also experienced rapid growth during this time.

Following more than a decade of growth and consolidation among large retail coffee brands, the specialty coffee industry remained fragmented. The number of businesses providing products and services in the specialty coffee industry doubled to more than 26,000 from 2001 to 2009. By then, the SCAA boasted 1,918 member businesses consisting of retailers, roasters, producers, exporters and importers, as well as manufacturers of coffee processing equipment involving more than 40 countries. Amongst members, the SCAA identified at least 369 independent roasters in 2009. The percentage of adults drinking specialty coffee had grown from 3.3% to more than 17% in the past 10 years (Exhibit 9).

New Developments in the US Coffee Industry

The US had grown into the single largest consumer of coffee, buying close to 25% of total global output. Overall, US coffee sales had grown at an average rate of 23% every year since 2003 (adjusted for inflation) with retail coffee sales exceeding $6.5 billion in 2008. According to the National Coffee Association, 49% of Americans 18 years old or older drank some type of coffee beverage, and roughly three of every four cups of coffee consumed was made at home. Combined, Kraft Foods and Proctor & Gamble commanded greater than 50% share of all roasted coffee sold in the US and marketed numerous coffee brands covering a wide spectrum of price points within various segments. Yet these large companies were still losing share to smaller roasters. Starbucks had grown into the largest specialty coffee company, followed by Peet's Coffee and Caribou Coffee, but was increasingly competing against national fast food retailers interested in gaining market share. Both McDonalds and Dunkin' Donuts began selling their own brands of coffee and espresso drinks (Exhibit 10).[178]

Despite the growth in net sales, consumers were buying less coffee by volume and paying more per pound. In September 2007, the number of Starbucks customers fell in American stores for the first time in the history of the company, and in 2008 the company announced the closure of 600 stores. Consumers were increasingly paying premium prices with expectations of high quality, and given the economic downturn, it was anticipated that more consumers were brewing specialty coffee at home. Meanwhile, foreign markets with consumers who had historically preferred to drink tea, such as in England and much of Asia, represented the largest growing market segment for many US coffee companies.

In conjunction with the industry trend toward higher quality, coffee roasters and retailers were also promoting their coffees on the basis of sustainability. Walmart launched six coffees under the Sam's Choice™ brand as part of an expansion of eco-friendly and ethical products. Whole Foods sold its 365™ brand of coffee, noting fair trade practices and direct relationships with more than 40 growers. Kraft General Foods advertised that 30% of all the coffee beans that went into Yuban coffee were officially certified by the Rainforest Alliance. Starbucks promoted its Shared Planet™ program with stated goals for ethical sourcing, environmental stewardship and community involvement. Green Mountain Coffee Roasters, long recognized as an industry leader in environmentally friendly and socially responsible business practices, was ranked 11th on the Forbes 100 Fastest Growing Companies list in 2009. In Stell's opinion, "Most of the growth in the SCAA is around sustainability, so whether it's Fair Trade, Organic, Utz Certified or Rainforest Alliance, sustainability is what's really moving our industry."

---

178 The information in this paragraph comes from the following source: Mintel, "US Coffee Industry Report."

Certified Coffee

There has been significant growth in the number of sustainability related certification and eco-labeling initiatives in response to globalization. An increasing number of corporations operate globally yet environmental, labor and human rights regulations in developing countries often lag behind developed country standards. Scrutiny has perhaps been most intense within the food sector, given concerns over health and safety. Within the coffee industry, the concept of sustainability was initially focused on concerns around the environmental and social impacts of large-scale coffee production. The International Coffee Agreement of 1962 established a quota system that withheld coffee supplies in excess of market demand and also established quality standards in an effort to maintain stable prices and production. However, the initial ICA did nothing to address environmental or social concerns related to coffee production. There have been various renewals of the ICA, with the latest agreements of 2001 and 2007 focused on stabilizing the coffee economy through the promotion of coffee consumption, raising the standard of living for growers by providing economic counseling, expanding research and conducting studies on sustainability.

To address some of the shortcomings of the ICA, a number of worldwide coffee certification initiatives have been established to address what are commonly referred to as the three pillars of sustainability, covering economic, social and environmental development (Exhibit 11). According to Ambrocio, "Quality and sustainability come first, for the farmer and the consumers. Once that is achieved, farmers can differentiate themselves in a number of different ways to reach a better market, and one way they can compete is using certifications." Although each certification has unique criteria, they rely on verification by independent third parties to maintain transparency. One of the challenges now facing coffee certifications is balancing the need to maintain reliability and credibility while also keeping certification costs to a minimum so that growers are able to reap economic benefits from the premium or stable prices paid for their coffees. By 2008, certified coffees amounted to more than 390,000 metric tonnes of coffee exports, or close to 4% of the worldwide green coffee market.

Fair Trade

The concept of fair trade emerged more than 40 years ago through alternative trade organizations that offered products purchased directly from small producers in developing countries to consumers in developed countries. The first Fair Trade certification initiative began in 1988, triggered by a sharp drop in world coffee prices when the ICA failed to renegotiate price quotas. It was branded "Max Havelaar," after a fictional Dutch character that opposed the exploitation of coffee pickers in Dutch colonies. In 1997, the Fair Trade Labeling Organizations International (FLO) united Max Havelaar with its counterparts in other countries and became the international umbrella organization for Fair Trade, representing 17 Fair Trade labeling organizations. Fair Trade's mission is focused on economic and environmental sustainability for farmers and their communities, while guaranteeing a minimum purchase price and social premium to cover costs of production and investments in the community. The base price paid for Fair Trade coffees was USD $1.26 in 2009, with an additional $0.15 added for organic coffees. The Fair Trade standards ensure that employees who work for Fair Trade farms are able to work with freedom of association, safe working conditions and fair wages; importers purchase from Fair Trade producer groups as directly as possible, eliminating the middle man and helping farmers to compete in the global market; Fair Trade farmers and farm workers decide how to invest Fair Trade revenues; and farmers and workers invest Fair Trade premiums in social and business development projects such as scholarship programs and healthcare services. However, Stell, as well as others in the sustainable coffee movement, was concerned that a sufficient percentage of the price premiums were not making it past the coops to the farmers. In addition, only cooperatives of small farmers can participate in Fair Trade, excluding both large and small individual farmers who cannot get the certification on their own. In 2008, close to 66,000 metric tonnes of Fair Trade coffee was sold.

Organic

The organic movement began in 1973 as a farming and certification system, solely focused on environmental issues. The International Federation of Organic Agricultural Movements sets international organic standards while the US Department of Agriculture oversees the USDA National Organic Program that also sets guidelines for coffee roasters, who must be certified in order to market organic coffees. Organic certification is focused on regulating agricultural production practices with the aim of eliminating the use of synthetic chemicals that are common in pesticides, herbicides and fungicides. In order for coffee to be certified and labeled as organic in the U.S. it must be grown on land without synthetic pesticides or other prohibited substances for three years, have a sufficient buffer between the organic coffee and the closest traditional crop, and include a sustainable crop rotation plan to prevent erosion and the depletion of soil nutrients. The initial amount of capital needed to grow an organic coffee crop is less than traditional coffee production since it does not require the purchase of synthetic fertilizers and pesticides, but it typically yields a smaller crop and thus the farms tend to make less money relative to the size of their farm. While there is no set premium for organic coffees, the average price is roughly 20% above non-organic coffees and is closely tied to the quality of the coffee. Many small, family-owned coffee farms are organic by necessity since they can't afford chemical pesticides and fertilizers. However, these small farms also cannot afford to pay for inspections to achieve the certification, and therefore are unable to benefit by selling their beans for higher prices. One common criticism of organic certification is that it focuses solely on environmental criteria while ignoring the social and economic aspects necessary for sustainable business. As Isabela Pascoal, marketing manager with Daterra Coffee explained, "It is important to have organic coffee, but that doesn't mean that you can be sustainable." Other certifications focus on sustainability by establishing criteria related to social and economic as well as environmental factors. In 2006, approximately 67,000 metric tonnes of organic coffee was sold throughout the world.

Rainforest Alliance
The Rainforest Alliance is a non-profit, tax-exempt organization whose mission is to conserve biodiversity through the promotion of sustainability in agriculture, forestry, tourism and other businesses. In order to be certified, coffee farms must maintain or restore enough natural forest cover to achieve 40% shade coverage and there must be a minimum of 70 trees per hectare and at least 12 native species. The Rainforest Alliance social criteria focus on fair pay, health and safety benefits, and schooling for local communities. If farms do not meet these standards, they can still be certified if they have a plan to meet the goals and are taking active steps to implement the plan. The certification program is managed by the Sustainable Agriculture Network (SAN), a coalition of leading conservation groups in Belize, Brazil, Colombia, Costa Rica, Ecuador, El Salvador, Guatemala, Honduras, Mexico and the US. The first coffee farms were certified through the Rainforest Alliance program in Guatemala in 1995. A common criticism of the Rainforest Alliance certification is that as little as 30% of the coffee in a container can be grown under Rainforest Alliance criteria and the coffee can still carry the certification seal.

According to Leiva, Rainforest Alliance has been growing in popularity with many of the farmers that he has been working with, but it does come with a cost. "Rainforest Alliance has a very strict set of standards in regards to the way you manage the farm, the environment, obviously, the forest, how you treat the employees, safety issues with the workers, and it's getting very, very expensive to be certified. And every year, they want more and more and more changes in the farm, to a point that those changes are challenging the volume that the farm produces. If you cannot make significantly more money per pound of certified coffee, then the costs of meeting these standards are not worth the effort to the farmer." Gaining market acceptance and building perceived value through certification is necessary before consumers will be willing to pay more certified coffee. If the consumer won't pay a price premium, farmers have little incentive to invest the extra effort and money required for certification. In Leiva's opinion, "If you can see that the prices today are not as good, and the cost of certification is very high, the producers start questioning the real value of this investment." In 2008, approximately 62,296 metric tonnes of Rainforest Alliance certified coffee was sold.

Bird Friendly®

The Bird Friendly certification was started in late 1996 by staff at the Smithsonian Migratory Bird Center (SMBC). The certification's criteria are based on research focused on biophysical aspects of shade on coffee plantations. The SMBC requires that producers meet the requirements for organic certification first, and then meet additional criteria including canopy height, foliage cover (40% shade coverage), diversity of woody species, total floristic diversity, structural diversity, leaf litter, herbs and forbs ground cover, living fences, vegetative buffer zones around waterways and visual characteristics. The Bird Friendly certification does not address labor conditions. As Robert Rice with the SMBC stated in regards to the Bird Friendly certification, "It's a seal that just has a lot of scientific rigor behind it." The biggest challenge to Bird Friendly certification is the cost of obtaining organic certification, which can require years of effort and expense. In 2008, approximately 2,916 metric tonnes of Bird Friendly coffee was sold.

Common Code for the Coffee Community (4C)

The Common Code for the Coffee Community, also known as 4C, was established by the German Coffee Association (DKV) and the Deutsche Gesellschaft für Technische Zusammenarbeit (GTZ) with the goal of facilitating more sustainable coffee production. Building on best agricultural and management practices, the 4C code of conduct intends to eliminate the most unacceptable practices while encouraging ongoing improvement. 4C distinguishes itself from organic, Fair Trade, Rainforest Alliance and Utz certifications by relying on an internal monitoring system incorporated within the initiative's corporate business model, rather than certification of standards compliance by third parties. 4C has no set price premiums, allowing free negotiation between 4C members with price reflecting coffee quality and sustainable production practices and the standards it sets are the absolute minimum in all ecological, social and economic aspects. By December 2008, approximately 116,400 metric tonnes of 4C certified coffee was purchased by 4C members.

Utz Certified

Utz Certified, originally known as Utz Kapeh which means "good coffee" in the Mayan language, was founded in 1997 by Guatemalan coffee producers and the Dutch coffee roaster Ahold Coffee Company, and is one of the fastest-growing certification programs in the world. Utz Certified aims to implement a worldwide standard for socially and environmentally appropriate coffee growing practices, and efficient farm management. The program is focused on the mainstream market, and is open to all growers, traders, roasters and retailers across the entire supply chain. Utz Certified has a unique track-and-trace system, showing the buyers of Utz certified coffee exactly where their coffee comes from. As Illana Burk, Business Development Manager with Utz explained, a roaster can print a code on a bag, whereby the customers enter the code in and immediately track their coffee all the way back to the originating farm. The farm's story can be told and transparency ensured. The price for Utz certified coffee is determined in a negotiation process between buyer and seller, which the certification body does not interfere with. Utz certified has been criticized over weak environmental and social standards, the lack of pre-financing standards, and the lack of minimum guaranteed prices. Leiva says, "Utz was developed for European grocery chains. That's the seal that they developed for their own marketing purpose basically." Although Utz certification is not recognized worldwide it has slowly been gaining recognition in more countries, particularly in Japan where certification not only yields a premium, but also is necessary to meet the exacting standards of the Japanese consumers. In 2008, 77,478 metric tonnes of Utz Certified coffee was sold.

Direct Trade and Farm Friendly Direct (FFD)

Direct trade is a general term for coffees that are imported directly from growers, rather than purchased through brokers at auction. Through a direct trade relationship, individual terms and prices can be negotiated and growers typically receive a higher price since there are no middlemen taking a share of the price. Stell and his team firmly believed in the FFD program that started in

2001 at the La Hilda Estate in Costa Rica. The program evolved to include direct trade arrangements with farmers in Tanzania, El Salvador, Costa Rica, Sumatra (Indonesia), India, Papua New Guinea, Guatemala and Ethiopia. Direct trade with farmers in developing countries is nothing new, but Stell wanted to create a program that embodied his commitment to community and sustainability. The FFD program was based on paying above market prices for premium coffee, then paying an additional premium to finance projects that help improve the lives of farmers and their communities (Exhibit 12). Other direct trade models pay premiums above Fair Trade price to reward quality, but they may not have specifics on how that money is spent by the growers. In creating FFD, Stell strongly believed that direct trade not only resulted in higher quality coffee for customers, but also ensured long-term mutually beneficial business relationships between PRC and their farmers, as well as between the farmers and their community and natural environment. As the quality of coffee improved under direct trade, certain farmers were approached by other buyers, often offering higher prices. Stell and PRC never tied growers into exclusive sourcing contracts, believing that a variety of buyers benefited the growers in the long term. Farmers had the choice of selling to the highest bidders, but tended to stay loyal to PRC trusting that they were making a long-term commitment and paying stable prices over the long term.

Stell would typically sample different coffees from a broker until he found one that had the quality he desired. He would then patiently work on finding the original source of that coffee and begin establishing direct trade relationships with the grower. Each FFD project was then designed and implemented through a collaborative process between PRC employees, farmers and their communities to address some of the most pressing needs. Projects were evaluated by how closely they aligned with the United Nations Millennium Development Goals (Exhibit 13), the potential for improving farmers' lives, overall costs and the visibility of each project with its direct trade relationship. Once a project was undertaken, PRC remained engaged to ensure that the farmers and communities had access to the assistance and materials needed to complete each project. Most FFD projects were short-term in nature and typically completed within a one to two-year timeframe before the next project was developed and implemented. FFD projects included building a school, paying teachers' wages, constructing a water treatment facility (Exhibit 14), installing water pumps, implementing a soil and leaf analysis program, supporting a local foundation to fund community needs and planting trees.

There were challenges to the direct trade model. It took time to work through coffee brokers to trace the source of high-quality beans back to the farm, begin a dialogue with those farmers and then begin developing a relationship that could become part of the FFD program. Farmers were often skeptical of foreign companies, and tended to be more comfortable transacting business through local channels and coops. Stell also knew that his team was only able to travel to each farm at most once a year to meet with farmers and monitor ongoing FFD projects. Certain projects required expertise that was outside PRC's core business. In some cases, PRC collaborated with NGOs on FFD projects, relying on their experience, yet this option was not always available or feasible. Stakeholders began asking Stell for specifics on how much PRC invested in FFD projects. There were no internally mandated policies or formulas for determining how much money would be allocated to fund FFD projects. Likewise, PRC had no formal guidelines for selecting and structuring FFD projects nor any metrics defined for measuring the success or effectiveness of FFD projects. Kathleen Finn, a communications and marketing representative at PRC, believed that the FFD program should remain flexible and fluid, argued that "the program supports sustainability and in order to best do so, the program itself needs to be organic. Sometimes a farmer growing coffee in a developing country like Guatemala or in another part of the world may be doing very well in relation to the rest of their community that supports them, so as a result sometimes the funds from proceeds going to the FFD program are best spent with the community versus the farmer. At other times the farmer needs support to meet quality standards or to help become more environmentally and/or socially sustainable. As a result the program needs to be organic, flexible, transparent, and may need to change from crop-to-crop or farmer-to-farmer in order to meet local needs and be able to bring value to PRC and our clients."

Portland Roasting Coffee Company

Supply Chain

Through the FFD program, PRC worked to minimize the number of middlemen in the coffee supply chain. The broker and importer still played a role by assisting with the necessary functions of transporting, processing, storing, financing or importing. However, PRC negotiated a separate contract with these intermediaries, assuring that the price offered to the growers was not impacted. The containers carrying FFD Central American coffees were shipped into Oakland or Long Beach (California), FFD coffee from Papua

New Guinea was shipped into the Port of Tacoma (Washington), and FFD Tanzanian coffees were shipped directly into the Port of Portland (Oregon). PRC coffee that was not part of the FFD program was typically purchased on the spot market through brokers who import coffee into various ports in the US and sell to roasters throughout the US. Since coffee crops ripen at different times throughout the year, roasters must source coffee from different growing regions throughout the year to secure a sufficient quantity of fresh beans to meet annual demand.

PRC works with farmers to ensure their coffee is farmed following the best possible practices, and then takes on the responsibility of trying to maintain this high-quality coffee on its long voyage to Portland to be roasted. Storage and shipping conditions can make a big difference in the overall quality of a cup of coffee. Coffee may leave the processing mill at 12% moisture, but if the coffee isn't shipped right away, problems may result. Humidity is a critical variable, and if coffee absorbs too much moisture, particularly from exposure to humid environments when stored for long periods of time, it may take on a moldy overtone in the cup. The temperature of coffee during shipping can also have an impact on the quality of green coffee, since quick changes in temperature cause condensation and fermentation of the beans. Good circulation is needed to keep humidity and temperature levels constant. PRC might receive Guatemalan coffee from the farm to the loading dock in as little as three weeks, while containers from other sourcing locations might take upwards of three to four months to arrive.

Upon arrival at PRC's facility, unroasted green coffee was stored in a climate-controlled warehouse environment. Samples were taken from each lot and inspected for defects to ensure quality. Irregularities in quality can be attributed to the farm, the processing or shipping depending on the nature of the defects found. Having some defects in a lot is quite common and only becomes a concern if abnormally high. Such defective beans are set aside to help the PRC staff learn how to inspect coffee lots for quality. Although green coffee can last significantly longer than roasted coffee, for the same reasons encountered during shipping, it is important for sourced green coffee to be roasted in a reasonable amount of time. Coffee is stored in burlap bags marked with the necessary information about the coffee to keep coffees from being confused. Organic coffees are strictly kept separate from other coffees to conform to certification standards.

The coffee roasting process heats green beans to a specified temperature for a specified length of time. Roasting profiles for each coffee, designating target temperatures throughout the different time intervals in the roasting process, are carefully followed to highlight different flavors in the coffee and ensure consistency in the final product. PRC's roasting equipment is computer monitored so that roast profiles can be highly consistent while maintaining the uniqueness of each roast. However, even with all the metrics the computer records, skilled roasters would diligently oversee every stage of the roasting process. As subtle changes such as fluctuations in the ambient temperature or humidity can affect the final product, every roast is slightly different. Most machines maintain a temperature of about 550 degrees Fahrenheit. The beans are kept moving throughout the entire process to keep them from burning as they slowly roast. When the beans reach an internal temperature of about 400 degrees, they turn brown, sugars start to caramelize and the oils locked inside the beans begin to emerge. The hot roasted coffee beans are then quickly spilled out onto a tray where cooling fans return the coffee to room temperature.

Having been returned to a stable temperature, roasted coffee is then ready for bagging and distribution (Exhibit 15). At PRC, whole bean coffee for grocery distribution was packaged in bulk to fill store containers where customers fill their own bags. Whole bean coffee for sale in small bags was simply packaged and stored for distribution. Ground coffee was crushed to a specific size increment depending on customer preferences and their method of making coffee, then bagged and stored. Bagged coffees are contained in a sealed package with a valve to release gasses produced by the coffee as it ages. The packaging keeps out air and slows the process wherein coffee ferments or goes stale, but as gasses are let off, the coffee also slowly loses its flavor.

Marketing and Product Differentiation

PRC used a number of different channels to market their coffee and services. They take leading roles in a wide range of industry trade shows, conferences and sampling events. Through these channels PRC showcased their wide range of coffee blends and supporting products and services. PRC also worked with retailers on cooperative marketing efforts including customized labeling, storyboards, decorative packaging and colorful photography that highlighted the FFD program (Exhibit 16). PRC also delivered their message to consumers through their website containing information on company history, products, blogs, their media outreach, the FFED program and PRC's other sustainable initiatives. Marie Franklin, the National Sales and Marketing Director, believed that beyond the overall focus on quality, customer service and a focus on sustainability were two attributes that helped to differentiate PRC from their competition.

Because PRC is a smaller company relative to large scale roasters, PRC made every effort to provide superior customer service. PRC offered a wide range of training programs for the café staff that prepare coffee beverages, or baristas, along with technical support services for clients using PRC espresso and drip coffee equipment. PRC also offered a range of online training videos available to anyone interested in the art of coffee making. According to Franklin, "Staying close to your clients is the best way to make sure that you are meeting their needs." In the PRC tasting room, PRC educated clients on the flavor spectrum of different coffee varietals and provided hands on experience and training with equipment available for purchase. This ensured that PRC clients were experienced with the technology used to make coffee and equipped to deliver the highest quality product to the end consumer. The training sessions also provided PRC with a valuable opportunity to build personal relationships with café owners. Nick Doughty, general manager for Elephants Delicatessen in NW Portland, emphasized that his business was about good coffee and good people. By doing business with PRC, he was able to bypass the hype of some bigger name competitors, get high-quality coffee and the training and equipment that his business needed, all while working with people he enjoys.

One of the most important differentiators, according to Franklin, was the company focus on social and environmental responsibility. PRC was the first company to create a sustainability-based direct trade program, even though competitors have introduced direct trade programs. Paul Tostberg, owner of Coffee Culture in Corvallis, Oregon, stated that sustainability, quality and proximity were at the top of his list of reasons he chose to work with PRC. Paul believed that being a local company working closely with customers, providing thorough customer support services and creating special blends that his customers were looking for, were all qualities that set PRC apart from other coffee roasters. Telling the story of the FFD program, raising customer awareness and being recognized for sustainable practices that exceed the standards of conventional certifications was integral to PRC's marketing strategy.

Distribution Channels

Coffee Houses

PRC targeted small specialty coffee houses in hopes that they would serve PRC coffee to the increasingly sophisticated palettes of their clients, who are demanding high-quality coffee. However, these coffee houses were not an easy sell. Many of them purchased coffee in low volumes yet had high expectations. Not all coffee house customers choose suppliers for the same reasons. Quality was important to Diana Benting, purchasing manager for Portland Community College, who performed a blind taste test every five years to determine whom they will purchase from. Although she appreciated local businesses promoting sustainable practices, if a new coffee didn't pass her taste test, it would not be considered. Although Benting had her own criteria for selecting companies to purchase coffee from, her students had a whole separate set of motives. According to Benting, many college students don't care so much about the brand or company policy, instead it is all about location. Time is always a premium, especially on campus. If the campus coffee house is the most conveniently located place to purchase a cup of coffee between classes, then that is where students will go, regardless of brand.

Customer service was also important to small coffee houses. Rico from the Coffee Lounge in Portland, purchased coffee from PRC for four years before he decided to switch to another roaster. As with any small business, an entrepreneur's time is money, and there is never enough. The additional support in customer service offered by the new roaster, at a minor cost difference and with similar quality, was enough to lure him away from PRC's business. That is not to say all of PRC's clients feel the same. Most of PRC's clients opt to do business with them because of the additional services they get. Doughty stated that one of his driving motives for selecting PRC was the additional training, sales and technical support the company offered him. As a small company, it was easier for PRC to maintain a personal touch with their clients, reacting quickly to and anticipating customer needs. Cooperative marketing, on-site training, custom labeling and personal attention are all valuable services for small businesses. These services do not come cheap however. One of the disadvantages to being a smaller roasting company is having less capital to work with. Every minute spent with an existing customer, no matter how important, is a minute that could have been spent looking for new customers and building new relationships.

Hotels & Restaurants

Many high-end hotels provided specialty coffee in rooms and restaurants as a way to enhance their visitors' experiences. PRC targets boutique hotels across the country. These boutique hotels believe that the quality of the coffee they offer their guests is just one reflection of a high–quality experience. Given the plethora of specialty roasters now in the business, and the dispersed nature of these hotels, it is not an easy market to penetrate. Franklin targets several larger boutique chains to reduce the cost of cultivating clients, lower costs of goods sold, and increase the volume of sales per client, while also seeking one-of-a-kind bed and breakfast establishments.

Portland Roasting recently won the account for supplying coffee to the Burgerville fast food restaurant chain across the NW. This is a very high profile and high–volume account for PRC. PRC supplies coffee to a number of other restaurants in the NW, and are actively pursuing accounts with boutique restaurants committed to supplying their customers with local, sustainable, and/or high–quality products, as well as higher volume accounts with chain restaurants who are also becoming more interested in providing quality, sustainable produced coffee.

Institutions

From the beginning, local institutions throughout Oregon were a strategically important market segment for PRC. The company created key relationships with several of the largest universities in Oregon including Portland State University, Portland Community College and Oregon State University. These clients purchased large volumes of coffee from PRC, but also put their products in front of a high-priority market — young and conscientious consumers. In addition, PRC also sold coffee and services to churches, large food distributors such as Food Services of America, casinos and medical centers such as Oregon Health and Science University. These clients were generally consistent, reliable and advertised the PRC brand in highly visible markets, providing exposure and marketing value beyond the direct purchasing of coffee and other products.

Grocers

PRC also sold a high volume of coffee to supermarkets and grocery stores. PRC had created a pilot marketing and sales campaign in partnership with Fred Meyer (a division of Kroger), one of Oregon's largest supermarket chains. This gained PRC an unprecedented amount of floor space to create a unique shopping experience for the coffee consumer (Exhibit 17) and provide consumer education about PRC's coffees and the FFD program. PRC hoped that Fred Meyer would expand this program, along with PRC's shelf space, into hundreds of stores across the Pacific Northwest. PRC also worked with other smaller, gourmet food markets and grocers including Zupan's Market and New Seasons, both of which had great potential for expansion.

Competitors

Wholesale Roasters

Although PRC had an innovative business model, they were certainly not the only specialty coffee company to purchase directly from farmers, roast beans to exacting standards and sell to a variety of retailers. Wholesale roasters represented the largest segment of specialty coffee providers in the industry. Unlike PRC, many wholesale roasters also opened retail storefronts which helped to introduce the public to their coffee, build strong brand recognition and provide an otherwise unavailable opportunity to have direct interaction with their consumers. Within Portland, PRC was competing against numerous other roasting companies including Stumptown Coffee Roasters, which also sourced single origin coffees from farmers around the globe and roasted the beans locally.

Retailer Roasters

There had been a recent rise in the number of small specialty and boutique coffee roasters. These micro roasters were often purchasing direct coffee either from farmers or coffee importers and then creating specialty roasts to meet the selective and demanding standards of their customers. Mike Ferguson from the SCAA noted, "This is one way for retailers to differentiate themselves from the competition, by having a wider variety of freshly roasted coffee." The SCAA estimates that there were well over 2,000 of these small specialty retail roasters, and they estimated that their numbers would continue to grow as consumers became more educated on the wide range of contributing factors that all come together to make a great cup of coffee. With a new generation of coffee loving students and young professionals joining the aging baby boomers, the market was strong enough to support a wide range of small niche retailers, as well as franchises. Some of the more successful retailer roasters had even been able to branch out their operations locally, regionally and even nationally.

Franchised Roasters

Some of the biggest players in the specialty coffee industry have been successful at not only directly sourcing their coffee, but also tapping into both the retail and wholesale markets across the country. Starbucks had been very successful in penetrating the institutional and wholesale markets by creating relationships with hotel chains, airlines and other large franchises like Barnes & Noble. The combination of these markets saw Starbucks capture more than 40% of the specialty coffee market.[179] Starbucks was not alone in trying to control this franchised market space, and any competitor to Starbucks was a competitor to PRC. Although not a roaster, McDonalds had recently added specialty coffee to their menu, and with thousands of locations across the country, massive economies of scale and a reputation for affordable convenience, McDonalds became a threat to the specialty coffee industry.

Volume Roasters

A small number of very large corporations dominated the coffee roasting industry for decades, creating some of the most recognized brands in the US. These large-scale roasters include J.M. Smucker Company (Folgers and Millstone), Nestlé (Nescafe and Taster's Choice), and Kraft Foods (Yuban, Maxwell House, Brim, General Foods International Coffee, Gevalia, Kenco, Maxim and Sanka). Not nearly as demanding in the quality of the coffee they source, these large roasters often sourced their coffee from very large producers in Mexico, Brazil, Columbia and other countries. Many of these companies also purchased the lower quality portions of a crop from high-end producers. Sales of conventional ground and whole bean coffee have been concentrated amongst these very few brands. Folgers controlled 38% and Maxwell House controlled 33% of ground coffee sales in 2007.[180] Historically, these volume producers have held the largest share of the market, but their growth had been slowing as consumers moved toward higher quality. Yet these volume producers exerted huge influence on the coffee industry due to their tremendous purchasing power, and were slowly implementing more sustainable practices.

Substitutions

The most obvious substitute for coffee is tea. According to the Tea Association of the United States, in 2007 the wholesale US industry value for tea was $6.85 billion. In many parts of the world tea is not only has a larger market but also has maintained stronger cultural roots making it very difficult to supplant. Despite this fact specialty coffee began to make some inroads into well-known tea drinking countries including England, China, and Japan. There has also been a rapidly growing market in highly caffeinated sodas and energy drinks, often referred to as functional beverages. From 2004-07, sales of energy drinks more than doubled from $1.1 billion to $2.5 billion.[181]

---

179   Wikinvest, "Starbucks."
180   Mintel, "US Coffee Industry Report."
181   Mintel, "Energy Drinks—U.S."

PRC's Commitment to Sustainability

Sustainable values played a part in every decision at PRC with regard to its customers, farmers, products and employees even going beyond the FFD program. Beginning in 2006, an in-house environmental team was tasked with finding environmentally friendly alternatives for all of its operations. As a result, PRC encouraged composting, recycling, using post-consumer office paper and the company-wide use of earth-friendly cleaning products. Employees were encouraged to ride bikes to work and PRC had even contracted with B-Line, a sustainable urban delivery service, to offer bicycle deliveries of coffee beans and supplies to Portland clients (Exhibit 18). One of PRC's two delivery vans ran on biodiesel and the company had declared that all new vehicle purchases would also be powered by biodiesel. The company began working with Trees for the Future with the aim of becoming a carbon neutral company through the purchase and planting of 16,900 trees.

But Stell wanted to have an even larger impact on the environment, and in 2007 began distributing Ecotainer to-go cups. These cups had an inside lining of bio-plastic made from corn, and an outer layer of paper harvested from trees managed in accordance with Sustainable Forestry Initiative guidelines.[182] All of the bulk coffee the company sold to groceries and all of the consumer bulk bags were 100% compostable. Under the proper conditions, these cups and bags can break down into water, carbon dioxide and organic matter. Finally, in 2009, PRC sponsored a Walk for Water, which raised funds to benefit Water for All, a non-profit organization dedicated to bringing clean water to families in sub-Saharan Africa. The inaugural event raised $28,000 to fund two wells in Yirgacheffe, Ethiopia, a coffee-growing region in Eastern Africa. Such efforts led to the company receiving the 2005 SCAA Sustainability Award and recognition from the City of Portland with the 2007-2009 RecycleWorks Award. PRC signed the Global Compact in 2005 and since then consistently promoted the Millennium Development Goals on cups, product packaging and the company website.

The Future of Farm Friendly Direct

As the pilot announced the final approach into Bujumbura, Stell glanced out of the window and down at the city on the shore of Lake Tanganyika. He

---

182   Portland Roasting, "Ecotainer."

was confident that the next direct trade relationship would be established in Burundi, and had no doubt that the FFD program could positively impact the quality of life for farmers and their surrounding community. However, he was less confident that the FFD program in its current form would provide PRC with the necessary competitive edge needed to secure regional accounts with large retailers in the US. Although Stell believed that the FFD program was unique to the coffee industry and superior to mainstream certification programs in many ways, consumer awareness of FFD was relatively low compared with Fair Trade, Organic, Rainforest Alliance and Bird Friendly labels. FFD lacked the credibility that certification provided as there were no established criteria for FFD projects and the impacts were not verified by an independent third-party. Stell had considered building more structure into the FFD program by implementing written guidelines and creating a proprietary FFD label. If PRC decided to go this direction, what criteria should be used to verify compliance, measure results and ensure credibility? Should PRC also invest the resources necessary to implement some form of verification, or rely on messaging to reassure consumers of the positive impacts of FFD programs on sustainability? From a marketing standpoint, in what other ways could the FFD program be leveraged to build the PRC brand and compel quality conscious coffee consumers to seek out and purchase FFD coffees versus other direct trade options? Stell unbuckled and prepared to exit the small plane. He had some tough decisions to make when he returned to Portland although any revisions to the FFD program would have to wait. The immediate priority for Stell and his team was to win the Fred Meyer account.

Exhibits

Exhibit 1: Portland Roasting Company Product Packaging

Exhibit 2: Portland Roasting Company Sourcing

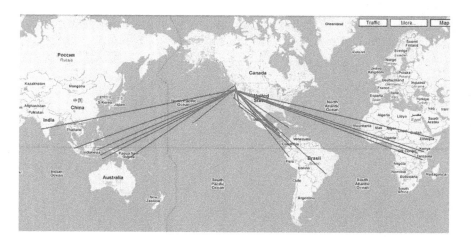

Exhibit 3: Portland Roasting Company Sourcing Data

Appendix 3 – Portland Roasting Company Sourcing Data

Portland Roasting Coffee Imports in Pounds per Year

Farm Friendly Direct Coffee	2003	2004	2005	2006	2007	2008
Costa Rica FFD	36836	39716	49389	58361	79053	87,207
Ethiopian FFD	28859	35776	42309	57990	74,649	31,407
Guatemala FFD	61173	72753	88746	109023	145,795	171,353
New Guinea Madan Estate FFD	0	0	0	24800	102,051	153,499
Sumatra Organic FFD	8437	15399	24524	25452	24777	31,963
Swiss Water Processed FFD	0	0	0	16,236	60,125	74982
Non Farm Friendly Direct Coffee	**2003**	**2004**	**2005**	**2006**	**2007**	**2008**
Bolivian Organic	39	836	0	0	0	0
Brazil	1902	4039	8127	10061	15128	21,185
Brazil Top Sky	0	0	0	411	1478	621
Colombian	8988	8527	10574	15185	17145	18,711
Colombian Decaf	19831	20320	19453	16026	2905	2509
Costa Rica Organic	281	5146	7073	5333	5798	7893
Costa Rica Decaf	46	0	0	0	0	0
El Salvador	1854	2410	5186	3011	2263	1625
Cup of Excellence - El Salvador	0	0	0	0	0	22
El Salvador Organic	0	0	0	0	0	989
Ethiopian Organic	732	1956	2282	5310	4592	3106
Guatemala Decaf	0	0	0	0	0	111
Guatemala Organic	6805	9233	12660	4862	0	0
India Monsooned Malabar	46	656	29	23	0	0
India Arabica	0	0	0	0	2778	3752
India Robusta	0	0	0	0	0	3154
Indonesian Robusta	4419	697	3774	1424	0	0
Jamaica Blue Mountain	54	86	105	47	15	21
Kauii	237	497	258	179	0	0
Kenyan AA	297	504	616	317	0	33
Kenyan PB	0	0	0	0	0	18
Kona	77	122	163	111	385	396
Mexican Chiapas	8935	9948	1091	0	0	0
Mexican Organic	431	1179	979	132	0	0
New Guinea Amuliba	8197	65	0	0	0	0
New Guinea Kinjibi	16620	27,275	50348	37714	185	0
New Guinea Red Mtn	0	0	0	8268	0	0
New Guinea Organic	3980	11478	12729	13108	9960	11966
New Guinea Peaberry	0	0	0	0	0	1984
Peru Selvanica	1642	8790	2411	5599	0	0
Peru Inkaico	0	0	0	462	241	0
Peru Organic	1601	4314	5453	12982	16,061	19566
Red Sea	344	491	0	0	0	0
Sumatra	68638	76289	53370	59021	66,325	85,566
Sumatra Decaf	12067	15780	18202	15159	1607	2035
Swiss Water Processed Colombian	486	1875	1430	1248	462	0
Swiss Water Processed Espresso Decaf	1280	1470	2478	2105	0	0
Swiss Water Processed Komodo Organic	264	132	0	0	0	0
Swiss Water Processed Mexican Organic	1764	3512	5512	3168	0	0
Swiss Water Processed Peru Organic	1905	1053	0	0	0	0
Swiss Water Processed Sumatra	1683	5335	3728	2376	1703	1,868
Swiss Water Processed Guatemala	0	0	0	0	1010	1870
Swiss Water Processed Ethiopian	0	0	0	702	264	0
Timor Organic	493	2074	228	0	0	132
Ugandan AA	25230	30262	28139	18109	38062	4950
Cascadia Blend Swiss Water Processed	0	240	948	1386	0	0
Celebes Toraja/Sulawesi	0	126	988	175	1307	1230
Tanzanian	0	0	4983	33831	0	34,063
Tanzanian PB	0	0	0	0	0	1,352
Honduras Organic	0	0	195	0	0	152
Cup of Excellence - Honduras	0	0	0	0	0	13
Salvador Organic	0	0	1560	66	0	0
Nicaragua Organic	0	0	0	15814	21,103	26,619
Cup of Excellence - Nicaragua	0	0	0	0	0	17
Rwanda	0	0	0	0	9867	18,500
Total Green Beans Processed (lbs)	338,476	422,365	472,045	587,593	709,101	828,448
% of total FFD	40%	39%	43%	50%	69%	66%
% of total organic	8%	13%	15%	15%	12%	12%

Exhibit 4: Portland Roasting Company Organization

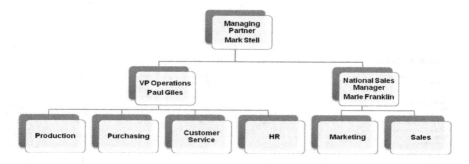

Exhibit 5: Portland Roasting Company Revenues

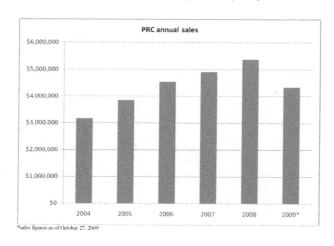

*sales figures as of October 27, 2009

Year	Sales (USD)
2004	$3,160,070.04
2005	$3,842,704.08
2006	$4,548,318.39
2007	$4,910,049.78
2008	$5,368,632.85
2009	$4,333,022.32*

*sales figures as of October 27, 2009

Exhibit 6: Coffee Cherry Cutout

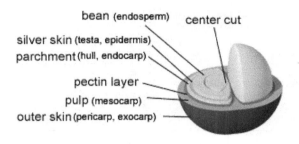

Exhibit 7: Coffee "C" Price History

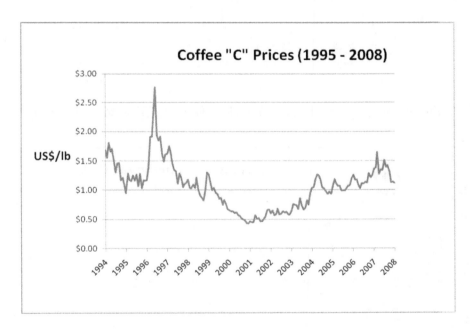

Exhibit 8: Growth of Starbucks Stores

Year	1995	1996	1997	1998	1999	2000	2001	2002	2003	2004	2005	2006	2007	2008
Total US Retail Stores	676	1004	1364	1755	2217	2976	3780	4574	5201	6132	7302	8896	10684	11567
Company Operated	627	929	1270	1622	2038	2446	2971	3496	3779	4293	4867	5278	6793	7238
Licensed	49	75	94	133	179	530	809	1078	1422	1839	2435	3168	3891	4329
Total International Retail Stores	1	11	48	131	281	525	929	1312	2024	2437	2939	3544	4327	5113
Company Operated	1	9	31	66	97	173	295	384	767	922	1133	1374	1712	1979
Licensed	0	2	17	65	184	352	634	928	1257	1515	1806	2170	2615	3134
Total Stores Open at Fiscal Year End	677	1015	1412	1886	2498	3501	4709	5886	7255	8569	10241	12440	15011	16680

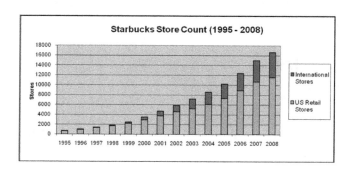

Exhibit 9: Coffee Market Historical Data (SCAA Market Data)

Specialty Coffee in the USA 2008

SPECIALTY COFFEE ASSOCIATION

CONSUMPTION
Percentage of adults drinking specialty coffee:

DAILY

1995	1996	1997	1998	1999	2000	2001	2002	2003	2004	2005	2006	2007	2008
2.7%	2.9%	3.0%	3.3%	4.9%	N/A	14%	13%	12%	16%	15%	16%	14%	17%

WEEKLY

2001	2002	2003	2004	2005	2006	2007	2008
30%	28%	27%	36%	35%	36%	37%	34%

OCCASIONALLY

2001	2002	2003	2004	2005	2006	2007	2008
62%	59%	54%	56%	60%	63%	68%	62%

Cups per day, specialty coffee drinkers:

2001	2002	2003	2004	2005	2006	2007	2008
2.45	2.49	2.29	2.27	2.55	2.34	2.49	2.63

Source: National Coffee Association Annual Drinking Trends Study. Visit www.ncausa.org

DOLLAR SIZE OF MARKET (in Billions)
Total sales of specialty coffee, beverage, whole bean and ground at retail (YE07)

2001	2002	2003	2004	2005	2006	2007
$8.30	$8.40	$8.96	$9.62	$11.05	$12.27	$13.50

Source: SCAA, Mintel Group (excludes Walmart)

ESTIMATED NUMBER OF OPERATING UNITS

1991	1992	1993	1994	1995	1996	1997	1998	1999	2000
1,650	2,250	2,850	3,600	5,000	6,700	8,400	10,000	12,000	12,600

2001	2002	2003	2004	2005	2006	2007
13,800	15,400	17,400	19,200	21,400	23,900	25,700

Source: SCAA, Mintel Group

Exhibit 10: Competitive Advertising from McDonalds and Dunkin' Donuts

Exhibit 11: Coffee Certification Comparisons

Initiative	Fair Trade	Organic	Utz Certification	Rainforest Alliance	Bird Friendly	4C
Mission	Ensure equitable trading arrangements for disadvantaged smallholders who are organized into cooperatives.	Create a verified sustainable agriculture system that produces food in harmony with nature, supports biodiversity and enhances soil health.	Set the world standard for socially and environmentally responsible coffee production and sourcing.	Integrate productive agriculture, biodiversity conservation and human development.	Conduct research and education around issues of neo-tropical migratory bird populations, promoting certified shade coffee as a viable supplemental habitat for birds and other organisms.	To achieve global leadership as the baseline initiative that enhances economic, social and environmental production, processing and trading conditions to all who make a living in the coffee sector.
Year Established	1970s	1973	1997, 2001 - 1st cert.	1992, 1996 - 1st cert.	1997	2007 1st cert.
History & Development	Began as "Max Havelaar" in The Netherlands in the 1970s. Now there are several national Fair Trade chapters organized by the Fairtrade Labeling Organization (FLO) in Germany. TransFair is the US chapter.	Begun around 1973 as a farming movement and certification system. Developed into internationally recognized system with production throughout the world and annual sales above $20 billion.	Begun in 1997 as initiative from industry and producers in Guatemala, became an independent NGO in 2000. First certified farms in 2001.	Begun in 1992 by Rainforest Alliance and a coalition of Latin American NGOs, the Sustainable Agriculture Network (SAN). First coffee farm certification in 1996.	Founded in 1997 with criteria based on scientific fieldwork. Operated out of the SMBC office initially, it currently involves 10 organic certification agencies as the eventual managers of the program.	Begun in 2003 by GTZ and DKA. Certified first farms in 2007.
Market Focus	All markets	All markets	All markets	All markets	All markets	Mainstream Markets
Scope of Program	Economic and environmental sustainability for farmers and their communities. Minimum price and social premium to cover costs of production and investments in the community. Organic premium for organic coffees. Small-producer organization's empowerment.	Organic farming and processing practices.	Sustainability; economics, ethics and environment. Worker safety.	Sustainability; economic, ethics and environment.	Certification aimed at the production of the coffee agro ecosystem.	Sustainability; economic, ethics, and environment.
Code Elements for Coffee Production	Social, economic, environmental, democratic organization of cooperatives.	Environmental, farm production and processing standards.	Social, environmental, and efficient farm management.	Social, environmental, worker safety and efficient farm management.	Biophysical criteria of the shade component, provided that the farm is certified organic.	Social and environmental.
Scope of the Code	Baseline and progress criteria. Continuous improvement required through progress requirements. Applies to democratically organized cooperatives formed by small scale farmers.	Federal standard with practices for producers and handlers applies to all organic product sold in the US.	Baseline criteria with field-tested indicators. Applies to farms and coops of all sizes. All countries possible. Continuous improvement required.	Baseline and advanced criteria with field-tested indicators. Applies to farms and coops of all sizes. Continuous improvement required.	Organic certification as a condition for BF certification. Certification applicable to estate farms and cooperatives. Annual inspections linked to organic inspection.	Baseline criteria; indicators under development. Applies to farms and coops of all sizes. Every country. Continuous improvement expected.
Standard Setting Body	Fairtrade Labeling Organizations International	International Federation of Organic Agricultural Movements	Utz Certified	Sustainable Agricultural Network	Smithsonian Migratory Bird Center	Common Code for Coffee Community Association

Monitoring Body	Autonomous non-profit certifier.	Private certifiers regulated by state and accredited by NGO.	Private third-party certifiers approved by Utz Certified.	Certification by member organizations.	Private certifiers approved by initiative.	Private certifiers approved by initiative.
Inspection Frequency and Accuracy	Annual inspections by independent and annually trained Fair Trade inspectors.	Annual inspections for certified entities. USDA accreditation required for certifiers of organic product sold in US.	Independent auditors accredited to ISO 65 standard. Annual audits.	At least annual audits by teams of biologists, agronomists, sociologists and other specialists trained, authorized and monitored by the Rainforest Alliance.	Annual, linked to organic inspection. Inspection/certification arranged/provided by a USDA-accredited organic certification agency.	
Traceability/ Chain of Custody	Yes, traceability from roaster to producer.	Yes, required by federal statute and historic standards. Organic products traceable from retailer to producer.	Yes, traceability from roaster to producer. Traceable to retailer via internet-based system.	Yes, traceability from roaster to producer.	Yes, traceability from roaster to producer.	
Production Strategy	Small farmers	Mostly small farmers, some plantations	Mostly plantations, some small farmers	Mostly plantations, some small farmers	Mostly small farmers, some plantations	
Environmental Standards	Standards regarding reduction in agrochemical use, reduction and composting of wastes, promotion of soil fertility, avoidance of GMOs.	Standards that bar the use of synthetic herbicides, fungicides, pesticides, GMOs and chemically treated plants.	Standards for protection of primary and secondary forests.	Standards for ecosystem and wildlife conservation, integrated crop management, and integrated management of wastes.	Requires organic certification. Additional standards for shade cover, canopy structure, secondary plant diversity, stream buffers.	Bans use of pesticides under Stockholm convention, bans destruction of primary forest or other protected areas.
Price Differential to Farmers	Yes. All purchases must be at or above the floor price.	Yes. Differential set by the market.	Yes. Differential set by the market.	Yes. Differential set by the market.	Yes. Differential set by the market.	
Price Premium Associated with Code.	Price floor of $1.21/lb and social premium of $0.10. Additional $0.20/lb for organic coffee.	US $0.015-0.20/lb	US $0.01-0.12/lb	Estimated at US $0.10-0.20/lb	US $0.05-0.10/lb	None specified. Prices reflect the quality, including the quality of the product and the Common Code quality of sustainable production and processing practices.
Fees to Buyers	Licensed roasters pay US $0.05-$0.10/lb. Importers must provide pre-harvest financing when requested by coop.	Vary by certifier from $700-$3,000/year.	US $0.01/lb	None	Importers pay $100/year. Roasters pay US $0.25/lb	Annual membership fee dependent on import levels.
Fees to Producers	Cost of auditing and reinspection fee.	Vary by certifier.	Auditing costs.	Auditing costs plus annual fee based on size of farm.	Cost of added days at inspection.	Annual membership fee dependent on production levels.

Source - SCAA

Exhibit 12: Farm Friendly Direct Projects

Year	Country	Amount(USD)	
2009	World Water Day Tanzania	$28,000.00	Internship and pump donated
2009	Costa Rica	$4,200.00	Teacher's salary
2009	Papua New Guinea	$8,000.00	Women's literacy and book drive
2008	World Water Day	$16,000.00	Pump sponsor Ethiopia
2008	Costa Rica	$4,200.00	Teacher
2008	Carbon Neutral El Salvador	$2,000.00	Planted trees
2008	Guatemala	$3,000.00	Yield project with Andres
2008	Sumatra(Indonesia)	$500.00	School uniforms
2007	Guatemala	$3,000.00	Yield project Andres
2007	Tanzania	$2,000.00	Agronomy Kit
2007	Costa Rica	$4,200.00	Teacher
2006	Costa Rica	$4,200.00	Teacher
2005	Costa Rica	$1,000.00	Internet setup and computer donated
2005	India	$500.00	School for the blind in Karnataka
2004	Papua New Guinea	$5,000.00	School built
2003	Guatemala	$12,000.00	Built water treatment for farm
	Total	$97,800.00	

Exhibit 13: United Nations Millennium Goals

The Millennium development goals are an UN initiative to address eight international development issues with a total of 21 target goals by 2015. They were adopted in 2000 by UN member states in recognition of the need to assist developing world nations in terms social, environmental and economic issues.

Goal 1: Eradicate extreme poverty and hunger
- Halve the proportion of people living on less than $1 a day (ppp).
- Achieve increased employment for women, men and young people.
- Halve the proportion of people who suffer from hunger.

Goal 2: Achieve universal primary education
- Provide primary education for all children by 2015. Increase enrollment. Increase completion of primary education. Increase literacy.

Goal 3: Promote gender equality and empower women
- Eliminate gender disparity in education. Equalize men/women rations in education. Equalize men/women wage disparity. Equalize men/women representation national political assemblies.

Goal 4: Reduce child mortality
- Reduce mortality rates of children under 5 by two-thirds. Increase proportion of 1-year-olds immunized against measles.

Goal 5: Improve maternal health
- Reduce maternal mortality ration by three-fourths. Increase proportion of births attended by health professionals.
- Achieve universal access to reproductive health.

Goal 6: Combat HIV/AIDS, malaria and other diseases
- Halt and reverse the spread of HIV/AIDS. Increase knowledge about HIV/AIDS. Increase condom use for high-risk populations. Increase orphan/non-orphan school attendance ratio.
- Achieve by 2010 universal access to treatment for HIV/AIDS.
- Halt and reverse the incidence of malaria and other major diseases. Increase preventative care and treatment. Decrease malaria and tuberculosis death rates.

Goal 7: Ensure environmental sustainability
- Reverse loss of environmental resources. Integrate principles of sustainable development into national policies and programs.
- Reduce biodiversity loss. Reduce CO_2 emissions. Reduce consumption of ozone depleting substances. Reduce percentage of water resources used. Reduce number of species endangered. Increase percentage of protected areas. Increase percentage of land covered by forest.
- Halve the proportion of people with sustainable access to water and sanitation.
- Achieve a significant improvement in the lives of slum dwellers. Decrease percentage of urban populations living in slums.

Goal 8: Develop a global partnership for development
- Further develop an open and fair, rule based and regulated trading and financial system.
- Address the special needs of less developed nations through debt relief development assistance, and financial policies.
- Address the needs of both landlocked and small island developing countries.
- Address the need to deal with the debt problems of developing countries. Make debt sustainable through national and international measures.
- Provide access to affordable essential medicine in developing countries.
- Make available access to new technology, especially information and communication technology.

Exhibit 14: Farm Friendly Direct in Action

The Clean Water and Balanced Plant Nutrition Project in Guatemala

At the urging of respected plantation owner and grower, Miguelina Villatoro del Merida, PRC invested proceeds from the Farm Family Direct pogram in a much needed water treatment facility at her Finca El Paternal farm. The fermentation process is important in the development of the flavor of the coffee, due in part to the microbiological processes that take place, but it results in wastewater containing organic matter like pectin, proteins and sugars that result in a decrease in pH. The high acidity of this effluent may deplete the life supporting oxygen of the water as it then flows into streams or other bodies of water, potentially impacting human health and aquatic life if discharged directly into surface waters.

The facility that PRC built for Miguelina sends leftover water from coffee production through a series of filtering tanks that removes much of the organic matter. The water can be reused several times, and then clean water is returned to the river free of contaminants. Other growers throughout the region now tour the state-of-the-art facility in order to learn about the benefits of water treatment and conservation. According to Miguelina the clean water facility has not only saved the farm thousands of gallons of water that they can now reuse for other agriculture, it has also helped them comply with the very rigid standards of the Rainforest Alliance.

Since completing the wastewater treatment facility, PRC has begun another project to improve plant health and yield at Finca El Paternal, working in collaboration with Karnataka Coffee Estates and Ramaday Micronutrients in India who have used micronutrient applications successfully in many other locations.

Exhibit 15: Portland Roasting Company Coffee Distribution

Oregon Network

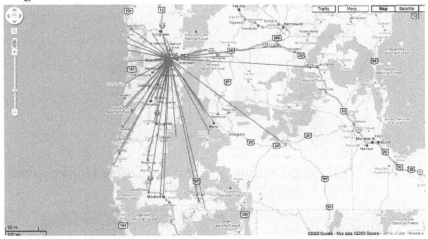

Nationwide Network

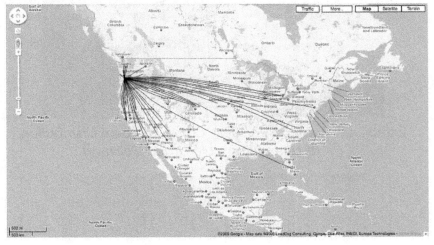

Exhibit 16: Farm Friendly Direct Marketing Images

Exhibit 17: Portland Roasting Company Coffee Display (Fred Meyer)

Exhibit 18: Portland Roasting Company Local Distribution (B-Line Sustainable Urban Delivery)

Bibliography

International Coffee Association. "Total production of exporting countries, Crop years 2003/04 to 2008/09." 2009. http://www.ico.org/prices/po.htm.

Mintel. "Energy Drinks—U.S." July, 2008.

Mintel. "US Coffee Industry Report." 2009.

Pendergrast, Mark. *Uncommon Grounds: The History of Coffee & How it Transformed Our World.* New York, NY: Basic Books, 1999.

Portland Roasting. "Ecotainer." 2009. http://www.portlandroasting.com/sustainability/ecotainer.

Wikinvest. "Starbucks." 2009. http://www.wikinvest.com/stock/Starbucks_%28SBUX%29.

SEQUENTIAL
Sustainability and Growth in the Biofuels Business

By Dave Garten, Jacen Greene, Carolyn Niehaus, and Devdeep Aikath

SeQuential Case Study

Introduction

Tyson Keever, SeQuential's CEO, had just returned to his desk after a full day. The morning had started with an operations review at SeQuential's biodiesel plant in Salem, Oregon. Heading north from there, Tyson stopped at a few restaurants that supplied SeQuential with used cooking oil, where he talked to the owners and operators to hear feedback about SeQuential's services and how the company could make the restaurants' operations smoother.

By lunchtime, Tyson was back at SeQuential's Portland headquarters for a stream of one-on-one meetings with his leadership team. First, Tyson and the HR Director met over lunch and discussed how to improve employee turnover, on-boarding, and employee engagement following a series of mergers and acquisitions. Following that, Tyson met with the CFO about funding and structuring the next round of system improvements for the company's CRM and ERP, which were needed to support SeQuential's rapid growth. Finally, Tyson had a one-on-one with the Sales and Marketing Director to discuss her vision for building a stronger SeQuential brand. After this set of internal meetings,

Tyson just made it to his last session of the day with a team of MBA students who were evaluating the company's strategy.

This full and diverse schedule was typical for Tyson, and at the end of the day he was left considering the complexity of SeQuential's business. SeQuential was a vertically integrated company, and its operations included collecting used cooking oil (UCO), servicing restaurant grease traps, refining the UCO into biodiesel, and selling biodiesel, biodiesel blends, and by-products from its production plant. While the current plant was performing well, and UCO collection and grease trap service contracts had doubled with the recent acquisitions and were still increasing, Tyson wondered how SeQuential could continue to grow while staying true to its environmental mission. Using UCO as the main biodiesel ingredient meant that SeQuential required few virgin materials for biodiesel production, unlike most competitors who used virgin soy, corn, palm, or other crops to produce biodiesel.

SeQuential's annual strategic planning process was underway. Tyson planned to coordinate with his leadership team and board on refreshing SeQuential's five-year plan and receiving early feedback about the annual operating plan. Should the company expand the plant? What would be the smartest path to build the UCO collection and grease trap servicing business? How would the 2016 elections, with Republicans taking control of the White House and retaining control of Congress, affect the broader economy and government incentives for sustainable fuels? What was the most effective way to differentiate SeQuential's products and services? How could the company achieve all of these objectives while reducing turnover, increasing efficiencies, and maintaining a strong and committed culture of sustainability?

SeQuential History and Leadership

Tyson thought back to his visit to the production facility in Salem, and reflected on just how far the company had come since its origin as a club of biodiesel enthusiasts making fuel in a garage.

History

SeQuential was formed in 2005 as the result of a joint venture between Q Bio and Pacific Biodiesel, two biodiesel pioneers. The venture was fueled by a desire to provide a source for regional, sustainable energy. Q Bio, based in Eugene, Oregon, imported railcars of biodiesel and sold the fuel directly to consumers from the back of a truck. Pacific Biodiesel, based in Hawaii, specialized in designing and building community-scale plants that converted UCO into biodiesel.

In 2005, SeQuential completed construction on a one-million-gallon per year production facility in Salem, Oregon. The company quickly learned that this scale of operations was not sufficient to fulfill demand, nor was it large or efficient enough to be profitable. In 2008, the company built a much larger plant on the same property. The new plant was designed to produce five million gallons of biodiesel per year, with a higher yield and more valuable by-products.

In 2008, one of SeQuential's smaller UCO suppliers, a plumbing company, exited the UCO collection business and, as an experiment, SeQuential decided to take over the company's operations. This first acquisition became a testing ground for a new vertical integration model. SeQuential's board then decided it was important to take more significant steps toward full vertical integration of UCO collection. Because the business operated in a commodity market, SeQuential leadership felt it would be prudent to at least partially secure one of the major variables in their company's production process. As a result, SeQuential acquired Standard Biodiesel's UCO restaurant accounts in the Pacific Northwest.

While the Standard Biodiesel acquisition provided a substantial portion of SeQuential's UCO needs, the company had expanded its plant's capacity past the original design through continuous improvements to equipment and flow. In 2016, the plant produced more than seven million gallons of biodiesel, requiring even more UCO than in prior years.

The success of the initial acquisition prompted company management to pursue several additional acquisitions of UCO collection companies in Washington, Idaho, Nevada, and California. The acquisitions added restaurant grease trap cleaning services to SeQuential's product portfolio, though the majority of UCO accounts still received their grease trap cleaning services from other companies. SeQuential integrated the acquired collection companies into a network of depots that received, treated, stored, and transported feedstock to the Salem, Oregon plant.

Leadership

When the founding companies, Q Bio and Pacific Biodiesel, formed SeQuential, they each appointed a member to the board, which oversaw SeQuential's General Manager. Additional capital required for the 2008 plant expansion added a third board member in order to represent the plant's largest investor. In 2012, a request from minority shareholders to strengthen the board through the addition of two independent directors was approved and executed, creating a five-person board. The board was actively involved in running the company and often took on projects to support the leadership team.

SeQuential was headed by Tyson Keever, one of the original founders of Q Bio. In 2008, Tyson became the General Manager of SeQuential, a role which later transitioned into CEO. As CEO, Tyson led the company through a number of transitions and acquisitions, and successfully moved SeQuential from its startup phase to a period of ongoing growth. As SeQuential grew, the company brought in new talent and worked to add depth to the leadership team. Tyson had a COO and CFO as direct reports, with directors in transportation, operations, human resources, and sales and marketing (Exhibit 1). The company made several acquisitions in 2016 and its rapid growth, combined with the integration of these businesses, exposed gaps in the company's management team, core processes, and systems.

Mission

Tyson's morning tour of the Salem, Oregon biodiesel plant had him watching SeQuential-branded trucks roll in with UCO and others roll out with biodiesel. The company's strategy of vertical integration was key to its role as a regional player in the Pacific Northwest, but Tyson also considered the role environmentalism played at SeQuential (Exhibit 2). SeQuential's mission, "To build a better energy model by making responsible, local, bioproducts," emphasized the company's commitment to a more sustainable energy future, as represented by its business model and commitment to using few virgin materials in the production of biodiesel (Exhibit 3).

Biofuel: Industry, SeQuential, and Competitors

Tyson was proud of SeQuential's UCO-based biodiesel and the company's growing production expertise, but he wondered how that expertise compared to SeQuential's competitors' and whether the company was taking full advantage of the plant, brand, and team capabilities.

Biofuels Industry

Biofuels, or fuel made from biomass, had been in use as a petroleum-fuel substitute for transportation for more than 100 years. In 1900, a demonstration of Rudolf Diesel's newly-invented diesel engine at the World Fair ran on peanut oil, demonstrating the capacity of the internal combustion engine to run on non-petroleum-based fuel.[183]

Biodiesel: Biodiesel was a hydrocarbon chain intended to be a replacement for, or mixed with, diesel fuel. Vegetable oils, such as canola, rapeseed, soybean, and sunflower, along with animal fat and cooking grease, were converted into biodiesel through a process called *transesterification*. This process resulted in the creation of biodiesel and small amounts of glycerin and other by-products (Exhibit 4). The resulting biodiesel was used as-is in vehicle engines or mixed with petroleum-based diesel to create a biodiesel blend. [184]

Biodiesel mixes were described on a blending scale, so that B100 indicated pure biodiesel, while B20 was a mixture of 20% biodiesel and 80% petroleum-based diesel. Because biodiesel contained compounds that crystallized or "gelled" in colder temperatures, mixes with lower biodiesel levels, like B20, were often used when seasonally appropriate. B100 reduced carbon dioxide (CO_2) emissions by 75% compared to petrol diesel; higher biodiesel proportions were more environmentally sound. Many diesel engines could run on B100, but this capability depended on a vehicle's make and model. However, concerns about low temperature gelling and biodiesel's higher flashpoint led auto and engine manufacturers to recommend limiting biodiesel blend to B5 in many diesel vehicles. [185]

Renewable Diesel: Renewable diesel was a relatively new product that, while made from the same ingredients as biodiesel, used *hydrotreatment* to create a chemically distinct fuel.[186] Renewable diesel could be used as-is in many diesel engines and met the diesel specification ASTM D975.[187,188] The hydrotreatment process did not create glycerin by-products. Renewable diesel facilities required significant capital expenditures to build and operate. Often, renewable diesel was made from virgin feedstocks, which came from crops grown on plantations that supplanted tropical rainforests. These virgin feedstocks were then shipped to the U.S. from around the world.

Ethanol: Ethanol was the chemical name for ethyl alcohol, the same alcohol used in spirits. It was made from crops such as corn, sugarcane, and sweet potatoes and was often mixed with gasoline, rather than diesel. Ethanol was about 30% less energy-dense than gasoline.[189] In the US, most gasoline was blended

---

183   "History of Biodiesel Fuel."
184   The information in this paragraph came from the following source: "Biodiesel Fuel Basics."
185   The information in this paragraph came from the following source: "Biodiesel Benefits."
186   "California Renewable Diesel Multimedia Evaluation."
187   "Hydrogenation-Derived Renewable."
188   "New Biodiesel Specifications."
189   "Ethanol Fuel Basics."

with at least 2% ethanol, as required by U.S. Environmental Protection Agency (EPA) regulations. Ethanol generated between 19% and 48% less CO_2 than traditional gasoline when analyzed using a full life-cycle approach. The average U.S. consumer sometimes confused biodiesel and ethanol, although they were separate products made from distinct feedstocks. In 2008, for example, a controversy in the U.S. over the environmental effectiveness of ethanol hurt all biofuel sales, including SeQuential's UCO-based biodiesel. [190, 191, 192]

SeQuential and Biodiesel

SeQuential's biodiesel was made from UCO, which was supplied and transported to the Salem, Oregon plant by SeQuential's collection system. SeQuential's regional depots shipped UCO to Salem, where it was stored in large tanks at the facility. The plant was run 24/7 by a team of trained employees who repaired problems and performed routine maintenance. Many systems and procedures had been standardized into a set of Standard Operating Procedures (SOPs) that were widely referenced and continuously improved.

SeQuential sold biodiesel to a variety of business customers, including international petroleum companies, regional fleet customers, retailers, and regional distributors. Large fossil fuel multinationals, like British Petroleum, purchased biodiesel to mix with conventional diesel to satisfy renewable fuel obligations with national or state governments. Regional distributors ("jobbers"), such as Tyree Oil, purchased SeQuential biodiesel for blends for their retail and fleet customers.

Some regional fleet customers, such as the Organically Grown Company and the City of Portland, purchased biodiesel from SeQuential to fuel their vehicles. These customers were mission-aligned with SeQuential and valued the company's sustainable sourcing model. The city of Portland, Oregon developed a pilot virgin fuels program with SeQuential and farmers in Eastern Oregon. In this pilot, Oregon farmers grew canola seed that was crushed into canola oil and was then processed into biodiesel at SeQuential's facility. This canola-based biodiesel was used to power vehicles throughout the City of Portland's Water Bureau fleet. The participating farmers concluded that they could earn more money selling canola oil for human consumption than as a biodiesel feedstock, so the pilot was discontinued. However, the process demonstrated the collaborative power of biodiesel production within the regional economy.

Local retailers, like Leathers Fuels, purchased biodiesel from SeQuential

190   "Ethanol Vehicle Emissions."
191   "How much ethanol is in gasoline, and how does it affect fuel economy."
192   Garrett, Jerry. "Corn Ethanol: Biofuel or Biofraud?"

and sold blended B20 diesel at their stations, where they had the option to brand their biodiesel pumps with the SeQuential logo. SeQuential was more directly involved in two biofuel gas stations through one of its founding companies, Q Bio. Both stations were located in Eugene, Oregon, where the SeQuential brand was licensed to Q Bio and the biodiesel was supplied by SeQuential. These stations were considered among the most sustainable refueling centers in the U.S., and each had a wide selection of biofuel and petroleum blends, electricity generated by solar power, and a market that featured organic foods (Exhibit 2).

Tyson and the SeQuential board considered expanding the company's direct-serve model, which had grown to deliver about one-half of the company's biodiesel. SeQuential made its biodiesel available at the Salem refinery and at a leased tank in a major petroleum terminal in Portland, where retailers could buy blends of biodiesel, pre-mixed with diesel. This convenience brought in up to $0.20 per gallon more for the biodiesel blend than sales through other channels.

Biodiesel Competitive Landscape

In 2016, the National Biodiesel Board was comprised of more than seventy member companies controlling 166 plants across the U.S.[193] Across a fragmented industry with a few large and many small to medium players, about 1.26 billion gallons of biodiesel were produced in the U.S. in 2015.[194, 195] Imported biodiesel represented about one-third of the market that year, or about 670 million gallons, according to the Environmental Protection Agency.[196]

The largest producer of biodiesel in the U.S. was the Renewable Energy Group (REG), which produced 375 million gallons of biodiesel in 2015 and generated revenues of $1.4 billion.[197] They operated a network of eleven biodiesel plants, which had a total operating capacity of more than 450 million gallons per year.[198] This expansion occurred primarily through the acquisition of biodiesel production facilities that were often in financial distress. REG plants used UCO and virgin oils to make biodiesel, and they held long-term supply contracts from a number of feedstock providers.

---

193   "Biodiesel: America's Advanced Biofuel."
194   "Monthly Biodiesel Production Report."
195   "USA Plants."
196   "Tax Incentive Action Page."
197   Renewable Energy Group, "Form 10-K, Annual Report."
198   Hulen, Anthony. "Renewable Energy Group Closes Acquisition of Sanimax Biodiesel Plant."

Archer Daniels Midland (ADM), an international, publicly-traded food processing company with annual revenues of $67.7 billion in 2015, was also a leading producer of agro-based biodiesel in the U.S. ADM owned an 85-million-gallon capacity plant in Velva, North Dakota; a 70-million-gallon unit in Lloydminster, Canada; a 54-million-gallon unit in Rondonopolis, Brazil; and other joint ventures in the U.S. and worldwide. ADM generated about $6.8 billion in revenues from biodiesel and ethanol production in 2015. [199, 200]

Cargill Foods, another leading food processing firm, was one of the largest private companies in the world, with $120 billion in revenues in 2015. The company had two U.S. plants, which produced biodiesel from soybean oil in Iowa and Missouri. Each plant had a capacity of 56 million gallons. Biodiesel production was only a small component of Cargill's overall production business.[201]

The largest worldwide producer of renewable diesel was the Finnish company Neste, which produced more than 420 million gallons of renewable diesel in 2014.[202]

Used Cooking Oil Collection: Industry, SeQuential, and Competitors

As Tyson continued to ponder his day of meetings, he reflected on his visit to the restaurant chain supplying some of SeQuential's UCO. SeQuential's business model was different than most of the players in the biodiesel industry—not only did SeQuential make biodiesel, but its vertical integration supplied the company with the UCO feedstock used to make biodiesel. Tyson considered where SeQuential stacked up in the industry and whether the company's actions were sufficient to stay competitive.

Used Cooking Oil Industry
Used Cooking Oil collection was a $1.9 billion industry. Since 2000, the industry had experienced growth nearly every year, and was expected to grow through 2020. A significant factor in the growth of the market was an increase

---

199   The information in this paragraph came from the following source: "USA Plants."
200   The information in this paragraph came from the following source: Nickel, Rod and Chris Prentice. "ADM Cuts Biodiesel Output as Industry Hit by Weak Margins."
201   The information in this paragraph came from the following source: "USA Plants."
202   The information in this paragraph came from the following source: "Neste Oil Claims World Leadership in Biofuels from Waste, Residue."

in UCO prices as the demand for biodiesel established more value for the commodity.[203]

UCO was almost pure fat, and was obtained by draining restaurant fryers and other cooking vessels on a regular basis.[204] UCO collectors often provided restaurants or food processors with containers of varying capacities into which the facilities could manually transfer and store UCO. A more capital-intensive UCO collection process was a direct plumbed system, where UCO was automatically transferred from a fryer directly to the collection bin after use. Manual transfer systems often had collection tanks ranging from 40 to 400 gallons in size, while the direct plumbed systems often had collection tanks with a 50 to 300-gallon capacity. The manual systems supplied the majority of the UCO.

Collection involved removing the UCO from the storage tanks on site. This service was accomplished through the use of a pumper truck. Sometimes access was simple, but other times accessing the narrow alleys in urban areas was difficult. Historically, restaurants had paid service providers to haul away the UCO, but beginning around 2005, entrepreneurs who saw UCO as a valuable resource for biodiesel production started paying restaurants for the resource. This repurposing of a waste product became standard procedure. The price paid to restaurants often depended on the commodity indices for UCO.

A secondary service provided by UCO collectors involved collecting oily water stored in a grease trap, which was a system used by most restaurants to prevent oil from entering the sewer system. The grease trap cleaning was a fee-based service that UCO collectors often used as a secondary revenue stream. The grease trap fluid contained small amounts of UCO.

If the UCO collection bin overflowed or was improperly handled, the UCO could spill and create a safety hazard. As a result, UCO collectors kept track of the rate of use for each facility and balanced collection times to maximize efficiency. The payment received by the restaurant for the UCO was often insignificant when compared to the restaurant's overall business. Therefore, the main value added to a restaurant was the service of having its UCO safely and expediently removed.[205]

Hotels and restaurants generated between 50 to 100 gallons of UCO per month, with food processors also contributing to UCO production. This led

---

203   The information in this paragraph came from the following source: Witter, Dave. "Cooking Oil Recycling in the U.S."
204   Ibid.
205   The information in this paragraph came from the following source: "National Weekly Ag Energy Round-Up."

to an overall world-wide market of about three billion gallons of UCO produced each year.[206] In 2015, about 70% of the UCO went into the production
of biofuels, primarily biodiesel with a small fraction to renewable diesel.[207]

The Jacobsen (the "Jac") was a commodity index for UCO and animal fats
(collectively referred to as yellow grease). It was used by the industry to establish the buying and selling relationships for UCO, which helped standard-
ize feedstock transactions for the industry. Yellow grease indices were created
on a regional basis. The historical Jac demonstrated the volatile nature of the
commodity, with a strong correlation to prices of petroleum and virgin soy oil
(Exhibit 5). The higher the price of UCO, the more valuable collection operations became to SeQuential. The spread between diesel's NYMEX index and
UCO was another important determinant in the profitability of the biodiesel
business (Exhibit 6). The larger the spread, the more profitable the biodiesel
business became.

SeQuential and UCO Collection

As access to its main ingredient was key to the production process, SeQuential
ran its own collection business through a subsidiary, SeQuential Logistics. The
acquisitions of UCO collectors helped SeQuential establish a strong presence
on the West Coast base in the UCO business. The logistics of servicing thousands of restaurants were complex, and Tyson had plenty of work ahead of
him to ensure that SeQuential successfully grew the efficiency and scope of
the collection business.

As SeQuential's team on-boarded UCO and grease trap customers from
their acquisitions, they were able to more than meet the supply needs of the
plant. SeQuential worked to integrate these customers into the company's existing collection system, which took several months to fully normalize. Many
of the restaurant routes SeQuential inherited from its acquisitions had used
hand-drawn maps and route calculations. SeQuential implemented an elec-
tronic GPS-based logistics and routing system called RoadNet, which provided
route optimization. However, because each customer was unique, it was crucial that pickup routes contained driver notes, such as "the bin is located inside the premises and cannot be accessed on weekends." Drivers made many
stops as they traveled along the routes and tracked this individual information.
Driving the pumper trucks and servicing the accounts was a difficult job, and
driver turnover was high.

---

206   "Learn About Biodiesel."
207   Witter, Dave.

Through detailed data collection, SeQuential designed and ran variable collection routes that optimized the UCO pickup so that containers were emptied when full, rather than on a particular day of the month. SeQuential's leadership team estimated that production patterns of their restaurant customers were learned over the course of several months, and pickup frequency was optimized accordingly. Pick-up frequency ranged from two or three weeks, to once every other month. SeQuential also provided grease trap cleaning services, which typically required routes distinct from UCO collection due to the larger average volumes of the grease traps. By providing grease trap cleaning service to a portion of its accounts, SeQuential was able to receive an additional revenue source and better serve the customer, although this did not provide a significant amount of UCO for biodiesel production. SeQuential believed that there was potential to grow this part of the business. Less than 20% of SeQuential's UCO restaurant accounts also contracted the company for grease trap services, and most of the grease trap business came with the recent acquisitions. Pricing of this service varied depending on capacity and accessibility, but a monthly grease trap service price was often $100 or more, with perhaps half of that contributing to the bottom line.

SeQuential believed that an important way to differentiate themselves was to provide superior customer service. Some customers considered price first when making a decision about who would collect their UCO, but after experiencing sub-par customer service, customers would accept a lower price per gallon for clean and timely collection. SeQuential observed this first hand as customers unsubscribed and re-subscribed to its services.

Improving efficiency while also improving service levels was a major challenge. Although SeQuential had modernized its logistics with RoadNet, the rapid growth from the acquisitions put a great deal of stress on the system and the team. The company found that driver productivity had a great deal of variance, about half of which could be explained by route density. For example, some of the best drivers serviced more than twenty-two locations per day, while others barely serviced ten or twelve. The remaining explanation was related to gaps in standardization and management of the drivers, vehicle fleet, and facilities.

Additionally, the fleet needed to be further standardized and modernized in order to meet the efficiency and service level requirements expected by SeQuential's new customers. Also as a result of the acquisitions, SeQuential had a number of depots, which spread operations out over several facilities. With a modest capital investment of several hundred thousand dollars, a central oil collection and drying facility was estimated to save up to $0.10-0.20 per gallon.

Over one-half of SeQuential's employees were drivers. With lower petroleum prices, the demand for drivers in North American oil fields had dropped, making it a little easier to hire drivers, but turnover in 2016 had skyrocketed as a result of SeQuential's recent acquisitions. The company believed that it needed to reduce driver turnover significantly to improve efficiency and reduce HR costs.

The original goal of vertical integration had been to secure feedstock for the plant, but as the UCO collection business grew, SeQuential saw the potential to increase margins as collection costs dropped below the Jacobsen Index. With the recent acquisitions, the company's collection costs had achieved that turning point, even in a volatile market. The company's variable costs of collecting were even lower, so the growth of new accounts was worthwhile. This intrigued Tyson. With better marketing of SeQuential's story, would 20% account growth per annum be possible for his team? At the same time, the high churn rate of customers given the frequency that restaurants went out of business added unpredictability.

UCO Competitive Landscape

The UCO collection industry was fragmented. Many of the lower volume oil collectors started out as a small business, essentially one person with a truck. These businesses made informal arrangements with a handful of local hotels and restaurants to collect their used cooking oil. Other players were large companies that had sophisticated logistics systems and collected UCO from thousands of locations. As the demand for UCO increased, these companies began to acquire and consolidate some of the smaller players.

The three largest players in the U.S. market were Darling Ingredients, Baker Commodities, and Valley Protein. Each company had been in business for a number of years and, in recent years, had used acquisitions to grow their business. They collected a diverse set of waste and by-products from food processors, restaurants, bakeries, and delis which were then refined and rendered into products that were sold to a variety of end markets in the chemical, feed, and fuel markets. UCO collection and grease trap services were a substantial portion of the portfolio and represented perhaps 20-40% of the company's revenue streams.[208]

Darling Ingredients, Inc., a Texas-based publicly traded company, led the

---

208   The information in this paragraph came from the following source: Witter, Dave.

field in UCO collection with about $462 million in segment revenue in 2015 and $3.4 billion in worldwide revenue. They accounted for 23.8% of the total UCO market share in 2015. Like other suppliers, Darling's UCO was used primarily for the production of biodiesel and renewable diesel (in a joint venture with a subsidiary of Valero, Inc.). Additionally, Darling used UCO for the manufacture of various chemicals and as a livestock feed additive.[209]

The second-largest player was Baker Commodities, a private, California-based company that specialized in rendering and grease removal services. They supplied the biodiesel, chemical, and livestock industries with UCO. Baker controlled about 8.8% of the market share and had an estimated $166 million in segment revenues in 2015.[210]

The third largest UCO collector in the U.S. was Valley Proteins, a privately-held company based in Virginia that focused the majority of its operations on the East Coast. Most of its UCO went toward providing food for livestock and pets. Valley Proteins controlled about 7.8% of the market with an estimated $148 million in segment revenue in 2015. [211]

By-Products of Biodiesel: Industry and SeQuential

Tyson believed that one of the advantages of biodiesel production was that by-products could be resold or repurposed. This helped the company minimize waste and align with an environmental goal of closed-loop operations.

By-Products of Biodiesel Production Process

The main by-products of biodiesel production were glycerin, free fatty acids, and methanol.[212] The methanol could be recovered and reused in the system to make more biodiesel, leaving the glycerin and free fatty acids for other uses.

Because the free fatty acids produced as a by-product of biodiesel production could be burned as a heat source, they were most often sold as boiler fuel.[213] Biodiesel-produced boiler fuel was a high-quality product, but faced significant competition, because almost anything with some carbon content could be turned into a low-cost boiler fuel. Matching customer need to biodiesel-based boiler fuel quality was an important element for successful boiler fuel sale.

---

209 Ibid.
210 Ibid.
211 Ibid.
212 "Biodiesel Production and Distribution."
213 "Boiler Fuel."

The glycerin produced in biodiesel production was useful in a variety of applications, depending on the purity of the glycerin. Uses included compost material, feed stock, and propylene glycol. Facilities that produced highly-refined glycerin could pursue a wider range of uses for glycerin, including the cosmetics industry. [214]

SeQuential and By-Products

By 2016, SeQuential's production efficiency had exceed 95%, reducing the amount of by-products produced. SeQuential's glycerin and boiler fuel were more refined than most. This generated a strong revenue stream for a handful of industrial customers. As SeQuential continued to improve its conversion efficiency, yielding more biodiesel, fewer by-products were available for sale.

Government Policy

While Tyson considered the biodiesel industry and SeQuential's role in each sector, he also thought about the impact that government policy had on SeQuential's business. Government policies had been a substantial driver of the industry, but following the establishment of a Republican White House, Senate, and House of Representatives, would they continue? How well would the company be situated should the level of support change?

Federal Renewable Fuel Standards

The U.S. government had implemented policies to ensure a viable market for renewable fuels. This was motivated by a goal of reducing greenhouse gas emissions from petroleum, and a desire to attain greater independence from imported fossil fuels (Exhibit 7).

The minimum demand set by the federal government was in the form of the U.S. Renewable Fuel Standard (RFS2). Created in 2005, RFS2 was a national policy requiring a specified volume of fossil fuel to be replaced by one of four types of renewable fuel. The minimum demand set for "Advanced Biofuel," the broader category biodiesel fell under, was 7.25 billion gallons for 2016 and 15 billion gallons by 2020. [215] This standard helped biodiesel producers by creating a predictable market in which to sell biodiesel, by obligating fossil fuel refineries and importers to use a required amount of renewable

---

214   The information in this paragraph came from the following source: "New Uses for Crude Glycerin from Biodiesel Production."
215   "Program Overview for Renewable Fuel Standard Program."

fuel mixed with their petroleum products. This requirement created a strong source of revenue for biodiesel producers.

When renewable fuel was produced or imported, each gallon (or batch) of that fuel was tagged with a 38-digit number, called a Renewable Identification Number or RIN (Exhibit 8). When biodiesel was sold or blended, the RIN assumed monetary value and became detached from the gallon or batch of the fuel. Fossil fuel refineries were required to fulfill their renewable fuel quotas either by turning in RINs associated with the biodiesel they purchased to blend with diesel, or by paying a penalty. Consequently, refiners either produced their own biodiesel and created and turned in their own RINs or, more commonly, they purchased RINs from renewable fuel manufacturers like SeQuential.

Depending on the source and type of the fuel, the RIN had a value that varied directly with the environmental benefit of the associated renewable fuel. SeQuential obtained a high value for its RINs because of the lower carbon footprint of biodiesel. For every gallon of biodiesel produced, SeQuential earned 1.5 RINs. Under the RFS2 program, RIN values for biodiesel made from UCO and virgin vegetable oils were treated equally.

The significant value associated with the emerging RIN market tempted scam artists. Houston-based Green Diesel sold $48.5 million from biodiesel RINs that were never produced. Rodney Hailey of Maryland sold $9 million worth of bogus RINs before being caught.[216]

In 2011, Genscape, a company that had provided real-time monitoring technology to energy companies, created the first RIN verification service and set up a voluntary program created with input from a National Biodiesel Board task force.[217] This fee-for-service model helped verify the authenticity and value of RINs. SeQuential was an active subscriber to Genscape's service to ensure that its customers knew that its RINs were legitimate.

Federal Tax Credits

Tax credits were available to the biodiesel industry in two ways: a tax credit of $1 per gallon for consuming pure B100 biodiesel, or a credit of $1 per gallon for blending B100 biodiesel to create a 1% biodiesel or higher mixture that was subsequently sold or utilized.[218] Credits were provided to the blender instead of the producer, which allowed foreign producers to access credits derived from U.S. taxpayer income if the product was blended in the U.S.

---

216   The information in this paragraph came from the following source: Parker, Mario, Jennifer A. Dloughy, and Bryan Gruley. "The Fake Factory That Pumped Out Real Money."
217   "RIN Integrity."
218   "Federal Laws and Incentives for Biodiesel."

Unlike certain tax incentives for the petroleum industry or other renewables, these credits were not permanently written into the tax code.[219],[220] The U.S. Congress had been inconsistent year to year in their legislation of when the tax credit would be available, and occasionally even passed legislation to apply it retroactively. For example, when the Federal tax credit ended in 2010, there was a 42% drop in biodiesel production and thousands of jobs were lost.[221] Another gap occurred in 2015, when no tax credit was in place until the U.S. Congress passed legislation in early 2016 that applied retroactively to 2015 biodiesel sales. That measure also covered biodiesel sales through 2016, but renewal was uncertain given the incoming administration's stated opposition to climate change initiatives.

State Renewable Fuel Standards

California: Some state and local governments also established unique renewable fuel standards and incentive programs. The California Air Resources Board implemented a Low Carbon Fuel Standard (LCFS), which encouraged production and use of cleaner fuels and the reduction of greenhouse gas emissions within California. As laid out by the LCFS, each producer submitted a certified fuel pathway for carbon intensity (CI), which documented the carbon footprint of their fuel. The LCFS mandated that total CI should be reduced by 10% by 2020 and set annual targets for producers to meet.[222]

In-state refineries generated an environmental deficit with a higher-than-target CI, which was overcome either by producing or blending renewable fuels, or by purchasing credits. Renewable fuel producers also generated credits when they produced and sold low-CI fuels. The amount of credit depended on how much the CI overage was balanced out by the renewable fuel. For example, diesel has a CI of 94.71 and biodiesel has a CI of 11.76.[223] In order to reach the LCFS target of 94.60, diesel producers had to either blend equivalent volumes of biodiesel or purchase credits. One credit equaled one metric ton of CO_2 emitted, and in September 2016, one LCSF credit was worth about $0.91 per gallon of biodiesel.[224]

Oregon: In 2016, the Oregon Department of Environmental Quality (DEQ) launched the Clean Fuels Program to reduce the carbon intensity of

---

219   "Tax Incentive Action Page."
220   "Tax Advantages."
221   Witter, Dave.
222   The information in this paragraph came from the following source: "LCFS Pathway Certified Carbon Intensities."
223   "Carbon Intensity Lookup Table – California."
224   "Ethanol & Biodiesel Information Service."

transportation fuels by 10% percent over the following ten years.[225] This initiative emulated California's model, but the market evolved slowly through 2016.

In addition, the Oregon DEQ mandated that all diesel fuel sold in the state must be blended with at least 5% biodiesel.[226] In 2015, this equated to about 35 million gallons of biodiesel, or 5% of the 700 million gallons of diesel used in the state that year.[227] In 2010, the City of Portland mandated a 10% percent biodiesel requirement that was temporarily suspended in favor of a 5% percent mandate, as the higher percentage was deemed infeasible due to technical and economic factors.[228]

Challenges for SeQuential

As Tyson prepared to leave the office, he thought back to the discussion he had with the MBA students about SeQuential's sustainability strategy. He knew that this was an essential and motivating part of the company's mission and model, but he wondered how it factored into the other challenges SeQuential faced. How should sustainability best be integrated into the fabric of the company in a way that supported the mission without constraining growth?

The Need for Growth

Tyson knew that economies of scale in the collection and biodiesel business mattered. The company had seen improved results through organic growth and acquisitions, but rapid growth was a challenge to the culture and mission of the company. What was the best way to continue this growth? Should they pursue another plant expansion, or expand grease trap servicing and UCO collection as part of an expanded upstream integration strategy? How could they keep SeQuential's staff aligned and motivated? How could the company continue to create a stronger infrastructure and better customer service?

As SeQuential continued to grow, the continued acquisition of new businesses was a possibility, but would have an impact on company culture and operating procedures. How could the company continue to work toward becoming an integrated organization that would remain competitive in a changing market landscape?

---

225   "Oregon Clean Fuels Program."
226   " Oregon Laws and Incentives for Biodiesel."
227   "Petroleum and Other Liquids."
228   "Bio-Fuel Memorandum."

Government Policy

From the beginning, SeQuential had worked with policymakers at the local, state, and federal level. Given the inconsistency of legislation, changing political priorities, and unpredictable outcomes at all levels, SeQuential needed to carefully consider its plans and strategies. What could SeQuential do to maintain a favorable environment for UCO-based biodiesel? Could SeQuential maintain profitability without government programs? How would the market react to changes in government regulation?

Market Identity, Branding, and Sustainability Philosophy

In 2016, SeQuential modernized and unified its brand after acquiring a series of UCO companies. While the rebranding gave SeQuential a unified message and appearance, Tyson wondered how SeQuential could continue to differentiate itself in the market. What indicators could be used to develop a superior service model? How could SeQuential connect with customers who supported its environmental mission? How central should sustainability be to its messaging?

Sustainability was an embedded value at SeQuential, given the product's superior environmental footprint. Through the use of UCO as feedstock, SeQuential contributed to a more sustainable energy future. Could the company's sustainability philosophy contribute to its bottom line, or would it hinder profitability? How would SeQuential stay competitive while also staying true to its mission? Should SeQuential pursue external verification, like B Corp Certification, to strengthen its branding and commitment to social, environmental, and economic sustainability? B Corp Certification had become increasingly popular and well-known among consumers, but could be time-consuming for staff and expensive for larger companies.

Conclusion

As he got in his biodiesel-powered car, Tyson revisited the topics he had considered through the day as he ran SeQuential. A host of challenges to ongoing growth faced him, from managing the staffing and logistical challenges of the company's new acquisitions and mergers, to evaluating the importance of customer service and branding to their clients, to navigating the uncertainty of political change. What actions could he take to ensure that SeQuential remained competitive and true to its mission, while fulfilling its potential for growth and profitability?

Exhibits

Exhibit 1: SeQuential

Source: SeQuential.

Exhibit 2: SeQuential's Value Chain

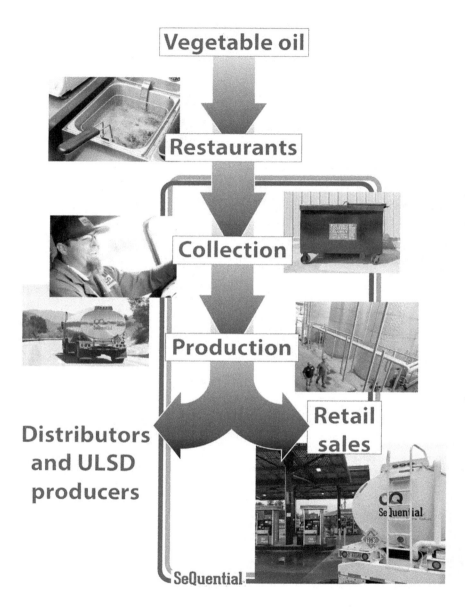

Source: SeQuential.

Exhibit 3: SeQuential's Mission Statement

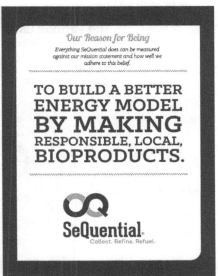

Source: SeQuential.

Exhibit 4: Transesterification Process

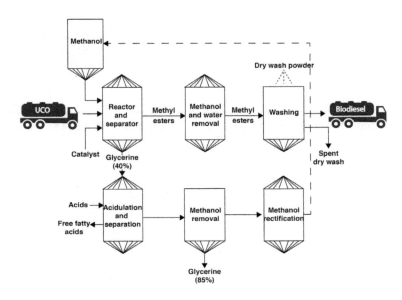

Exhibit 5: Used Cooking Oil Report

The various uses of Used Cooking Oil
(source: *IBISWorld report, December 2015*)

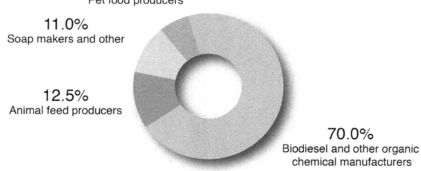

6.5%
Pet food producers

11.0%
Soap makers and other

12.5%
Animal feed producers

70.0%
Biodiesel and other organic
chemical manufacturers

Comparison of biodiesel feedstock amounts
(source: *U.S. Energy Information Administration, July 2016*)

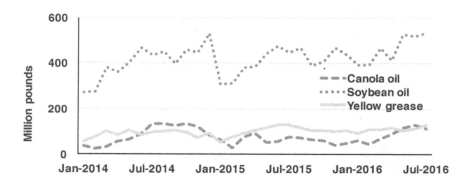

Exhibit 6: NYMEX vs. Yellow Grease Index

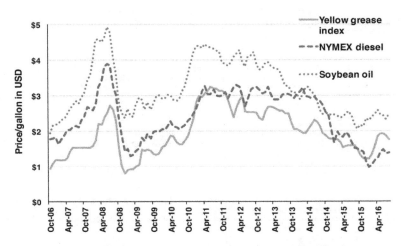

The NYMEX ultra-low sulfur diesel index is an important consideration for pricing biodiesel, while cost of feedstock such as used cooking oil (yellow grease index) and soybean oil make up most of the variable costs.

Source: The Jacobsen, October 2016.

Exhibit 7: Government Policies Related to Biofuel

Energy Policy Act of 1992
- Directed studies on alternative fuels to be undertaken
- Sets guidelines and requirements for the Secretary of Energy
- Authorizes several avenues by which the federal government can finance alternative energy research
- Sets a timeline for the adoption of certain alternative energies as well as rules for fleet program purchases of alternative fuel vehicles

Energy Policy Act of 2005
- Increased Power of congress to regulate the biofuel industry
- Directed the Secretary of Energy to conduct R&D to demonstrate the commercial application for bioenergy
- Increased duties for Secretary of Energy and Secretary of Agriculture in regard to biomass feedstock development including development of the feedstock themselves
- Development of conversion technology for cellulosic biomass
- Diversification into areas like cogeneration
- Funding for education and outreach regarding biofuels
- Tax credit for investment in alternative motor vehicle technology
- Tax credit for installation of refueling system that dispenses at least 85% ethanol by volume
- Requires FTC to monitor the ethanol industry for price-setting and anti-competitive behavior
- Provides for funding for anyone involved in the development of biofuels or related technology
- Established the Advanced Biofuel Technologies Program
- Funds demonstration projects to develop conversion technologies for cellulosic biomass

Energy Independence and Security Act of 2007
- Sets requirements for the Corporate Average Fuel Economy (CAFE) to encourage use of more fuel efficient vehicles.
- Any vehicle using 20% biodiesel is eligible for a CAFE credit
- Secretary of Energy establishes grant program for alternative biofuels that emit at least 80% less GHG than current fuels
- Sets aside funding to study the effects of biodiesel on engine performance and durability
- Sets aside funding to evaluate and develop a fuel production and distribution infrastructure
- Sets a expressed wish" that renewable resources provide at least 25% of all U.S. energy needs

The Food, Conservation, and Energy Act of 2008 (aka The Farm Bill)
- Increases funding for advanced biofuel research
- Biomass Crop Assistance Program
- Support production of dedicated cellulosic feedstock
- Assist agricultural and forest land owners in collection and transport of eligible material for use in biomass conversion facilities
- Biorefinery Assistance Program
- Grants and loans for development, construction, and retrofitting of commercial-scale refineries to produce biofuels
- Requirements for funding and evaluation of these programs
- Provides a tax credit for fuel blenders using certain cellulosic feedstock
- Reduces tax credit for ethanol blenders
- Extends the ethanol import tax to the end of 2010

Public Law 110—353
- This is the act that established the Troubled Asset Relief Program
- Included the Energy Improvement and Extension Act of 2008
- Extends and increases income and excise tax credits for biodiesel and renewable diesel fuels
- Extends the tax credit for alternative fuel and fuel mixtures

American Recovery and Reinvestment Act of 2009
- Provides funding to the Department of Energy for:
- Research into energy efficiency and renewable energy
- Advanced Research Projects Agency - Energy
- Other energy research
- Speeds up timeline for deployment of renewable energy and electric power transmission projects

Renewable Fuel Standard (started by the EPA 2005 and expanded by EISA 2007)
- Gives power for regulating fuel quality, blend, and safety to the EPA
- Mandated that the U.S. use 36 billion gallons of renewable fuel annually by 2022
- Mandated that 21 billion gallons of advanced biofuels be used by 2022
- Mandated that 1 billion gallons of biomass-based biodiesel be used by 2012

Source: Biofuel.org.uk, October 2016.

Exhibit 8: Renewable Identification Numbers and Biodiesel

Lifecycle of RINs
(source: *EPA*)

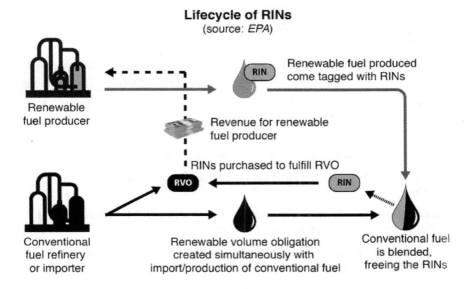

RIN price history
(source: *The Jacobsen, October 2016*)

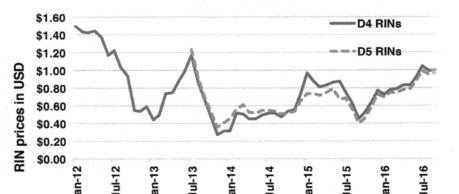

Biodiesel falls under both D4 (biomass-based diesel) and D5 (advanced biofuels) categories. Revenue from RINs depend on both the number of RINs per gallon for the fuel type (1.5 for biodiesel, for example) and the market price per RIN of the category applied.

Bibliography

Alternative Fuels Data Center. "Biodiesel Benefits." U.S. Department of Energy, 2012. www.afdc.energy.gov/fuels/biodiesel_benefits.html.

Alternative Fuels Data Center. "Biodiesel Fuel Basics." U.S. Department of Energy, 2012. www.afdc.energy.gov/fuels/biodiesel_basics.html.

Alternative Fuels Data Center. "Biodiesel Production and Distribution." U.S. Department of Energy, 2012. www.afdc.energy.gov/fuels/biodiesel_production.html.

Alternative Fuels Data Center. "Ethanol Fuel Basics."U.S. Department of Energy, 2012. www.afdc.energy.gov/fuels/ethanol_fuel_basics.html.

Alternative Fuels Data Center. "Ethanol Vehicle Emissions." U.S. Department of Energy, 2012. www.afdc.energy.gov/vehicles/flexible_fuel_emissions.html.

Alternative Fuels Data Center. "Federal Laws and Incentives for Biodiesel." U.S. Department of Energy, 2014. www.afdc.energy.gov/fuels/laws/BIOD/US.

Alternative Fuels Data Center. "Hydrogenation-Derived Renewable." U.S. Department of Energy, 2012. www.afdc.energy.gov/fuels/emerging_green.html.

Alternative Fuels Data Center. "Oregon Laws and Incentives for Biodiesel." U.S. Department of Energy, 2014. www.afdc.energy.gov/fuels/laws/BIOD/OR.

Agricultural Marketing Service. "National Weekly Ag Energy Round-Up." United States Department of Agriculture, 2016. www.ams.usda.gov/mnreports/lswagenergy.pdf.

ASTM Standardization News. "New Biodiesel Specifications." *ASTM International Standards Worldwide*, 2008. www.astm.org/SNEWS/ND_2008/D02E0_nd08.html.

Biodiesel: America's Advanced Biofuel. "RIN Integrity." 2012. biodiesel.org/policy/rin-integrity.

Biodiesel: America's Advanced Biofuel. "Tax Incentive Action Page." 2016. http://biodiesel.org/policy/fueling-action-center/tax-incentive-action-page.

Biodiesel Magazine. "Neste Oil Claims World Leadership in Biofuels from Waste, Residue." March, 2015. http://www.biodieselmagazine.com/articles/324835/neste-oil-claims-world-leadership-in-biofuels-from-waste-residue.

Biodiesel Magazine. "USA Plants." 2011. www.biodieselmagazine.com/plants/listplants/.

California Environmental Protection Agency Air Resources Board. "Carbon Intensity Lookup Table – California." 2016. www.arb.ca.gov/fuels/lcfs/121409lcfs_lutables.pdf.

California Environmental Protection Agency Air Resources Board. "LCFS Pathway Certified Carbon Intensities." 2016. www.arb.ca.gov/fuels/lcfs/fuelpathways/pathwaytable.htm.

Extension. "New Uses for Crude Glycerin from Biodiesel Production." 2015. articles.extension.org/pages/29264/new-uses-for-crude-glycerin-from-biodiesel-production.

Garrett, Jerry. "Corn Ethanol: Biofuel or Biofraud?" Wheels: The Nuts and Bolts of

Whatever Moves You, *The New York Times*, September 24, 2007. wheels.blogs.nytimes. com/2007/09/24/corn-ethanol-biofuel-or-biofraud/?_r=0.

Hulen, Anthony. "Renewable Energy Group Closes Acquisition of Sanimax Biodiesel Plant." *Business Wire*, March, 2016. http://www.businesswire.com/news/home/20160316005770/ en/Renewable-Energy-Group-Closes-Acquisition-Sanimax-Biodiesel.

Nickel, Rod, and Chris Prentice. "ADM Cuts Biodiesel Output as Industry Hit by Weak Margins." *Reuters*, February 25, 2015. www.reuters.com/article/ usa-adm-biodiesel-idUSL1N0VZ1W520150225.

Oil Price Information Service. "Ethanol & Biodiesel Information Service." 2013. www. opisnet.com/images/productsamples/EBISnewsletter-sample.pdf. Accessed 6 Oct. 2016.

Pacific Biodiesel. "History of Biodiesel Fuel." 2014. www.biodiesel.com/biodiesel/history/.

Paratherm Corporation. "Biodiesel: America's Advanced Biofuel." www.biodiesel.org/home.

Parker, Mario, Jennifer A. Dloughy, and Bryan Gruley. "The Fake Factory That Pumped Out Real Money." *Bloomberg*, July 13, 2016. www.bloomberg.com/ features/2016-fake-biofuel-factory/.

Piedmont Biofuels. "Boiler Fuel." 2011. www.biofuels.coop/about/parkmap/boiler-fuel.

Portland Water Bureau. "Bio-Fuel Memorandum." The City of Portland, Oregon, 2014. www.portlandoregon.gov/bds/article/289142. 6 Oct. 2016.

Renewable Energy Group, Inc. "Form 10-K, Annual Report." 2016. investor.regi.com/secfil-ing.cfm?filingID=1628280-16-12666&CIK=1463258.

State of Oregon Department of Environmental Quality. "Oregon Clean Fuels Program." 2016. www.deq.state.or.us/aq/cleanFuel/docs/Bulletin-AdoptedPhase2Rules.pdf.

The Energy Exchange. "Tax Advantages." 2016. www.enex.com/word/tax-advantages-2/.

United States Energy Information Administration. "How much ethanol is in gaso-line, and how does it affect fuel economy." April 6, 2016. www.eia.gov/tools/faqs/faq. cfm?id=27&t=4.

United States Energy Information Administration. "Monthly Biodiesel Production Report." 2015. www.eia.gov/biofuels/biodiesel/production/table1.pdf.

United States Energy Information Administration. "Petroleum and Other Liquids." 2016. https://www.eia.gov/dnav/pet/pet_cons_refoth_c_SOR_EPD2DM10_mgalpd_a.htm.

United States Environmental Protection Agency. "Learn About Biodiesel." 2016. www3.epa. gov/region9/waste/biodiesel/questions.html.

United States Environmental Protection Agency. "Program Overview for Renewable Fuel Standard Program." 2015. www.epa.gov/renewable-fuel-standard-program/program-overview-renewable-fuel-standard-program.

University of California Davis and Berkeley. "California Renewable Diesel Multimedia Evaluation." California Environmental Protection Agency, 2010. www.arb.ca.gov/fuels/multimedia/renewabledieseltieri_dftfinal.pdf.

Witter, Dave. "Cooking Oil Recycling in the U.S." *IBIS World US*, January, 2016. clients1.ibisworld.com.proxy.lib.pdx.edu/reports/us/industry/currentperformance.aspx?entid=5810.

TROPICAL SALVAGE'S GROWTH STRATEGY
From Recession to Expansion

Oikos Case Writing Competition 3rd Place (Social
Entrepreneurship Track), 2011

By Scott Marshall, Ph.D., Lisa Piefer, and Erin Ferrigno

Tropical Salvage Case Study

Introduction

*"[Tropical Salvage] demonstrates that business can adjust its values and practices
to become a part of the solution to social and environmental challenges, while remaining responsible to the financial bottom line."*
— Tim O'Brien, Founder and President

Tim O'Brien, founder of Tropical Salvage, was preparing for another warehouse clearance sale of his unique, handcrafted hardwood furniture. It had
been an enormously challenging year and it was important to reduce inventory before the next container arrived from Indonesia. The market for fine furniture had begun to decline steadily in early 2008 following the stock market
crash of the prior September. The company survived a difficult period, but not

without suffering a decline in sales. O'Brien had spent ten years building a sustainable business model based on environmental stewardship, worker empowerment and unique, high quality product. As the economy recovered, O'Brien believed Tropical Salvage needed to pursue an aggressive expansion strategy.

Although the warehouse clearance sale was occupying O'Brien's mind, he was excited about the prospect of implementing a bold growth strategy for the coming years. The two most significant strategies for growth focused on diversifying product offerings beyond hardwood furniture and opening branded retail stores in the United States. Many fundamental business challenges, including brand awareness, financing and operational efficiency, had to be overcome to make these strategies effective. However, O'Brien was confident that the highly vertically integrated structure, unique product designs, cost-competitive sourcing and deeply engrained social mission of Tropical Salvage provided the leverage to overcome these challenges.

As O'Brien considered how best to expand, he prepared to markdown the remaining inventory from his last shipment. Are his growth plans overly ambitious while the economy is so uncertain? Does it make sense to extend his product line beyond the hardwood furniture for which Tropical Salvage is known and has experience manufacturing? Is it financially sound to expand into branded retail at this time? Perhaps most importantly, are the trends in "conscientious" consumerism significant enough to support the growth of a values-driven, sustainability-inspired business like Tropical Salvage?

Tropical Salvage

Headquartered in Portland, Oregon, Tropical Salvage is a private manufacturer of distinctive handcrafted furniture made from salvaged, or rediscovered, hardwoods. O'Brien established the company in 1998 to utilize underemployed, yet highly skilled Javanese woodworkers and a nearly inexhaustible supply of salvageable (non-virgin) tropical timber from around Indonesia. Combining these resources provided O'Brien the capability to create unique furniture products whose sale can profitably advance positive social and environmental change.

Tropical Salvage has become largely vertically integrated. The company operates timber salvaging operations and designs and builds furniture in Indonesia and markets and wholesales the furniture in North America. In addition to selling its products to wholesale customers, Tropical Salvage invites consumers to purchase goods directly from its Portland shipping and receiving warehouse. Despite the business challenges of bootstrapping a young company and operating in Indonesia, for over ten years Tropical Salvage has steadily added to its production capacity and may now be poised for expansion.

Indonesia: Systemic Connections of Economy, Communities and the Forest

Indonesia has extremely high levels of biodiversity. It is home to about 10 percent of the world's flowering plant species, 12 percent of the world's mammals, 16 percent of the world's reptile and amphibian species, 17 percent of the world's birds, and at least 25 percent of all of the world's fish species.[229] On the islands of Borneo and Sumatra are the last remaining Sumatran tigers, orangutans, pygmy elephants and Sumatran rhinos and are a key source of freshwater to Borneo and Sumatra's 56 million people. It is not possible to overstate the extent to which the long-term viability of Indonesians, the archipelago's flora and fauna and the country's economy are systemically linked and delicately balanced.

It has been conservatively estimated that at least 20 million people depend on Indonesia's forests for their livelihoods.[230] Wood-based industries' contributions to Indonesia's GNP rank second to petroleum, generating approximately US$7 billion in formal revenues and perhaps another US$1 billion in informal revenues associated with illegal logging and unreported exports.[231]

Logging in Indonesia's forests played a significant part in boosting the country's economic status from the late 1960s until the Asian Financial Crisis in 1997. Commercial and illegal logging practices during President Suharto's "New Order" drove Indonesia's economy but severely diminished a substantial portion of its tropical forests, placing the country's environment and economy in jeopardy. Although a number of regulations mandated government control of Indonesia's forests during Suharto's presidency, it was not until more recently that forest conservation became seriously regarded. Illegal logging practices have decreased as a result of this frame of mind, but they are still responsible for much of Indonesia's forest loss and violent crime rate.

---

229   Case, Fitrian, and Spector, "Climate Change in Indonesia: Implications for Humans and Nature."
230   Sunderlin and Resosudarmo, "Rates and causes of deforestation in Indonesia: towards a resolution of the ambiguities."
231   "Generating economic growth, rural livelihoods, and environmental benefits from Indonesia's forests: A summary of issues and policy options."

In addition to logging jobs with commercial firms, residents rely on the forests for fuel, construction materials, water supply, soil nutrients for farm systems, and shelter and shade for crops and animals. Non-Timber Forest Products (NTFPs) such as game, medicines, fruits, and nuts have deep cultural significance and other NTFPs, such as rattan, charcoal, resin, and seeds are traded locally and internationally.[232] Indonesians rely on income and benefits from over ninety other NTFPs.

Indonesia's widespread deforestation (Exhibit 1) has led to massive environmental, social and economic disruption. The intense deforestation rates that have occurred over the years pose a significant threat to the country's economy and its residents' livelihoods. Most employees in the wood products industry will face unemployment if the area can no longer sustain commercial forestry. Forest loss is also diminishing the area's biodiversity; aside from the direct endangerment of native trees and plants, wild orangutans, sun bears, and clouded leopards are only a few of the species that face extinction in the next ten to twenty years. Of course, the aforementioned NTFPs are also threatened by forest loss; without forest products, Indonesians would experience increased poverty and health risks. Because of these systemic connections, the effects of forest loss are becoming more severe and compound the difficult economic and social conditions in Indonesia. Unfortunately, in the minds of most Indonesians, the immediate benefit of income from logging still outweighs its negative long-term effects.

The town of Jepara, on the north coast of Central Java, is well known globally for its handcrafted hardwood furniture and woodworking. Over 15,000 furniture workshops, showrooms, log parks, sawmills, warehouses and ironmongers are located in Jepara, making it a localized network, or "industrial cluster." The industry's success garnered political support to accommodate the growing volume of furniture exports. For instance, roads were paved and are maintained in order for container trucks to move wood and furniture in and out of the area from other significant parts of the island. At its height, Jepara's hardwood furniture industry employed about 170,000 workers and firms competed fiercely for both inputs and markets.[233]

There are a number of companies and organizations responding in numerous ways to Indonesia's deforestation. Home Depot, for example, cut its purchases of Indonesian lumber by more than three-quarters since 2000. Many

232   "Sustaining Economic Growth, Rural Livelihoods, and Environmental Benefits: Strategic Options for Forest Assistance in Indonesia."
233   The information in this paragraph comes from the following source: Roda, et al., Atlas of Wooden Furniture Industry in Jepara, Indonesia.

companies, including IKEA, require that their hardwood supplies be harvested from Forest Stewardship Council (FSC) certified forests. As O'Brien sees it, FSC-certification is a step in the right direction but still ultimately results in trees being cut down. So, Tropical Salvage is addressing deforestation concerns through its own unique business model. In time, it seems likely that other large companies will follow suit and discontinue the purchase of illegally obtained wood.

Tropical Salvage: The Inspiration and Start-Up

Having lived in and visited Indonesia over the course of nine years, O'Brien was familiar with the archipelago and felt personally attached to its culture when he became inspired to start Tropical Salvage. During a week of trekking in 1998, O'Brien encountered stunning biodiversity juxtaposed with wasteful exploitation of natural resources and underutilization of craft traditions. O'Brien saw that the impressive array of wildlife and fantastically diverse population of trees was, quite unfortunately, offset by vast areas of recently clearcut primary, or old-growth, forest. More than once he came upon areas that had been among the most biologically diverse locations on earth, reduced to an eerie, silent ruin of power-saw litter. For O'Brien, the experience was ominous and affecting.

As his travels continued through cities on the islands of Java, Bali, Lombok and Sumbawa, O'Brien noticed old wooden structures being replaced by more secure structures built from concrete and rebar. In many instances no plan existed to re-use the old beams, boards and poles. Old, hand-hewn wood derived from mature, wild-grained, tropical hardwood trees was fueling simple cooking fires. The idea for Tropical Salvage struck – salvaging wood from deconstructed buildings can be a significant source of raw material for hardwood furniture production.

As the wheels for his new business venture turned in his head, O'Brien began to view Indonesia a little differently. Travel in population centers made him acutely aware that the high deforestation rates have devastating effects, not only on the environment, but also on the social and economic climate. Depletion of the forests was not only leaving wildlife homeless, but was also putting millions of Indonesians out of work. O'Brien started Tropical Salvage based on a conviction that "a reasonable and promising market-oriented strategy can contribute to positive change in a part of the world beset by extraordinary challenges."

The Tropical Salvage Business Model

O'Brien knew that earning and maintaining the respect of Indonesians, especially in Java, would be important to the success of his business model. One day by chance, he was fortunate to meet Agus Rafiqkoh, a likeminded, well-connected and trustworthy businessman. After many lengthy conversations, the two of them set out to actualize Tropical Salvage.

Rafiqkoh, Partner and the Director of Indonesian Operations, had worked in Jepara's wood furniture production industry for eight years prior to meeting O'Brien. He now plays a number of critical roles in Tropical Salvage's Indonesia operations: hiring employees, designing new pieces, directing production, and locating and coordinating wood salvage projects. He is skilled in networking and admits to approaching most new interactions with the business in the forefront of his mind. Brought together by rather random circumstances, O'Brien and Rafiqkoh have developed a strong partnership and friendship, based on shared philosophies, trust and commitment. It is this relationship in particular that serves to anchor Tropical Salvage and has permitted it to overcome the many obstacles faced since its inception.

Both social and environmental mission objectives were implemented at the onset of business in 1999 with eight employees working in a two thousand square foot rented space. O'Brien was excited about the market back then, but was also uninformed of it. After a number of setbacks, he still marvels in the company's utter existence. Today, the company's operations in Indonesia have grown into a salvaging operation and production facility that employs 85 people, including wood salvagers, millers, kiln operators, artisan furniture-makers and carvers, and finishers, some of whom quite likely used to be employed in the illegal logging industry. Tropical Salvage employees are compensated with benefits and wages twenty percent higher than the local industry average and the company has been instrumental in developing the Jepara Forest Conservancy, which protects land for reforestation, economic opportunity and educational purposes.

Sourcing

Tropical Salvage uses only salvaged, or rediscovered, wood to build its line of furniture. So far the company has worked with wood from around 55 different species of trees including teak, acacia, jackfruit, and ingas. O'Brien claims to be a pioneer in using ingas for constructing hardwood furniture and much of what the company finds and uses is this particular specie. Although, and perhaps because, they carry the heaviest weight with consumers, primary forest teak trees have possibly the saddest story of depletion. Today these fast-growing hardwoods are grown on plantations and tend to be cut after just ten years. This is half the time it takes for teak to fully mature. Because mature teak has become increasingly rare, much of the teak used by Tropical Salvage comes in the form of old objects used for outdoor purposes, such as boats.

Fortunately for Tropical Salvage, the company's business model has not yet required it to compete for raw materials. Most of the wood the salvaging crews retrieve is without value in Indonesia. The beauty is that, through years of experimentation, Tropical Salvage has determined how to give new life to the wood so that it becomes valuable again, in the form of furniture. One piece of Tropical Salvage furniture might consist of several species of wood aged from thirty to thousands of years. O'Brien and many of Tropical Salvage's customers feel that the effects of nails, seasoning cracks, bore holes, wild-growth grain, and mineral deposits in the finished products are a wonderful testament to the wood's historical richness.

The company estimates that the supply of salvageable wood in Indonesia is inexhaustible for meeting its own demand. Tropical Salvage has already discovered and surveyed multiple wood salvage sites in Sumatra, Kalimantan and Sulawesi. When it discovers salvageable wood, the company pays for short-term "rent" of the land immediately surrounding the site. If the salvaging process compromises crops or other NTFPs, it will pay the landowner to replace them after the process is completed. Well known as the authority on wood salvaging in Jepara, the company is often contacted by government officials when salvageable wood is discovered. However, as other producers adopt salvaging methods, Tropical Salvage may face competition for rights to salvage in certain areas.

Using hard labor, basic winch systems and limited heavy machinery, the company applies five principle wood salvage strategies on the island of Java. It reclaims wood from demolition sites where old buildings, houses or bridges have been razed or deconstructed. Old fishing boats and truck roofs are also used. It salvages old, wild growth trees from rivers and lakes (Exhibit 2), as well as those that have fallen off logging barges or were felled by floods and landslides during the rainy season. The company also uses diseased or unproductive plantation coffee, cacao, and fruit trees. And finally, unique to the company, since 2003 it has mined entombed trees from beneath the ground (Exhibit 3).

Manufacturing

After the wood is salvaged it is transported to a storage yard in Jepara and cut into boards. Currently, Tropical Salvage contracts primary milling of the wood it salvages. This makes sense in a very soft market where wood processing facilities are operating at a fraction of capacity. From here it moves to the production facility where it is treated for insects and placed in a kiln for drying. Discovering the optimum adjustments for the kilns in order to dry the numerous species is an ongoing challenge, but has gotten much easier with years of experience. The unique expertise that Tropical Salvage has developed in drying a vast array of species serves the company well and provides it with a competency that competitors find difficult to imitate. From the kiln, millers, artisan furniture-makers, carvers, and finishers construct the furniture that makes up Tropical Salvage's product offerings, including dining tables, chairs, benches, drawers, armoires, cabinets, buffets, shelves, desks, beds, side tables, media stands, coffee tables, and console tables (Exhibit 4).

Warehouse employees receive specification guidelines from Rafiqkoh in order to assemble and finish the furniture; each piece passes through many hands to complete the process. The greatest challenge during the manufacturing process is determining how to put together the different species and grain patterns to create attractive finished products. Rafiqkoh also handles quality assurance, making sure each piece is built to Western standards. The product catalog includes roughly 150 different models, but the company also builds one-of-a-kind custom pieces and furnishings built to commercial specifications. O'Brien and Rafiqkoh keep the catalog fresh by introducing at least one new design with each container shipment, about four times a year.

By offering steady employment, Tropical Salvage positively affects an area distressed by high rates of poverty, underemployment and unemployment. In addition, the company offers benefits such as paid vacations and health care. Tropical Salvage is committed to its employees and respects their rights to fair wages, health, and safe work environments. The company became a member of the Fair Trade Federation in 2003; all of its products are Fair Trade certified, a result of which being that wages are 20 percent above the local standard.

Distribution

Containers are loaded with finished Tropical Salvage products (Exhibit 5) in Jepara and shipped to North America. These containers take anywhere from 25 to 40 days to arrive and come directly to the main warehouse in Portland, Oregon or to Ten Thousand Villages Canada's receiving warehouse and distribution center. From these receiving locations, the products are dispersed to each Ten Thousand Villages store location in Canada and wholesale retailers in the United States.

Tropical Salvage has only a few employees in its Portland, Oregon headquarters, which is home to a receiving warehouse and small showroom that manages wholesale sales and distribution and some retail transactions. Independent contractors are occasionally brought in to assist with unloading containers or to make local deliveries.

Customers in Portland have the option to come to Tropical Salvage's warehouse location to buy products directly at standard retail prices. As a furniture manufacturer, Tropical Salvage is able to offer products at wholesale prices to its retail partners, but can also gain higher margins by selling at regular retail prices in its own warehouse location.

ECOpdx, also located in Portland, Oregon, is the company's largest local wholesale customer. Tropical Salvage has a number of other wholesale customers including: Small Planet Trading in Hood River, Oregon and Kizuri in Spokane, Washington. The Banyan Tree in Portland sells Tropical Salvage furniture to customers on consignment.

Beyond the local market, Ten Thousand Villages Canada is a key retail partner for Tropical Salvage. Ten Thousand Villages Canada has truly embraced the Tropical Salvage business model and its products. In fact, the Fair Trade retailer took the initiative to create a hard-copy "Tropical Salvage" catalog for its customers. This strong retail partner regularly stocks a number of furniture pieces and has arranged to receive direct container shipments of specifically selected pieces. In addition to the local partners and Ten Thousand Villages Canada, Tropical Salvage caters to other retailers across the United States for occasional wholesale orders.

Partnerships

Tropical Salvage initiated its business model without deliberate attention to partnerships outside of its supply chain and manufacturing operations. In the refinement and actualization of its sustainability-inspired mission, Tropical Salvage found NGO partnerships to be a critical resource. NGO partnerships bring expertise and credibility that have, according to O'Brien, permitted Tropical Salvage "…to hasten development and expansion of the model."

Since 2007, Tropical Salvage has been a leader in the creation of a conservation, education and reforestation project in Kunir, a village community in Jepara experiencing the widespread effects of overdependence on unsustainably harvested teak forests. The Jepara Forest Conservancy (JFC) shows how ecological restoration integrates with and positively influences cultural, social and economic conditions. For instance, with the help of Tropical Salvage, Kunir has recently adopted a number of Etawah goats, which are highly valued and produce exceptionally nutritious milk. Not only will this provide nutrients directly to the community, it will eventually result in improved economic conditions. JFC's restoration efforts have also had a positive effect on the area's native wildlife; its work is crucial in saving the Lutung monkey species.

Tropical Salvage collaborates with The Institute for Culture and Ecology (IFCAE) to maintain the JFC. IFCAE, a 501(c)(3) nonprofit organization, seeks to improve human and environmental conditions through applied research, education, and community improvement projects. Through its cross-sector partnership with IFCAE and the creation of the JFC, Tropical Salvage is able to fully realize its social mission objectives. The JFC provides a recreational botanical park for the community, educational facilities for school children and community members, and a model for alternative, economically sustainable land uses for local landholders. O'Brien firmly states that, "such collaborations are very important to Tropical Salvage's current and future business model," partially because Tropical Salvage does not have in-house expertise to overcome many of the challenges that arise in developing its mission. And, both O'Brien and Rafiqkoh do not consider the partnership with IFCAE and the creation of the JFC as optional; rather these efforts are at the core of the market-based strategy that seeks to reverse the destruction of Indonesian forests and the communities that depend on them.

The Hardwood Furniture Industry

Hardwood furniture is a sizable global industry, requiring intense labor and natural resources (Exhibit 6). Between 1995 and 2000, trade in furniture grew by 36.5 percent, faster than world trade as a whole (26.5 percent), and, also in that time, became the largest low-tech sector.[234] Indonesia ranks fifth among the world's fifteen major furniture exporters (Exhibit 7). Sixty-two percent of all furniture exports are wooden, which includes both solid wood and flat-pack, or ready-to-assemble, furniture made by both craft-based firms and large-volume producers.

The United States is not a major exporter of hardwood furniture. In fact, in the last 10 years the U.S. has become a major importer. In 2000, U.S. hardwood furniture manufacturing was a $13 billion industry employing over 135,000 individuals.[235] In 2006 the industry had shrunk to US$8.6 billion in revenue and

---

234   United Nations Industrial Development Organization, "The Global Wood Furniture Value Chain: What Prospects for Upgrading by Developing Countries?"
235   The Gale Group, Inc., "Industry Report: Wood Household Furniture, Except Upholstered, NAICS 337122."

63,066 employees.[236] These numbers reveal the significant decline in the U.S. industry over a relatively short period of time. Between 1997 and 2005 U.S. demand for furniture grew by 27 percent,[237] but the market share was captured by imports whose outsourced labor and production costs are much lower than those in the U.S. For example, China's household furniture imports to the United States increased 78 percent between 2003 and 2007,[238] and rose a total of 525 percent between 1998 and 2005.[239] Currently, nearly 70 percent of hardwood furniture purchases in the U.S. are imported products; about half of those are manufactured in China. Amidst this global competition, hardwood furniture has remained the largest sector of the U.S.-manufactured furniture industry.

The growth in demand for furniture occurred while the U.S. real estate market flourished from 2001 to 2006, due to favorable mortgage interest rates. Furniture sales are closely related to the state of the real estate market, which includes new and resale housing sales as well as home remodeling. The real estate market's sharp downturn in 2008, correlating with the U.S. financial crisis, resulted in a decrease in sales for numerous industries, including hardwood furniture. The effects of this downturn are noticeable throughout Jepara; a city that, before the recession, had been teeming with foreign business people buying furniture. Many warehouses and showrooms in Jepara now stand empty as a result of this decreased demand.

Another important trend in the furniture industry is consumers' shift from considering furniture a lifetime or even generation-to-generation investment to deeming it disposable and easily interchangeable. Often sold by big-box retailers and warehouse stores because it requires less inventory space, ready-to-assemble (RTA) composite wood furniture has proven to be the answer to consumer demand. A report by Mintel/Simmons NCS revealed that people in older age groups bought less RTA furniture. But older people buy less furniture and younger, more mobile, people buy more furniture in general and embrace RTA furniture, stand-alone furniture stores selling high quality, fully-assembled furniture have faced increased competitive pressures. This shift was likely brought on by increased frequency in relocation and less immediate disposable income. Because RTA furniture sells on average for less than half the price of comparable assembled furniture, price is a major driving factor in the increased demand for RTA items.

---

236   U.S. Census Bureau, "FactFinder."
237   Wood Digest, "U.S. Wooden Household Furniture."
238   Kaiser, "Furniture demand falls, ripples felt worldwide."
239   Business & Company Resource Center, "Industry Report: Nonupholstered Wood Household Furniture Manufacturing."

Although RTA furniture has increased in popularity, some providers of solid hardwood furniture continue to successfully compete in the furniture industry. The wood furniture industry is structured as a buyer-driven value chain with few scale- or technology-entry barriers in production. The consequence of this structure is that lead or governing firms that set prices, delivery schedules and quality standards are located at the apex of the chain; that is, among the buyers. The top two furniture retailers in the United States, WalMart, Inc. and Ashley Furniture,[240] both carry solid wood pieces. In addition to distributing its products to a range of specialty and department stores, Ashley Furniture sells its products in over two hundred branded retail stores called Ashley Furniture HomeStores. Williams-Sonoma is third in total sales and focuses exclusively on high quality, premium furniture. It owns Pottery Barn and Ethan Allen. Both Williams-Sonoma subsidiaries have built their reputations on consistent high quality, distinctive product and store designs and standalone branded retail stores. The next tier of competitors includes Cost Plus World Market and Pier 1 Imports, both of which sell mid- to low-end furniture.

There are only a few, smaller competitors that offer hardwood furniture with explicit social and environmental missions. The Wooden Duck in San Francisco uses reclaimed timber from pre-1920 structures to manufacture and sell household and office furnishing. The Wooden Duck's sales are primarily in San Francisco and the surrounding area. Environment Furniture is headquartered in Los Angeles and has showrooms in New York, Atlanta and Orange County. It salvages wood from Brazil as well as from forests certified by the Forest Stewardship Council and the Sustainable Forest Initiative. It offers uniquely designed, premium products for the home.

These two companies, as well as Tropical Salvage, are well-positioned to take advantage of a more recent trend impacting the tropical wood and hardwood furniture industry. The trend entails regulatory and non-regulatory initiatives to limit imports from non-sustainably managed tropical forests and promote sales from sustainably managed tropical forests. The Lacey Act, The Rainforest Alliance's SmartWood program (Exhibit 8), The Sustainable Furnishings Council, and The Prince's Rainforest Project were all launched between 2007 and 2009. By restricting importation of illegally harvested tropical timber – whether raw logs or in finished product – and by encouraging consumers to buy sustainability-based certified furniture, these developments seem to provide ample opportunity for socially-minded businesses in this industry

---

240   Mintel Reports, "Home Furniture – U.S."

to expand. In fact, with growing consumer awareness of environmental issues, eco-friendly furniture is no longer a niche market. It is increasingly common for wood products to be manufactured with Forest Stewardship Council-certified wood and environmentally friendly finishes. Recycled materials are also gaining popularity. Although less common in the industry and not well recognized as an issue by the marketplace, there is significant opportunity for furniture companies to focus on social issues, such as labor conditions and wages. All facets of sustainability will gain importance over the coming years as both governments and consumers demand greater transparency of environmental and social impacts.

O'Brien knows that his craft-based company must produce affordable, high-quality furniture products to effectively compete. His unique business model – combining low raw material and production costs with a clear and compelling social mission – helps mitigate some of the current industry trends and competitive risks faced by other companies. Tropical Salvage's profit margins remain high because the company controls the majority of its value chain. Furthermore, Tropical Salvage has a clear sustainability–oriented brand, which provides an authentically differentiated position in the marketplace.

Challenges to the Business Model

"The road to the vision has been a lot more fun and a lot more difficult than I expected it to be. Both the risks and rewards have been a thrill and have brought true happiness."
— Tim O'Brien

Although O'Brien is confident in his expansion plans for Tropical Salvage, the company has had, and continues to have, its share of challenges. In the beginning, O'Brien needed to learn the Indonesian culture and language. It was important for him to be able to communicate his philosophies and vision first-hand. Furthermore, because the company's wood salvaging techniques were groundbreaking in the region Tropical Salvage had to work to determine proper and effective kiln times for the 55 different woods to be utilized. Today O'Brien's knowledge of the language and culture, his partnership with Rafiqkoh, and the company's salvaging and dry-kilning techniques are considered to be the company's key competitive advantages.

Operations
Distance contributes greatly to the challenge of quality control. North

American consumers expect unique designs and exceptional quality in high-end hardwood furniture and O'Brien is not able to oversee warehouse operations year-round. Rafiqkoh has developed good insight into North American consumers and is charged with managing the furniture designs and quality standards. One of the most recent issues the company has encountered involves the presence of boring insects in certain pieces of recently fallen wood. Tropical Salvage lost some sales as a consequence and had to add a permethrin treatment for the wood at the production facility.

Expanding salvage operations presents another challenge for Tropical Salvage. The expense of setting up operations at a new site on the island of Kalimantan has been much higher than originally anticipated; mechanized systems are necessary to recover the wood and it is more difficult to move the wood across the Java Sea to the Jepara warehouse. There is an abundance of quality salvageable wood in Kalimantan's rivers and O'Brien is confident that the volume of wood recoverable from this new site will more than compensate for the additional expense. However, as Tropical Salvage continues to seek out additional sources of salvageable wood around the Indonesian archipelago, it will need to ensure efficient salvage and transport processes to maintain the margins that are key to its expansion efforts.

Inventory

Tropical Salvage also must deal with unreliable shipping schedules. Due to traffic in Indonesian and U.S. ports or extreme weather, a container can be delayed by several weeks. Such delays have been costly, particularly when working with commercial clients facing deadlines of their own.

Tropical Salvage also lacks a formal computer-based system to track and control its incoming and outgoing inventory. While the current informal approach has been sufficient for the small warehouse in Portland and its retail partnerships, this is a challenge that will become more evident with the introduction of one or more branded retail locations. O'Brien understands that he will need to be able to accurately evaluate a store's sales turnover and support the retail staff's forecasting and inventory management processes. Further, tracking inventory will help O'Brien understand the customers in a given location and place appropriate orders for the future.

Marketing

Increased demand for its furniture is necessary in order for Tropical Salvage to expand its operations and social and environmental missions. While untapped prospects and channels of distribution remain, determining the most effective ways to market the product line and mission is essential. O'Brien considers this his greatest challenge.

Tropical Salvage serves three core audiences: B2C retailers, commercial businesses, and consumers. Each audience requires a unique message. Creating the appropriate marketing approach for each group will involve learning about their needs and values. For example, commercial business prospects include both restaurants and offices. Determining the messages that resonate and which materials will get noticed for these two segments of the commercial business market is critical.

While the demand for sustainably sourced furniture increases, the majority of Americans remain unaware of the effects of illegal logging and deforestation. Because Tropical Salvage produces high-quality furniture while at the same time promoting social and environmental sustainability, the marketing must blend and balance two notions that perhaps consumers have yet to associate. Images are exceptional tools for telling a story and are an asset to Tropical Salvage, whose business model allows direct access to sourcing and restoration sites. By emotionally connecting consumers to its products through images of Tropical Salvage's work in Indonesia, the company may be able to offer a persuasive marketing message. But to what extent should Tropical Salvage take responsibility for educating its audiences on the effects of illegal logging and deforestation? And could too much emphasis on the mission deter certain prospective customers?

Although the hardwood furniture market is fairly saturated, O'Brien believes there is an opportunity to continue to supply the Lifestyles of Health and Sustainability (LOHAS) market segment (Exhibit 9). LOHAS consumers are passionate, environmentally and socially responsible and tend to be early adopters who can be used as predictors of upcoming trends. They are also influential over friends and family, are more brand loyal than other consumers especially to companies whose values match their own, and most importantly, are willing to put their money behind their beliefs and values.[241]

It is roughly estimated that a third of Portland's population practices a LOHAS perspective; O'Brien knows that most of his customers in the Portland warehouse are LOHAS consumers. These consumers share many of Tropical Salvage's values, focusing on health and fitness, the environment, personal development, sustainable living, and social justice19. These consumers are educated and informed, and many have traveled abroad to less developed destinations which increased their awareness of social, environmental,

---

241   French and Rogers, "Understanding the LOHAS Consumer: The Rise of Ethical Consumerism."

and health-related issues on a global scale. About one in every four adults in the United States, roughly 41 million, falls into this market segment; this US$209 billion market is shaping future consumer trends. O'Brien can incorporate his existing knowledge of the target customer into the marketing message; however, he still needs to determine how to reach this target market with his value proposition.

The Business Expansion Plan of 2010

It is obvious to O'Brien that expansion is necessary in order to sustain Tropical Salvage's growing business. In response, he has devised an extensive expansion plan to move toward branded retail stores, and has numerous other ideas and new products in mind.

O'Brien sees forward vertical integration of the company into branded retail stores as the first step toward growth. In remaining loyal to his retail partner, EcoPDX, O'Brien will seek retail space outside of Portland. Seattle is an obvious choice for the first market that Tropical Salvage will enter with a branded store. Because of its proximity to Portland, O'Brien can be as involved as is necessary to find a location, hire a team to maintain the store, and create a strong storefront. Further, he will be able to supply a Seattle location through his existing Portland warehouse and a third-party trucking company. Exhibit 10 provides the estimated annual operating expenses for the Seattle-based store, including on-going and one-time expenditures. Although the new store represents a significant financial commitment for Tropical Salvage, the financial projections (shown in Exhibit 11) suggest that this expansion plan could be quite successful.

Fortunately, Tropical Salvage has not acquired any debt during the recession, but O'Brien needs to decide how to proceed with the financial outlay required of opening a retail store. Venture capital financing or a small business loan seems to be the most appropriate options, but O'Brien has not yet settled on one over the other.

It may make sense to incorporate some of O'Brien's other expansion ideas into his branded retail store strategy. Some new products that he would like to introduce include: sustainably sourced bamboo and rattan, coffee, tea, spices, and textiles (including pillows and cushions). Offering a more diverse product line may, in fact, be necessary for a successful retail location. The diversity of sustainability-oriented products will draw more people into Tropical Salvage storefronts to increase opportunities to sell higher-end — and often higher margin — furniture. Tropical Salvage could acquire these products through its relationship with JFC, further benefiting the residents of Kunir and fulfilling the company's mission.

The Future of Tropical Salvage

As O'Brien prepared signs for the warehouse clearance sale, he thought about different ways to arrange his furniture in a retail store. He believed that strong displays would draw more customers and increase demand so that he could expand his sourcing operations and employ more people. He was also confident that he could introduce new merchandise to complement Tropical Salvage's furniture, which would greatly benefit the small communities in Indonesia working with the company.

O'Brien still questioned the best financing option for his expansion plan however. Does it make sense to appeal to investors or continue down his financially independent path? Further, is he in a secure enough position to take on expansion while the economy's future is so unclear? He worried that if his expansion efforts failed, Tropical Salvage's social mission could be compromised. He also wondered whether he should consider The Rainforest Alliance's SmartWood Certification in order to increase visibility to consumers in the LOHAS market. This question was part of the larger challenge of how to effectively communicate the value of Tropical Salvage to its target customers. What marketing efforts would best serve his plans? O'Brien had a lot of thinking and work to do before he would be able to jump into branded retail stores successfully.

Exhibits

Exhibit 1: Indonesian Forests

Forest Cover Loss in Indonesia, 2000-05

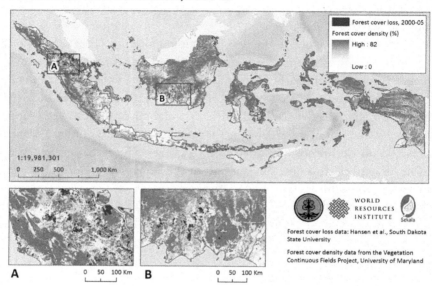

Forest cover loss data: Hansen et al., South Dakota State University

Forest cover density data from the Vegetation Continuous Fields Project, University of Maryland

Indonesia Forest Area

Classification	Area			Annual change rate				Total change		
					1990-2000		2000-2005		1990-2005	1990s vs 2000s
Period	1990	2000	2005	1990-2000	2000	2000-2005	2005	1990-2005	2005	2000s
Units	ha	ha	ha	ha	%	ha	%	ha	%	%
Total forest area	116,567,000	97,852,000	88,495,000	-1,872,000	-1.7	-1,871,000	-2	-28,072,000	-24.1	17.65
Other wooded land				0		0		0		
Primary forests	70,419,000	55,941,000	48,702,000	-1,447,800	-2.06	-1,447,800	-2.59	-21717000	-30.8	0
Plantations	2,209,000	3,002,000	3,399,000	79,300	3.59	79,400	2.64	1190000	53.9	-26.3

All data derived from the Forest Resources Assessment and the State of the World's Forests published by the U.N. Food and Agriculture Organization (F.A.O)

Exhibit 2: Wood Salvaging

River salvage site in Bundu (Java, Indonesia)

House deconstruction site

Exhibit 3: Tropical Salvage Wood Salvaging Methods

Deconstruction wood	Indonesia is replacing a number of its buildings and structures with concrete and rebar; deconstruction wood is very common. Teak was used in many of the deconstruction projects Tropical Salvage comes across. Old doors and shutters from deconstruction are often used in Tropical Salvage's armoires and wine cabinets.
River and lake salvage	Years of severe weather and volcanic activity in Indonesia have knocked down a number of trees that have been swept into rivers. Low water levels in the dry season make it easy to find these trees; the wood is pulled out of rivers and lakes, cut into two-meter lengths and brought to the sawmill.
Flood and landslide salvage	Trees and houses fallen victim to landslides are a result of illegal logging. Deforestation eliminates the soil's protective canopy, increasing the likelihood of landslides during Indonesia's rainy season.
Plantation "waste"	Coffee and cacao trees are not typically used in furniture, but Tropical Salvage has learned to use them in their furniture designs. These woods are traditionally burned when they are culled from a plantation.
Entombed wood	Entombed wood exists as a result of volcanic eruptions hundreds of years ago. These trees became entombed in bogs and aged below ground, deep enough so that oxygen has not decomposed them. The rainy season erodes the soil around the bogs and brings the entombed wood closer to the surface. While the logs are entombed, they absorb minerals from the soil to add density to the wood; the woods are very hard and very heavy. Tropical Salvage can sometimes make tabletops with a single plank of wood that still holds the shape of the tree's trunk.

Exhibit 4: Jepara Production Warehouse

Exhibit 5: Tropical Salvage Finished Products

Exhibit 6: Wood Furniture Industry Value Chain

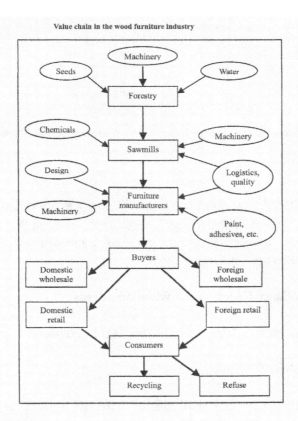

Source: Global Wood Furniture Value Chain: What Prospects for Upgrading by Developing Countries

Exhibit 7: Top 15 Furniture Exporters (2000)

Table 1   Global furniture trade—top 15 net exporting countries (US$ million)[a]

Country	Gross exports 2000	Net exports 1995	Net exports 2000	Net exports percentage change 1995-2000
Italy	8,359	7,595	7,395	-3
China	4,582	1,671	4,412	164
Canada	5,179	685	2,044	198
Poland	2,191	1,180	1,815	54
Indonesia	1,518	819	1,498	83
Malaysia	1,596	826	1,491	80
Denmark	1,900	1,687	1,209	-28
Mexico	3,315	468	1,173	151
Thailand	949	712	909	28
Spain	1,453	523	531	2
Slovenia	586	409	461	13
Czech Rep	780	148	445	201
Romania	445	472	377	-20
Sweden	1,298	510	338	-34
Brazil	496	212	333	57
Total of rest	22,742			
Total [b]	57,388			

Source: Global Wood Furniture Value Chain: What Prospects for Upgrading by Developing Countries

Exhibit 8: Rainforest Alliance SmartWood Certification Program

Rediscovered Wood and Underwater Salvage: approves wood that is reclaimed in such a way to preserve the "integrity of the environment as well as the health welfare of workers and the community."

Rainforest Alliance Rediscovered Wood Standards

PART 1. REDISCOVERED WOOD ELIGIBILITY AND RECOVERY

1.1 Rediscovered Wood Classification

1.1.1 RWO systems shall ensure materials it reclaims for use as Rediscovered Wood qualify as coming from one of the RW categories defined in section D above.

1.1.2 RWO systems shall ensure materials obtained from suppliers and used as Rediscovered Wood qualify as coming from one of the RW categories defined in section D above.

1.2 Wood Recovery Source Information (for each source)

1.2.1 Each source of Rediscovered Wood shall be sufficiently documented to provide credible evidence that materials qualify as coming from one of the RW categories defined in section D above.

1.2.2. Source information including origin/recovery and classification under one of the RW categories defined in section D shall be demonstrated through the completion of the RW Source Information Form (Annex 3) or through equivalent documentation.

1.2.3 If Rediscovered Wood materials are purchased or obtained from a supplier, the RWO shall provide documented evidence that the source meets Rediscovered Wood requirements as defined in this standard.

1.2.4 A summary of the methods used for recovery of the Rediscovered Wood materials and potential impacts shall be developed and maintained.

1.3 Wood Recovery Impacts

1.3.1 Environmental impacts associated with recovery and on and off-site processing shall be identified and mitigated.

1.3.2 Worker safety conditions associated with the recovery operation shall meet legal requirements.

1.3.3 Any cultural, historic, or social impacts of the Rediscovered Wood recovery shall be identified/researched and reconciled.

1.4 Resource Rights and Use

1.4.1 All necessary documentation that accompanied the Rediscovered Wood source shall be in place, e.g., permits, deeds, demolition contracts.

1.4.2 Clear evidence of rights to the Rediscovered Wood source shall be demonstrated, e.g. permits, deeds, demolition contracts.

PART 2. CHAIN-OF-CUSTODY

2.1 Quality System

2.1.1 RWO shall define CoC system responsibilities and appoint staff positions, including the following:

a) One overall responsible person shall be designated for the CoC control system;
b) Individual responsible persons shall be designated for each part of the CoC control system (purchasing, processing, final storage, marking, sales documents, recordkeeping, etc.).

2.1.2 RWO shall develop and maintain up-to-date documented procedures and/or work instructions to ensure implementation of all applicable CoC standard requirements.

2.1.3 RWO shall develop and implement procedures for addressing non-conformances (corrective action requests, observations) identified by auditors.

2.1.4 RWO shall develop and implement procedures for internal auditing of its systems as related to CoC requirements in this standard and include the following:

a) Documentation to show when audits take place and audit results;
b) Provision for review of internal audit results by senior management staff; and
c) Provision for internal audits to occur at least annually.

2.1.5 RWO shall develop training requirements and implement training as follows:

a) All applicable staff and workers shall be trained according to the CoC procedures;

b) Record shall be kept to demonstrate training has taken place.

2.1.6 RWO shall define and document the product that will be tracked as Rediscovered Wood.

2.1.7 RWO shall develop and maintain records to document quantities of Rediscovered Wood product for the following:

a) Purchased as inputs/raw material;
b) Used in production;
c) Conversion factors;
d) Inputs and final products in stock; and
e) Final products sold with and without a Rediscovered Wood claim.

2.2 Purchasing and Receiving

2.2.1 If supplier is a Rediscovered Wood certificate holder, RWO shall verify the validity of the supplier's RW certificate.

2.2.2 RWO shall verify that material purchased and received is consistent with Rediscovered Wood categories.

2.2.3 RWO shall store Rediscovered Wood material as separate, secure units.

2.2.4 RWO shall use a distinguishing mark to identify Rediscovered Wood material. When supplier is not RW-certified, 1.2.2 and 1.2.3 requirements apply.

2.3 Processing

2.3.1 RWO shall keep Rediscovered Wood material physically separate during all stages of processing.

2.3.2 RWO shall use a tracking system or production records to document production of Rediscovered Wood material.

2.3.3 RWO shall ensure that any off-site processing that takes place at a subcontracted facility follows CoC procedures and is covered by a signed outsourcing agreement.

2.3.4 All material that cannot be identified as qualifying for Rediscovered Wood shall be kept physically separate from all other material until documented evidence of the Rediscovered Wood status is obtained.

2.4 Shipping and Sales

2.4.1 RWO shall store final Rediscovered Wood products as separate, secure units.

2.4.2 RWO shall use a distinguishing mark to identify final Rediscovered Wood products.

2.4.3 RWO shall include Rediscovered Wood claim information on sales invoices and shipping documents, including the following:

a) A description of the product as "Rediscovered Wood";
b) The quantity/volume for each product; and
c) The SmartWood Rediscovered Wood certificate code.

PART 3. REDISCOVERED WOOD CLAIMS AND PUBLIC INFORMATION

3.1.1 All on-product and off-product/promotional claims made by the RWO shall be in compliance with Rainforest Alliance Rediscovered Wood trademark requirements.

3.1.2 RWO shall have procedures in place and demonstrates submission of all on-product and off-product/promotional claims to SmartWood for review and approval prior to use.

3.1.3 RWO shall have procedures in place and demonstrates that all trademark review and approval correspondence with SmartWood is kept on file for a minimum of 5 years.

Source: http://www.rainforest-alliance.org/forestry.cfm?id=smartwood_program

Exhibit 9: LOHAS Market

LOHAS (Lifestyles of Health and Sustainability) populations are the ideal target customers for Tropical Salvage. A market analysis of the top six potential markets is below:

Market Analysis							
		2009	2010	2011	2012	2013	
Potential Customers	Growth						CAGR
Portland	3%	247,405	254,827	262,472	270,346	278,456	3.00%
Seattle	3%	384,741	396,283	408,171	420,416	433,028	3.00%
San Francisco	3%	473,369	487,570	502,197	517,263	532,781	3.00%
Boston	2%	351,000	358,020	365,180	372,484	379,934	2.00%
Chicago	2%	419,000	427,380	435,928	444,647	453,540	2.00%
Minneapolis	3%	424,807	437,551	450,678	464,198	478,124	3.00%
Total	2.67%	2,300,322	2,361,631	2,424,626	2,489,354	2,555,863	2.67%

Market Analysis (LOHAS Households)

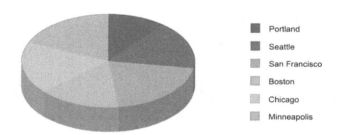

- Portland
- Seattle
- San Francisco
- Boston
- Chicago
- Minneapolis

Source: Tropical Salvage Growth Plan: August 2010

Exhibit 10: Estimated Annual Operating Expenses for Seattle Store

Category	Expense (US$)
On-Going Expenses	
Wages and salaries	$110,000
Lease	$80,000
Utilities (phone, broadband)	$12,000
Marketing	$50,000
State/local license and permits	$3,000
Container furniture shipments (5 shipments, 40' containers	$100,000
Computer and organizational/inventory software	$6,000
Information kiosk in storefront	$5,000
Miscellaneous supplies	$2,000
Travel	$5,000
Furniture maintenance tools	$3,000
Subtotal	$376,000
One-Time Expenses	
Delivery truck (used)	$8,000
Signage	$10,000
Expansion of production capacity in Indonesia	$20,000
Lighting system in storefront	$10,000
Subtotal	$48,000
Total	$425,000

Exhibit 11: Tropical Salvage Condensed Financial Data

Consolidated Income Statement Data	FY 2009	FY 2010	FY 2011	FY 2012	FY 2013	FY 2014
Sales	$470,000	$478,813	$863,480	$1,674,450	$2,881,364	$4,529,157
Gross Margin	$204,000	$282,682	$583,266	$1,212,062	$2,113,682	$3,435,952
Gross Margin %	43.40%	59.04%	67.55%	72.39%	73.36%	75.86%
Total Operating Expenses	$250,000	$288,420	$520,000	$903,000	$1,304,450	$1,719,900
Profit Before Interest and Taxes	($46,000)	($5,378)	$43,266	$289,062	$774,232	$1,716,052
Other Income	$77,212	$0	$0	$0	$0	$0
Retail Door Build Out & Remodel	$0	$0	$20,000	$20,000	$35,000	$0
Net Profit (Loss)	$31,212	($10,258)	$27,123	$200,762	$541,962	$1,201,237

Consolidated Balance Sheet Data	FY 2009	FY 2010	FY 2011	FY 2012	FY 2013	FY 2014
Current Assets						
Cash	$28,593	($10,598)	($16,933)	$52,207	$473,381	$1,652,700
Accounts Receivable	$5,000	$5,608	$10,113	$19,610	$33,745	$53,043
Inventory	$14,400	$48,859	$133,639	$257,027	$429,349	$524,416
Total Current Assets	$47,993	$43,868	$126,819	$328,844	$936,476	$2,230,159
Total Long-term Assets	$4,837	$3,517	$8,517	$6,517	$4,517	(16,483)
Total Assets	**$52,830**	**$47,835**	**$135,336**	**$335,361**	**$940,993**	**$2,213,676**
Accounts Payable	$5,000	$9,813	$50,641	$95,102	$158,772	$230,218
Total Current Liabilities	$5,000	$9,813	$50,641	$95,102	$158,772	$230,218
Long-term Liabilities	$45,197	$45,197	$45,197	($1)	($1)	($1)
Total Liabilities	$50,197	$55,010	$95,838	$95,101	$158,771	$230,217
Paid-in Capital	$0	$0	$20,000	$20,000	$20,000	$20,000
Retained Earnings	($28,579)	$2,633	($7,625)	$19,498	$220,259	$762,222
Earnings	$31,212	($10,258)	$27,123	$200,762	$541,962	$1,201,237
Total Capital	$2,633	($7,625)	$39,498	$240,259	$782,222	$1,983,458
Total Liabilities and Capital	**$52,830**	**$47,385**	**$135,336**	**$335,361**	**$940,993**	**$2,213,676**

Source: Tropical Salvage Growth Plan, August 2010

Bibliography

Business & Company Resource Center. "Industry Report: Nonupholstered Wood Household Furniture Manufacturing." Not dated.

Case, Michael, Fitrian Ardiansyah, and Spector, Emily. "Climate Change in Indonesia: Implications for Humans and Nature." 2007. World Wildlife Fund.

CIFOR. "Generating economic growth, rural livelihoods, and environmental benefits from Indonesia's forests: A summary of issues and policy options." 2004. Report prepared for the World Bank.

French, Steve, and Gwynne Rogers. "Understanding the LOHAS Consumer: The Rise of Ethical Consumerism." Not dated. The Natural Marketing Institute. www.lohas.com/journal/consumertrends.htm.

Kaiser, Emily. "Furniture demand falls, ripples felt worldwide." July 25, 2008. Reuters. http://www.reuters.com/article/idUSN2537252220080725.

Mintel Reports. "Home Furniture – U.S." 2008.

Roda, Jean-Marc, Philippe Cadene, Philippe Guizol, Levania Santoso, and Achmad Uzair Fauzan. *Atlas of Wooden Furniture Industry in Jepara, Indonesia.* 2007. CIRAD & CIFOR, Harapan Prima, Jakarta.

Sunderlin, W.D., Resosudarmo, I. A. P. "Rates and causes of deforestation in Indonesia: towards a resolution of the ambiguities." 1996. *CIFOR Occasional Paper* No. 9. CIFOR.

The Gale Group, Inc. "Industry Report: Wood Household Furniture, Except Upholstered, NAICS 337122." 2010.

United Nations Industrial Development Organization. "The Global Wood Furniture Value Chain: What Prospects for Upgrading by Developing Countries?" 2003.

U.S. Census Bureau. "FactFinder." 2007. http://factfinder.census.gov/servlet/IBQTable?_bm=y&-ds_name=EC0700A1&-NAICS2007=337122&-ib_type=NAICS2007&-_industry=337122&-_lang=en.

Wood Digest. "U.S. Wooden Household Furniture." 2000. Datamonitor Industry Market Research.

World Bank. "Sustaining Economic Growth, Rural Livelihoods, and Environmental Benefits: Strategic Options for Forest Assistance in Indonesia." December, 2006. The World Bank Office, Jakarta Indonesia.